CANNERY VILLAGE: COMPANY TOWN

K. Mack Campbell

© Copyright 2004 K. Mack Campbell. All rights reserved.

No part of this publication may be reproduced, stored in a retrieval system, or transmitted, in any form or by any means, electronic, mechanical, photocopying, recording, or otherwise, without the written prior permission of the author.

Printed in Victoria, Canada

cover photo: Tallheo Cannery, Canadian Fishing Co., Ltd.

National Library of Canada Cataloguing in Publication

Campbell, K. Mack (Ken Mack), 1930-
    Cannery village : company town / K. Mack Campbell.

Includes bibliographical references.
ISBN 1-4120-0965-0

    1. Salmon canning industry--British Columbia--History.
2. Canneries--British Columbia--History. I. Title.

HD9469.S23B75 2003   338.4 7664942 09711   C2003-904342-8

TRAFFORD

This book was published *on-demand* in cooperation with Trafford Publishing.
On-demand publishing is a unique process and service of making a book available for retail sale to the public taking advantage of on-demand manufacturing and Internet marketing.
On-demand publishing includes promotions, retail sales, manufacturing, order fulfilment, accounting and collecting royalties on behalf of the author.

Suite 6E, 2333 Government St., Victoria, B.C. V8T 4P4, CANADA
Phone   250-383-6864   Toll-free   1-888-232-4444 (Canada & US)
Fax   250-383-6804   E-mail   sales@trafford.com
Web site   www.trafford.com   TRAFFORD PUBLISHING IS A DIVISION OF TRAFFORD HOLDINGS LTD.
Trafford Catalogue #03-1334   www.trafford.com/robots/03-1334.html

10   9   8   7   6   5   4   3   2

Acknowledgements

I am hugely indebted to all those who took the time and interest to subject themselves to a taped interview of their personal reminiscences. They are listed in the Bibliography and their recollections form the essence of this book. And to those who allowed me to use their pictures, a special thank you.

And I want to express my appreciation for the even more extraordinary degree of support and encouragement I received from my good friends and fishing industry colleagues, Ian Bell-Irving, Jack Elsey, Ewen Macmillan, Donovan Miller, Eric Turnill and Peter Wilson. Their faith in the project was an inspiration.

Writing and publishing a book is a daunting experience, a consumer of time and like Fred Kohse's seine boat, a sleep robber. I extend my thanks to my wife Gwen for her patience over the past few years, and to my daughter, Kathy for her excellent technical assistance.

KMC

Table of Contents

	Page
Foreword	i

Chapter

1. Introduction 1
2. Cannery Village—Company Town 10
3. The Influence of Ethnic Factors 20
4. The Outlying Plants 30
5. The Multi-Purpose Plants 85
6. The Causes of Decline of the Outlying Plants 100
7. The Great Amalgamations 111
8. Supplying the Plants 121
9. Managing the Resources 131
10. The Lifelines 142
11. Decisive Decades 159
12. Not the Salmon Fishery 167
13. The Bell-Irvings and the Anglo-B.C. Packing Company 179
14. The Dormans of Bones Bay 188
15. The Ewen and Macmillan Families 196
16. The Francis Millerds 224
17. The Nilssens 229
18. The Inrig and Hogan Families 236
19. The Simpsons 254
20. A Few (More) Good Men 259
21. Glimpses of Cannery Life 281

Appendices

1. 1923 Surveys, British Columbia Fire Underwriters Association 299
2. Canneries and Hatcheries on the British Columbia Coast – 1932 ... 331

Bibliography 335

Foreword

This is not the first historical work on British Columbia's fishing industry, nor will it be the last. Much has been written about it over the years—some of it exhaustively comprehensive like Cicely Lyons' near-encyclopaedic *Salmon Our Heritage*—others specific to an area or to a particular coastal point—still others aimed at imparting a political or ideological slant to the development of the industry.

The Fraser River was the birthplace of the commercial fishing industry and its salmon runs, the most important in the province. In many ways, the industry there "spawned" the salmon canneries in the outlying areas. These became important in their own right and as a group, from time to time, out-produced the mighty Fraser. This history is about those upcoast canneries and the villages that supported them.

The genesis of this book can be attributed to Ian Bell-Irving. When I worked with the Fisheries Association of B.C., he and I had many conversations about the history of this wonderful industry that we were part of. When I was preparing to leave Vancouver to take over the Fisheries Council of Canada in Ottawa, Ian avowed that I should some day write a history of the salmon canning industry from the perspective of the people who were in it. To that end, he promised to save me some of the company records of Anglo-B.C. Packing Co. and of H. Bell-Irving and Co. He was as good as his word, and when I retired and returned to B.C. in 1993, we again talked about this project. I only regret that he passed away before he could read the finished product.

My objective from the beginning was to focus on the upcoast canneries. This was partly personal because I had worked in a number of them in the 1950s. It was also a practical decision, because the history of the canneries of the Fraser River and Burrard Inlet is a story of its own and in many ways different from that of the plants outside that area. But the main reason was that the canneries outside the metropolitan area came to represent a distinct, frontier culture that resulted from their isolation, their need for self reliance and their tenuous existence. And the overriding fact was that they have disappeared from the coast and that distinctive culture has died with them.

The story as written here is not complete, nor could it be, because every individual who worked in these places or who influenced them from a distance is part of it.

I had the advantage of knowing personally, a good many of the cannery "old-timers" who were still alive and they were good enough to record their reminiscences on tape. Many of these have been used in the following chapters—a type of oral history.

I had the additional advantage of having worked in some of the plants myself and of having visited most of the others on various occasions.

My first introduction to salmon canneries was a summer job in 1950, at Nelson Brothers big St. Mungo plant on the Fraser River, where the south pier of the Alex Fraser bridge now stands. When I graduated from the University of British Columbia in 1952 with my shiny new Bachelor of Commerce degree I was hired by Canadian Fishing Company's accounting department and shipped off immediately to Porcher Island in the mouth of the Skeena River estuary. During the next few seasons, I worked at Porcher, Goose Bay in Rivers Inlet, Margaret Bay in Smiths Inlet, Bones Bay in Johnstone Strait and briefly, at the Gulf of Georgia in Steveston.

I was then moved into Personnel and Industrial Relations and this led, in 1961, to becoming Manager of the Fisheries Association of B.C.

The connection with the outlying plants continued through my involvement with government regulations on the one hand, and on the other, with the industry's collective bargaining and collective agreements with the United Fishermen and Allied Workers Union and other industrial groups. But now the connection was with the plants of all the companies which were members of the Fisheries Association of B.C.

In 1973, I moved to Ottawa to manage the Fisheries Council of Canada, the national trade association of the Canadian fishing industry. The Fisheries Council of Canada was a federation of provincial fish processors' associations and the Fisheries Association of B.C. being a member, my connections with the B.C. industry continued until 1982 when I left the fisheries field. More or less by coincidence, the era of the upcoast canneries ended about this time and so it provided a natural time frame for my research and the history covered by this book.

One of the problems in describing past times is that standards in human relations change. It is necessary that history be told in the context of the times described but this may cause some concern or even resentment in present-day readers. An example of this is the racial factors that were at work in the first century of the salmon canning industry. Some of the names by which Native Indians were called originated with themselves, but came to be less than complimentary and even pejorative. I have used them when they were included in quotes from the early days and there is no intention at disrespect.

Speaking of names, the reader will not find the term "fisher" used in reference to those who fish. To me, a fisher is a four-footed fur-bearing mammal of the weasel family and will remain so. Fisherman in this work refers to all those who fished and includes the few women who made this their vocation.

Again I regret that many of the people who shared their memories with me have since passed away. There are many more who have stories to tell and I hope that, while I haven't had the opportunity to talk with them, they realize the importance of recording their memories and experiences in some way—for this is history.

Ken Campbell
Kelowna, B.C.
December 2003

Chapter 1

INTRODUCTION

The recorded history of British Columbia (B.C.) is very recent by any standards. It begins with the appearance of European explorers, Drake probably, then the Spanish sailing north from Mexico (they were in the vicinity of Nootka and off North Island in the Queen Charlotte Islands in 1774), then Cook in 1778, the Spanish again, this time out of Nootka which they occupied in 1789, then Vancouver in 1792/93/94, and the Russians from their coastal settlements in Alaska.

The thread of history that brings us to today began much earlier with the colonization of the area by the aboriginal peoples, themselves immigrants, who made their way from Asia, we are told, over an ice bridge or landforms across Bering Strait. What desperate conditions at home must have driven them to make such a migration? Or was it a gradual drift that took centuries to bring them to present day British Columbia? And were they the first humans here or did they, like the Europeans later, conquer or displace an earlier race? Are they really the First Nations or are they the Second or even the Third? The clues that anthropologists unearth and interpret for us haven't yet been able to tell us and possibly never will.

But in telling stories of our past, we have to start somewhere and that usually seems to be the beginning of recorded history, and that coincides with the arrival on our coast of European explorers. All history before that is called "pre-contact," and who and whatever was here at that time is aboriginal. Pre-contact history exists, but in traditional stories and myths that were passed down from one aboriginal generation to another and from the skimpy gleanings of historical scientists.

It is recorded that Francis Drake visited the Pacific coast of North America and landed in what is now California in 1579. He may have made it as far north as the Queen Charlotte Islands. Juan de Fuca's voyage in 1592, and the discovery of the "Straits of Anian," may have been apocryphal (he was a Greek explorer, whose real name was Apostolas Valerianos, and in the employ of the Spanish), and he failed to establish beyond doubt that he actually reached our waters. Nevertheless, his claim was good enough to convince Captain Charles Barkley who, in 1787, was the first Englishman to discover the Strait (Cook missed it), to name it Juan de Fuca Strait in his honour. But at best, these were visits without any significant follow-up or results. There was no attempt at colonization as the Vikings had done in Newfoundland, or at commerce as the British and French had done in the Newfoundland cod fishery. Even Perez, on his voyage from San Blas, Mexico in 1774 and Quadra, in 1775, did not land on the coast and managed only some inconsequential trading with the Indians.

So the recorded history of the B.C. coast really begins in 1778 with Captain James Cook's voyage and his landing in Nootka. His quest was the Northwest Passage, that elusive dream of several generations of Europeans who found the Americas a barrier to easy access to the riches of the Orient, which other European explorers had "discovered" for them. The realization that the riches in that barrier were far greater than those of Asia had not yet fully taken root, although the Spanish had certainly realized the value of the treasures of the lower latitudes.

Cook was an amazing mariner and his exploration of the coast from Oregon through Alaska, was nothing short of phenomenal. He had already visited Tahiti and New Zealand and discovered the Hawaiian Islands and he had mapped in detail the coasts of Newfoundland, our destined-to-be fellow bookend province with which we have so much else in common. His voyages here were shortly followed with territorial disputes with Spain and Captain Vancouver's voyage of exploration of the coasts of Washington, British Columbia and Alaska—all of which established Britain's claim to New Caledonia which included present day British Columbia.

But Cook's voyage was also the beginning of commercial activity—the trade for furs, especially of the sea otter and later the fur seal, which found a ready and lucrative market in China and attracted hunters and traders from several countries, especially the infant United States of America and what was now British North America or Canada.

The fishing industry was a natural fallout of this activity as the resources of the sea and rivers provided a ready source of food for the venturers and the coastal Indians found supplying them to be an easy source of the trade goods that they valued. Similarly, the forest industry began out of the need for materials for repair and building of ships for the fur trade. But the value of the fishery resource did not attract commercial entrepreneurs until well into the 19th century. The first export trade in fish was developed by the Hudson's

Bay Company (HBC) at Fort Langley when they shipped salted spring salmon in great tierces to Hawaii. The accepted date for the debut of this commerce is 1837.

The British Columbia commercial salmon fishery as we know it today had its beginnings after the Oregon Territory boundary settlement in 1846. And the birth of the salmon canning industry begins at Annieville on the Fraser River with Alexander Ewen and his partners in 1870. The first species to be sought were the spring salmon (king or chinook) and the first processing was by salting and curing. But the cannery building era was based on the sockeye and most of the first canneries were sockeye canneries. Coho were valued too, because of their colour, but being less oily than the spring and sockeye, they didn't can so well. The abundance of pink and chum salmon led the canners to develop markets for them as well, but this took some time and in the early years, these were considered scrap fish or "cheap fish". The lowly chum was used by the Natives to feed their dogs and for many years had to bear the sobriquet, "dog salmon". To this day, although all the species are caught and processed, the hierarchy of canning values remains with sockeye at the top, followed by pink and chum or keta. The attributes of spring and coho have placed them in the higher value fresh and frozen markets and prime sea run chums have made their own market as frozen silverbrights.

The Hudson's Bay Company built its first coastal establishment in the future British Columbia, at Fort Langley in 1827. HBC was fairly new to New Caledonia, having swallowed its arch-competitor the Northwest Company in the great merger of 1821. The merger established the HBC name on the Columbia River and in the Interior at the Northwest Company trading posts such as Fort McLeod, Fort George, Fort St. James, Fort Alexandria and Fort Kamloops. But the coastal fur trade in the Gulf of Georgia and Fraser River was in the hands of coasting traders from the U.S. and Britain. Fort Langley was meant to assert the company's rights to this trade.

It was a very isolated post and the staff was largely confined to the fort. To venture out, even to work the gardens that were necessary for sustenance, was risky because many of the Natives were not friendly. Many tribes from the lower coast and even from Vancouver Island came to the Fraser River to catch and cure the salmon. The main fishing posts were at the lower Fraser Canyon near present day Yale where the salmon could be easily caught by dip nets and snares. But those with no claim to these stations found the means of catching the salmon in the opaque waters of the lower river. Splitting and drying took place on the spot and some of these fish were traded to the fort. The runs were not always plentiful and in times of shortage, the supply was unreliable. In time, the Bay men were able to venture out and began to supply some of their own needs by netting both salmon and sturgeon in the nearby river.

In 1831, the company established Fort Simpson at Nass Harbour to forestall the southbound advance of the Russians from southeast Alaska. In 1834, they moved the fort to the site of present day Port Simpson. In 1833 they built Fort McLaughlin, which would become the site of the Indian village of Bella Bella.

Fort Victoria was established in 1843, in anticipation of the loss of the southern portion of the Oregon Territory to the United States. By that time the aboriginal Indians were losing their status as the dominant culture on the Fraser River and they would lose it altogether when the gold rush erupted in 1858.

The HBC were shipping their furs direct to China via the Sandwich Islands and many Hawaiians were crewmen on the ships. They developed a taste for Fraser River salmon and out of this grew a demand in the Islands for salted salmon, a taste which endures today. American whaling crews, wintering in the Islands were the other prime market for the cured salmon. (Many of the Hawaiians, known as Kanakas, settled near Fort Langley and became farmers and fishermen on the River. Kanaka Creek is named for them.)

Salmon was being canned in Saint John, New Brunswick in 1839. Canning food was a relatively new procedure then, invented in response to Napoleon's need for a reliable preservation system for food for his far flung armies. George and William Hume had experience in seafood canning in New Brunswick and Maine and in 1864, they started canning salmon in Eureka, California—the first commercial canning of Pacific salmon. But already, in 1865, the salmon runs on the Sacramento River were feeling the effects of pollution and habitat destruction from mining operations and in 1866, the Humes moved to Astoria where they were the first to can salmon on the Columbia River. They moved again to Puget Sound in 1877.

Canned salmon is, in many ways, the perfect product. It transforms a highly desirable but highly perishable food product into one which has a virtually unlimited shelf life without loss of its taste or nutritional qualities. The container has been improved over the years, but it is still a "tin can". There have been many improvements in the process, including mechanization and quality assurance, but the product is still a slice of salmon hermetically sealed and cooked in the can with nothing added but a pinch of salt. As in the 1860s, 140 years later, canning salmon is still the best way to preserve the huge quantities that are caught in a very short time frame. And nobody does it better than the B.C. fishing industry.

The first commercial salmon canning in B.C. is dated from 1870, when Alexander Loggie and his partners, David Hennessey, Alexander Ewen and

Annieville Cannery

James Wise built the first cannery at Annieville across from New Westminster on the Fraser River. Loggie and Hennessy were from New Brunswick and had some familiarity with canning. Alexander Ewen, by that time, had a retail fish and game enterprise in New Westminster. James Wise was a commercial fisherman who had already worked with Ewen in the fish and game business. James Symes had successfully canned a few dozen cases in two-pound cans on his kitchen stove in 1867, but this experiment did not survive commercially.

Outside the Fraser, the main salmon fisheries were focused on the Skeena and Nass Rivers, in Rivers and Smiths Inlets, on the Queen Charlotte Islands, on the east coast of Vancouver Island north of Seymour Inlet and the mainland inlets opposite, and on the west coast of Vancouver Island. In 1877, the first cannery outside the Fraser River was built at Woodcock's Landing on the Skeena River Slough by Northwest Fishing Co. It would become known as Inverness cannery.

Out of these modest beginnings, a distinctive way of life grew up on the coast of British Columbia that lasted for about 100 years. The coastal cannery way of life no longer exists. It rose with astonishing speed once it started and it ended the same way. Where once there were nearly 100 canneries, bustling, humming, vibrant and living—some for just a few weeks in the year—now there is almost nothing.

The family-owned or operated enterprise characterized the industry in the early years. Ewen Fisheries, J.H. Todd & Sons, Wallace Brothers Fisheries, Gosse-Millerd, R.V. Winch, Cassiar Packing, Canadian Fishing Co. and Nelson Brothers Fisheries were all family firms, notwithstanding some silent partners. Anglo-B.C. Packing Co. was a public company with its nominal head office and most of its shareholders in the U.K., but it was unmistakably the creature of the Bell-Irving family of Vancouver.

B.C. Packers was the only truly publicly owned company and it broke the mould by introducing professional managerial executives. Henry Doyle, its first president in 1902, could probably not be called a professional but William Barker, who succeeded him in 1904, was. And so was H.R. McMillan, who was elected to manage the Company in 1933 when the newly reorganized B.C. Packers Ltd. was suffering the first blows of the Great Depression and of the big salmon pack of 1930. He was succeeded as president in 1946 by John M. Buchanan who held the position until his retirement in 1964. The takeover of the company by George Weston Ltd. had far-reaching effects on the company (and on the B.C. industry), and led to its demise in 1999.

Salmon canning was always the main foundation of the fishing industry in B.C. But most of the other marine resources of the coast came to be utilized as well and other processes were added. Salmon salting and curing actually preceded canning as the most efficacious way to preserve the raw fish. And the very lucrative market in eastern United States and in Europe for mild-cured B.C. spring salmon supported a specialized production that was unexcelled anywhere. Freezing and cold storage was introduced before the end of the 19th century—where a power source was available—and this led to the combination plants and options for the best use of the raw product.

The halibut fishery, which began in earnest around 1880, soon came to rely on the freezing and cold storage plants and was the forerunner in long-distance transportation from the fishing grounds. It developed on its own in the early years, and in fact, one of the major salmon canners, The Canadian Fishing Co., Ltd. was, at first, a halibut company.

Herring and pilchard reduction plants for the manufacture of fish oil and high protein fishmeal also were single purpose in many cases, especially on Vancouver Island's west coast. But in time, the reduction plants became a part of the complex at combination plants.

The salmon populations of the North Pacific Ocean are one of Mother Nature's most wonderful phenomena. They return to the rivers and streams of their birth in North America and Asia and, given a fair chance, reproduce themselves year after year and century after century—a priceless renewable resource. In the eastern North Pacific, salmon have, in the past, inhabited virtually every coastal stream from central California to the Bering Sea. Many of these rivers have lost their salmon populations—from over fishing in some instances, but principally from habitat destruction resulting from mining, forestry, power and flood control dams, pollution from factories and cities, and here and there, from natural phenomena like landslides.

B.C.'s greatest salmon producer was always, and still is, the Fraser River.

And it is one of the main producers in the whole of the North Pacific. It was the birthplace of salmon canning here. The first canneries were built there, followed in short order by the upcoast or outlying plants.

There was money to be made, commensurate with the risks—and there were economic casualties, almost universally so in the Great Depression. But operations which were well located and with good management were consistently profitable. Fortunes were made simply because the operations were closely held—often family owned or by a few partners—so that the profits were distributed over only a few and because the capital investment was modest.

In the early days, the cannery provided the boats and nets and charged a rental for the season. The boats were powered by sails and oars and were towed to the fishing grounds near the cannery by steam tug. The nets were set and pulled by hand. In the main rivers like the Fraser and the Skeena, the linen nets were effective both day and night in the silty waters. But in the clear salt water fishing grounds, the early fishery was primarily a night time operation because the nets were visible to the fish. The dyed linen net was an innovation of the central coast in the 1920s and it was revolutionary in its effects. After the second world war, another revolution took place with the introduction of nylon nets that came from the manufacturer, dyed whatever colour was deemed to be the most effective for the area.

The rental boat system endured until the 1970s, but by then most boats and licences were privately owned by the fishermen themselves. When boat engines were introduced, the canneries, in their own interest, bought and installed them in their boats to be competitive for the supply of salmon—but sail still remained in a few places into the 1950s.

Salmon dominates the industry and the other species and fisheries are ancillary. But there is a halibut fishery and a herring fishery and a groundfish fishery and a shellfish fishery and a dogfish fishery, and there has been a pilchard fishery and even a tuna fishery and a whaling industry.

The fishing industry developed during a period when racial and ethnic differences were front and centre issues in the society of the day. And as the participants in fishing and processing were multi-racial—Native Indians, Chinese, Japanese and a full spectrum of European races including Celts, English, Scandinavians and Slavs—all the racial biases and conflicts manifested themselves in the cannery villages. The anti-Asian bias was the most virulent and it was strongest among the white and Indian fishermen. But it was dealt with surprisingly well (except during some of the early fishermen's strikes) until Canada went to war with Japan in late 1941.

There were some outstanding people in the industry over the years who influenced the way in which it developed and who led the battle to preserve the resources and to perpetuate their economic production. It was difficult to be involved in the fisheries, especially the salmon fishery, without becoming imbued with the conservation ethic. The level of commitment varied and it was probably motivated by the understanding that, treated with respect, the fishery resources would keep on producing *ad infinitum*, and that this was the key to economic returns.

There were always conflicts with other resource users—forestry and mining, for example—whose industrial activities impacted on fish habitat. The fish and power controversy of the 1950s and 1960s was one of the most serious of these conflicts and, in hindsight, was a defining period for public acceptance of the value of the fish resources. And it probably created a lasting realization of the importance of environmental values and their protection. And because the salmon resources were worth protecting, B.C.'s environment today is substantially in better condition than it would otherwise have been.

One of the most enduring and seemingly insoluble conflicts has been the American intercepting fisheries on the southern and northern extremities of our coast. Since the United Nations Law of the Sea Conference, there is now, a general international acceptance of the principle that salmon belong to the nation in whose rivers they spawn. Where intercepting fisheries occur in national waters, they are supposed to have some form of balance. It would be so much simpler if Canadian spawned salmon would come direct from international waters to Canadian waters on their migrations. But some of them don't, and this makes them vulnerable to U.S. fishing gear as they pass through American waters.

From the time that Point Roberts and Anacortes fisheries on Fraser River stocks began in 1896, it took over 30 years for negotiations for joint management and rehabilitation to bear fruit. While the Fraser enjoyed the benefits of the 1934 International Pacific Salmon Fisheries Treaty, interceptions increased in Alaska waters and were never satisfactorily resolved.

Prosecuting a fishery and developing a processing capability in the most remote parts of our very rugged coast, called for exceptional transportation facilities. The steamship fleets were the lifelines for the outlying plants. The development of coastal freight and passenger service was an outstanding feat, given the navigational hazards and the lack of navigational aids. It was regular, reliable and comfortable—even luxurious for first class passengers. Canadian Pacific Navigation Co., Boscowitz Co., Canadian Pacific Railway's B.C. Coastal Service, Union Steamships, Grand Trunk Pacific (CN), Waterhouse and Northland Navigation all provided service over the years and competed or cooperated with each other, depending on the mood of the day.

Wartime development of airports and post-war introduction of scheduled air services, spelled the beginning of the end for marine passenger services. And the closure of the canneries themselves brought an end to the regular freight services.

Radio communications, radio telephone and then micro-wave telephone systems ended the isolation of the outlying plants. But by that time, the cannery village culture was already doomed, as methods of handling and transporting raw fish were improved, enabling processing facilities to be concentrated near urban areas.

But in the meantime, the cannery life flourished and generations of British Columbians spent a good part of their lives in these coastal locations. To some it was heaven. To others it was close to hell. But for most it was something in between—something that was exceptional and special and a life experience that is no longer available. This story is about the outlying plants, the cannery villages which were an integral part of them and some of the people who made them work. All these canneries are gone and the way of life they created, is only history. In most cases, even the physical evidence is gone, that once there was a thriving community bent on the economic harvest of the sea. Modern day rules require that properties which are to be abandoned are to be returned to their original state as if the fact that they were there is a cause for reproach and should be expunged. So this history remains only in the memories of those who were there, and in dull and dusty archives.

Chapter 2

CANNERY VILLAGE—COMPANY TOWN

Of all the books and anthologies written about Canada's Pacific fishing industry, none has dealt in any comprehensive way with the dynamics of life in the upcoast plants and the villages that supported them.

The imperatives of dealing with a highly perishable product mandated the necessity of locating processing facilities close to the predictable routes of the salmon migrations. The realities of competition produced the cluster system of multiple canneries near the mouths of the main producing river systems—the Skeena and Nass, for example—in Rivers and Smiths Inlets, in Johnstone Strait and in the Queen Charlotte Islands. The establishment of the outlying plants began soon after canning started on the Fraser River, with the first cannery on the Skeena River at Inverness in 1877.

As the canneries were established, a community evolved which over a hundred years, rather quickly grew, flourished and then died, with scarcely a trace remaining. Although it was spread from one end of the coast to the other—from Victoria and Saanich in the south, to the Nass River in the north—the salmon industry was a community, with its members surprisingly mobile from plant to plant and company to company.

It was linked by the coastal steamships which provided a highway between its parts for fishermen and shoreworkers alike. The sea was the provider as it is today, but it was also the only road from place to place until the bush plane and the flying boat came into play. Even today, there is no road along the coast of British Columbia between Port Hardy on the northeast coast of Vancouver Island and Cassiar cannery at the mouth of the Skeena River. On the mainland coast, once past Lund, there is no highway connection to the interior and the south except at Bella Coola, Kitimat, Prince Rupert and Stewart.

Upcoast, "The Cannery" meant the actual processing plant, but it also meant the village that was attached to it and which provided the infrastructure that made the fishing operation and the processing operation work.

The first outlying canneries were simple affairs. A site would be chosen for its proximity to the fishing grounds, for a reliable source of fresh water which could be gravity fed to the plant, and for access to deep water with some shelter from the prevailing weather. In not all cases were all these criteria present. Deep water, for example, was always a problem on the Skeena, where the variation from high to low tide is as much as 24 feet. In most cases there, the littoral strip where pilings could be driven was very narrow. So at low tide, the mud flats were exposed and vessels at the dock could be high and dry until the rising tide freed them. Steamships would go dry at the wharves on the slough and they had to time their arrivals and departures, and the length of their stay, by the tides.

The fresh water was essential for canning and a site with an upland lake was invaluable. In some cases, like Butedale and Walker Lake, there would be enough head and volume to produce hydro electricity. But at most of the plants the water source was a dammed stream.

A typical cannery had the following elements:

The wharf or steamship dock: All the raw fish came over the front dock from the fishing vessels, the packers and scows, and all the finished product went out the same way. So these were substantial and roomy structures, built on pilings and accessing deep water. Attached to the wharves would be a series of floats, built on logs and kept in place by dolphin pilings, where the fishermen could tie up. Netracks were built on these floats so that the fishermen could spread their gillnets for mending the mesh and repairing the lines.

A section of the wharf would be devoted to bluestone tanks (large woodstave tanks), in which the gillnets would be treated on the weekend closed times in a copper sulphate solution to remove algae and river silt and to preserve them from the inevitable rotting. This was a necessity for the cotton and linen nets but less so for the nylon web which became available after World War II.

The cannery itself: It was usually long and narrow, two storeys, with acres of hip roof. Open floor space was essential and the typical cannery was built with timbers of extraordinary length and from 12" to 18" dimensions. Of course, the material was near at hand in the old growth forests and sawmills sprang up to supply the lumber.

The netloft: Next to the cannery, this was the most important building. Here the gillnets were selvedged and hung with leadline and corkline. For those canneries which had a seine boat fleet, the seines would be made up in the netloft and stripped and stored again after the season.

The netlofts were cavernous affairs with wonderful smells of cutch and tar and linen and nylon. The floors had to be smooth so as not to snag the web and they were often made of fine hardwood which would be polished to a high sheen as a result of the nets being dragged over them. This made for a great dance floor for the weekend dances which were a feature of many of the canneries.

The boiler house: Steam was essential for cooking salmon and still is. The steam boiler was a key part of the operation. In plants that could not generate hydro power, steam engines drove the machinery.

The early boilers were fired by cordwood and their appetites were voracious. One of the pre-season essentials was to secure an adequate supply of cordwood to feed the boiler and heat the houses. This job was usually contracted to locals. Later, the boilers were fired by bunker fuel, delivered by the oil company vessels and stored in huge tanks ashore. Lighting and power came, in time, to be provided by diesel generators.

The canloft: At first, the cans were made by hand at the cannery from tinplate imported from Britain. They were cut out with shears and the seams hand-soldered. Every cannery had a rusting pile of tinplate trimmings under the tinshop, where the waste would be dropped through a hole in the floor. Some of these remain to this day.

The can-making crew—usually Chinese—would arrive at the cannery well before the fishing season to make the cans for the anticipated pack. Because the process was slow and the integrity of the cans always in doubt, canmaking from the beginning was a candidate for mechanization. A number of the outlying plants had can manufactories and supplied the needs of other plants besides their own.

Anglo-B.C. Packing Co. invested in the Automatic Can Company in Sapperton as early as 1897. This plant could produce many times the number of cans that the hand makers could.

Eventually all cans came to be factory made. The cans were then shipped from Vancouver to the outlying plants with the ends and bodies separated. The bodies were partially collapsed to save shipping space and the cannery would have reform machinery in the canloft that would open up the bodies and attach the end. The cans would then be fed by runways, from the canloft, directly to the canning machinery on the canning floor below. The rattle and clatter of the cans was a trademark of every cannery and along with the rumble of moving belts, the whump of the vacuum machines, the hiss of escaping steam from the retorts, was part of a cacophony of noise unique to the canning of salmon.

The machineshop: Every cannery had to be self-sufficient in regard to repairs to boats and machinery. Each had a blacksmith shop in the early days, and later a machineshop with all the related tools and machinery. Some were quite elaborate as in the multi-purpose plants and provided a service to all comers. In some cases, as in Rivers Inlet, private machine shops served this need as well.

The gas station: Once gasboats were introduced, each cannery had to operate a gas station to fuel the boats. The major oil companies delivered marine fuel by tanker on a regular basis. At the seasonal plants, the gas float was usually operated by a high school or university student.

The store: Each cannery had a retail store for groceries and dry goods. They were sometimes much maligned for price gouging. Such accusations may have been justified in some cases, but the store operation was always a compromise between service to fishermen and the community and avoidance of loss. The store was meant to be a profit centre or at least, not a loss centre, but it often lost money. The problem was the cost of freight—for everything had to come in by ship—especially for perishables. A further problem was the difficulty in hiring competent staff for short seasons. In the multi-purpose plants, the stores were open year round; they served a broader geographic area and did operate profitably.

Each company issued gas coupons and store coupons to its fishermen on credit. The idea was that they should be used at the company's own premises but this wasn't workable and usually one company would accept another's coupons and redeem them from time to time. In Rivers Inlet at Duncanby and Dawson's Landings and at places like Alert Bay, where non-fishing company stores and gas stations operated, the company coupons were accepted as cash. One of the main reasons for the coupon system was that bootleggers only accepted cash, so the credit advanced by the company in this way had to be used for essentials.

On the Skeena River, before the turn of the century, Robert Cunningham issued his own currency—"Cunningham dollars"—which were stamped out of brass or bronze. They became a medium of exchange from Port Essington to Hazelton—no doubt a practice borrowed from the Hudson's Bay Company. Because of shortages of currency in those days, issuance of tokens by merchants and even hotels in remote parts of the province was commonplace.

The office: The office was the nerve centre of the operation. There the Manager would hold forth, along with the bookkeeper and probably some assistant bookkeepers, depending on the size of the enterprise. The accounts were kept in painful detail. Each fisherman would have an account that would record the advances made to him before and during the season and the charges he had incurred.

The fish ledger: The fish ledger held a special significance. It recorded every fish delivered to the company, by every fisherman, by species and weight. It was the ultimate authority on the credits he would have coming at the end of the season.

Over time, a very sophisticated system of catch records developed. Each fisherman was issued an official "fishbook" by the Department of Fisheries and each delivery he made had to be recorded in it. A copy went to the company he fished for and a recap to the Department of Fisheries. The collector or packer which took the catch from the fishermen had also to record the details of each delivery and report the totals to the Department. In this way, the daily catch of any given run was known and recorded. These statistics were the basis for estimating run size and managing escapement.

The office was also the communications centre once radio-telephones were introduced. During the Second World War and immediately after, a trained radio operator had to be employed. But this requirement was discontinued as the equipment became more user-friendly and the phones were handled by the manager and office staff. The radios were a constant background noise in most offices as the common bands were monitored in case the plant was called, and for clues as to what the fleet was doing and what other companies were up to. Staff were adept at hearing the calls that were important to them and ignoring the rest, as they went about their work.

The first aid room was also attached to the office and the bookkeeper was often the First Aidman. It had to meet Worker's Compensation Board standards and it could not be used for any other purposes. It was not unusual, however, that it would be the drinking room for the office staff or visiting dignitaries.

The messhouse: The messhouse was for the cannery crews and office staff living in the bunkhouses. The cook was usually Chinese, but not always, and there would probably be one or more bullcooks or flunkies, depending on the size of the crew. They usually had their quarters in or near the messhouse, rather than in the China House. When Namu was at its peak, the messhouse was a full-blown cafeteria operated by a catering company on contract.

The Manager's house: This would be the prime residence in the establishment—sometimes quite grand, considering the isolation of the sites. It was usually situated on the hill, if there was one (there usually was), with a good view of the cannery, the wharf and the water.

Staff houses: There were usually houses for key staff, especially if they were married. That would include the bookkeepers, netboss, foremen, storekeeper and perhaps key machinemen.

Bunkhouses: There was always at least one, and it housed the single men in the cannery crew, except for the Chinese who lived in the China House, and except for any employees who preferred to live in the Indian or Japanese villages.

Some plants would have a girls' bunkhouse to house the single women—usually high school or university students. They might have their own messhouse and probably a matron to oversee her charges. In one or two canneries, there were separate bunkhouses for single Japanese women. In at least one cannery, there was a separate bunkhouse for the girls from Sointula because there were some concerns among their elders about the morals of the other white girls.

The China House: This was a must for housing the Chinese cannery crew. It was managed by the Chinese foreman and was built to the specifications of the Chinese contractor. It was always a mysterious place and generally off-limits to non-Chinese. The amenities varied, but typically the sleeping arrangements were wooden bunks, three-high, closed in for privacy. There would be a cook and bullcooks who assisted him and did the housekeeping. This was an exacting task because the Chinese were meticulous about cleanliness.

The common room was the dining room and the games room where mah jongg and other gambling games were favourites. Smoking was universal and water-pipes were common. What they smoked in these besides tobacco was seldom discussed by them, but was a matter of constant conjecture by outsiders.

There would always be a pen nearby for the pigs which were fed from the kitchen slops. Usually there would be chickens and possibly ducks. If the climate were congenial, there would be a vegetable garden as well.

The Indian Village: The Indian fishermen and their families were provided with their own housing which, each year, took on the character of a full-fledged community. In many cases, the home village would be virtually deserted during the canning season as the bulk of the population migrated to the canneries. At some canneries, non-Indians were not very welcome in the village. This would not apply to the Manager or to the First Aidman, who would be in constant demand. But just as often, the Indian people struck up strong friendships with whites and visiting back and forth would be commonplace.

The Indian populations were not monolithic and great care had to be taken not to house members of certain tribes close to each other. In canneries with large Indian villages, weekends, when the fishermen were in port could be violent times and sometimes this would spill over to other parts of "town" outside the Village.

The Japanese houses: The Japanese fishermen preferred to live separately from others in the cannery village. They had separate housing, a communal eating area, a communal bath and, in some cases, their own netrack floats. There would be homes for married Japanese as well.

Virtually every establishment on the coast had these elements. The separation of living quarters was, in part, hierarchical, but it was primarily cultural. At the head of the pecking order was the cannery Manager, of course. He was followed by the bookkeeper, the foreman and the netboss, not necessarily in that order. The head bookkeeper was usually second in command by virtue of his involvement with the pack records and fishermen's accounts and his connection with the powers that be at head office (if there was one). But often, the 2-i-c would be the netboss, who arguably was the most important man in the operation from the fishermen's point of view.

The cannery machinemen came next. These were skilled employees who were treated well, primarily because they didn't grow on trees and because the operation couldn't run without them. In the early days, they were laid off in the winter like everyone else, but as the operation became more mechanized and the machinery more complex, the key machinemen became year-round employees. In some companies, they were able to be placed in winter production jobs, but in others, they enjoyed the sweet rewards of just having to be present every day, probably at Head Office in the south.

The next "layer" involved the white seasonal workers. They were mostly young women and men—students—sent up from the south or from Prince Rupert and housed in the bunkhouses. Often white fishermen's families would work in the cannery as well and they would be housed in the white fishermen's houses.

So this set-up is what created the unique cannery way of life. In turn, it was created and made possible by the commercial value of converting a very perishable product into a non-perishable state under the pressure of large volumes in a short time.

The cannery Manager was a very special person. He has been described as cock of the walk, king of the hill, supreme being, mayor of the town, arbitrator, father figure, feared tyrant, respected autocrat. There is no question that he had unique powers. His fief was the company property and his word was law. He represented the company in all its facets. But he did more—he was responsible for the people, who for whatever reason, lived at or visited the cannery village. In the small plants, this was relatively simple but in the large ones, like Namu and Butedale and Port Edward, it was a huge responsibility.

The company was supreme. It was the employer, landlord and storekeeper. And the cannery Manager was the personification of the company. At the same time, he had to exercise his power and authority in a benevolent way or suffer the wrath of those with nothing to lose. Most of the Managers were good at it.

In the days before radio-telephone communication, the Manager was completely in charge of his operation—free from daily influence from head office. He received his instructions before leaving Vancouver or Victoria in the spring and ran his operation as he saw fit through the season. Communications depended on the steamboat or on the Company's own boats. The steamboat method required a delay of at least a week, so dependence on the Manager's ability to make decisions and make do with resources at hand was paramount.

Some of the Managers were larger than life and became household names on the coast—A.E. Moorehouse at Namu, Hans Otteson at Wadhams, Ole Anderson at Good Hope, Bill Trotter at Margaret Bay, Ted Quisenberry at Tallheo, Billy Malcolm at Butedale, Robert Johnson at Inverness, Tom Wallace at Sunnyside, Clare Salter at Carlisle, Jack Dorman at Bones Bay, Henry Doyle at Mill Bay, Harry Robins at Port Edward and Cassiar, Ole Phillipson at North Pacific, and many more.

Entertainment or diversion at the canneries was a problem. In the first place, when the fishing was on and the cannery was running, there wasn't much leisure time. If the run was heavy, the hours would be long and tiring and the favourite leisure activity was sleeping. But there would be times before fishing started and even during the season, when time off was available and often it hung heavy on the crew. Those who liked the outdoors were ideally situated. The wilderness was literally on the doorstep and some of the best sports fishing in the world was in the waters leading to the canneries and in the lakes and streams nearby. Hunting was also available, for deer, moose, bear and birds. The scenery, of course, with the high mountains and deep fjords was incomparable, as it is today.

The main holiday for all the upcoast plants was the 24th of May. The cannery would be almost ready, the main salmon fishing season had not yet started and the weather was usually decent. And the whole crew would climb aboard one of the cannery tenderboats and head for a picnic on the beach. There are so many great beaches on the B.C. coast and most were unknown except to the fishing community. July 1st and even the American holiday, July 4th, were sometimes celebrated, but by then the fishing season would be in full swing and getting away from the plant was difficult.

Some of the plants were connected by trails or boardwalks and a hike through the woods was a common past-time. Carlisle and Claxton were joined this way, Greens and Brunswick, Port Essington and Brown's Mill. But most cannery workers never got past the front dock. The arrival of the weekly steamboat was always a time for excitement and the whole town would turn out to meet the boat—even in the middle of the night. The tuck shop would be opened and a lively business done in magazines, newspapers, candy and pop. Or the stewards would set up shop on the dock to avoid the necessity of having to police the shore people from wandering around the vessel.

Management made an effort to provide recreation opportunities for the employees. It was in management's interest to do so. There were card games and birthday parties. Some plants had recreation rooms or even gyms, where dances and basketball games would be held. In others, the netloft doubled as dance hall for weekend dances. Namu even had a bowling alley and Butedale was famous for its Christmas and New Year's celebrations.

But by and large, as in most isolated places, the main recreation was drinking. And the canneries had more than their share of alcohol abuse and alcoholism. The fact that liquor was not easy to get did not seem to hinder its use and may even have made it more desirable. There were no liquor outlets on the coast prior to prohibition in the 1920s, and after prohibition, the only outlet between Nanaimo and Prince Rupert was at Ocean Falls. Liquor had to be ordered ahead of time and delivered by the steamboat. The Manager would have a small stock and might provide a bottle to a fisherman who could be trusted to use it responsibly. But there was always a bootlegger. Often it would be one of the Chinese crew or an old time employee. Bootlegging had to be discreet, because it could be cause for dismissal. In any case, if the supplier was too well known, he ran the risk of having his supply raided and his own bodily safety compromised.

There were problems—mostly with fishermen in port for the weekend. The Native people had the most difficulty with drinking problems. Parties in the Village had a way of getting out of hand, sometimes with serious consequences. Once started, they were not easily stopped. The people generally policed themselves, but sometimes things would get out of control and long-held resentments would boil over. These might be inter-tribal where old rivalries or feuds would come to the surface. Or they might be the ever-present resentment of the white man's "theft" of Indian lands. It would be the Manager or the police constable, if there was one, who would have to bring order to the situation. And it was here that the personal respect for the Manager was so important.

Controlling the supply of liquor was a never-ending problem. If fishing was good, it was not unusual for fishermen to charter a plane to bring in liquor from Ocean Falls to say, Namu or Rivers Inlet. But home brew or moonshine was also a staple. There is a debate that says that Indians learned how to make alcohol from the white man. But most aboriginal peoples had discovered the process of fermentation and it seems unlikely that the Pacific coast natives had not. In any case, they knew how to make it in the canneries and in most, there was a batch going most of the time.

There is a story of the storekeeper at Margaret Bay—an elderly gentleman who had sold his business in the city and took the seasonal job for one year. He had no experience with the Natives and he came into the office one day in August looking very pleased. He told the Manager how industrious and forward looking the Indian ladies in camp were. They were already getting ready to make their Christmas cakes, because they had just ordered large quantities of candied and dried fruit to be delivered on the next steamboat!

The canneries on the Skeena Slough had a particular problem stemming from the ease of access to Prince Rupert. They sometimes took extreme measures, officials meeting the last bus from Rupert on a Saturday night, and confiscating any liquor destined for the Village.

But drinking problems were not confined to the Indian population by any means. Many a cannery manager or bookkeeper had his problems with strong drink as well. Butedale had an unusual number of recovering alcoholics because the Manager, himself a pillar of Alcoholics Anonymous, made a point of hiring them where their credentials fit the jobs at the plant. For the most part, this was a successful procedure because Billy Malcolm could keep his eye on them, but there were lapses and the Butedale First Aid cupboard contained treatment for DTs.

When the merger of B.C. Fishing and Packing Co. with other companies was being contemplated in 1924, some investigation of the management capabilities of the potential "mergees" was done. In regard to the Gosses, the report stated, "The active management of Gosse Millerd is in the hands of the younger Gosses, but their convivial habits affect their activities and it is reported that recently the Directors have intimated that unless there is speedy improvement in this respect, a change of management will be made." The habits must have improved because Robert Gosse was appointed president and managing director of the new company, B.C. Packers Ltd., when it was formed in 1928, and his brother Richard was named general superintendent.

Chapter 3

THE INFLUENCE OF ETHNIC FACTORS

There were and are a number of ethnic groups in the fishery. The first fishermen were the Native Indians. The Hudson's Bay Company used them to provide salmon for the first commercial operations at Fort Langley, just as they provided the furs. Later, as the fishery became organized on the Fraser and as it spread upcoast, the Indians were the first fishermen in boats provided by the canneries.

Still later came the Norwegians, Scots, Finns, Japanese and Yugoslavs. These groups tended to stick together and often were hostile to each other.

The Finns were from Sointula, the failed commune on Malcolm Island in Johnstone Strait. Every central area cannery had a group of Sointula fishermen and made sure they had a sauna bath to use on weekends.

Baths were a must for Japanese fishermen, too. The Japanese communal bath was integral to keeping that section of the fleet loyal to the company.

The Japanese were primarily gillnet fishermen.

The Yugoslavs were almost exclusively involved in the seine fishery—salmon, herring and pilchards.

The Norwegians and Scots were well represented in all fisheries—gillnet, seine and troll—and were less "tribal" than the others.

Much attention has been given to the treatment of different races in the salmon industry. And it is true that race and nationality figured prominently in the way of life in the canneries. Many of the fishermen were classified by ethnic groups and certainly race was significant in cannery divisions and in the accommodation provided for the plant workers. There was a sort of social stratification, but because of the seasonal nature of the business and the hectic pace of having to deal with huge quantities of a highly perishable product in a short time, social life figured far behind work. There wasn't much time for socializing.

To understand the divisions, it is important to remember the context of the times. When British Columbia became a Crown colony in 1858, "British" was a hugely relevant part of the name. The territory had been the exclusive domain of the HBC (aboriginal occupation notwithstanding), until the Fraser River and Cariboo gold rushes created a temporary population imbalance in favour of Americans and even Chinese. The Company was British and it was an extension of the British Empire and British imperialism. And of course, white British men were ethnocentric, and considered themselves supreme and most other races inferior, especially Asians and indigenous Indians. As late as confederation with Canada in 1871, even Canadians were not accepted as equal beings, whether of French or British ancestry.

It had taken only about 60 years from Captain Cook for the British to establish themselves as the dominant culture. But in the beginning they had been dependent on the Native Indians, even for sustenance as in the case of the early days at Fort Langley.

In the 1880s, before the completion of the Canadian Pacific Railway (CPR), the population of British Columbia was about 20,000 whites, 25,000 Natives and 4,000 Chinese. By the turn of the century there were still only 180,000 souls in the whole of the province.

The early cannery owners carried their racial biases without even questioning them. Added to that was the desire, even the insistence, of the main racial groups to be treated as separate units and to be segregated in housing.

For example, the Indians, who were typically the first fishermen involved, would be drawn to a cannery in their neighbourhood. They were a key part both of the fishing fleet and the cannery crew. The cannery manager usually would contract with a head man in the village for the fishermen he needed. Part of the deal would be that the cannery provided accommodation for the fishermen and their families and work in the plant for wives and, very often, children. So each cannery would have its Indian village and each season the Indians would move in from their home villages, complete with goods and chattels and dogs and kids. They considered this their place and did not tolerate a lot of influence from outsiders, including management.

There was racial discrimination in the plants, aimed primarily at the Indians and to some extent, at the Japanese. It was endemic in the society as a whole and was not a function only of cannery life. In fact, it might be said that over the years, the bringing together of the races in the canneries helped to mitigate the superior/inferior feelings that so many accepted as natural. British Columbians at the turn of the century, and for many years after, were more racially biased than politically correct. Indeed, in those years, the bias was politically acceptable.

The salmon canneries were generally the first involvement the coastal Indians had with the white man's industrial activities. In the fur trade, they were free agents and traded their furs to the fur trader. But in the canneries they were employees and for the first time were introduced to hours of work and standards of production. It was a huge cultural adjustment to which they adapted surprisingly well. The whites often treated them as children and they were naïve in the ways of the Europeans' world. But they accepted that as well.

As a group they had a reputation of being lazy and unconcerned with the white man's preoccupation with work schedules. The term "Indian time", similar to the "manana" concept of the Mexicans, was a given. And it was a great frustration for management when the Indians might decide that a funeral back at the home village during the canning season was more important than getting the fish into cans.

But these stereotypes were not the norm. Many were considered "good Indians", which meant they were more like the white man and had recognizable ambitions and were conscientious about what they did. The Indian women in the canneries were essential as fillers and lineworkers and could endure long hours without complaint. They held these jobs because they were good at them, because they were dependable and because they would train each other—not because it was inferior work. The same held true for network, where they became skilled hangers and menders.

The Indians came from their villages as families. The cannery was obliged to provide seasonal "villages" for them as part of the process of securing labour and fishermen. All the canneries did it; without this housing they wouldn't have the necessary help.

Chinese men were the backbone of the cannery labour force. They were known to be good workers who could be depended on for the long and uncertain hours of canning salmon. Each cannery had its Chinese crew. In its early days, B.C. often had a shortage of labourers and the Chinese represented a usually reliable, usually trouble-free pool. The first Chinese came with the gold rush from California. Then railway builder Andrew Onderdonk had received permission to bring Celestials over from China as labourers for the construction of the CPR through the Fraser and Thompson canyons. When the railway construction was finished, many of these men became the labour force for the canneries and lumber mills.

Because of language and cultural imperatives, the Chinese workers were provided through a middleman or contractor and were paid by him—a system that began in the late 1880s and continued until after World War II. The contractor would be paid a fixed price per case of product so that the cannery operator would know in advance his direct labour costs and would not have the trouble of maintaining a crew of individuals. Very often the Chinese contractor handled the payroll for non-Chinese labour as well, but usually was responsible for hiring only the Chinese. Part of this contract was separate accommodation for the Chinese men. So each cannery had its China House where the Chinese crew slept, ate and spent their leisure time. They had very little interaction with the other residents and there was always an air of mystery and even fear about what went on in the China House. There is little doubt that some of these men were newly immigrated, some illegally, and indentured to the contractor.

The Chinese were so much an integral part of cannery labour that when a mechanical butchering machine was invented, to do the work of the hand-butchers, it was named officially, the "Iron Chink". Chink was the derogatory term for Chinese, in general use in the bigoted white society both in the U.S. and Canada. Curiously, it was not often used in reference to Chinese in the B.C. canneries. You can speak to pioneers of the time and search what personal records exist, and seldom hear or see the term. The preferred terms were Chinese or Chinamen or Celestials.

One of the features of the China House in every plant was the pigs. Each year, the Chinese crew would go to the canneries before the fishing season in the area started, to prepare the cannery for processing. In the earliest days they would actually make, by hand, the cans for the season's production. So the Chinese crew were there early. They would travel by steamship from Vancouver, always in steerage class. And they would have a few adult pigs with them and probably a bunch of little ones. The adults would be slaughtered first and the young ones raised on the slops from the kitchen. The off-loading of the pigs at the cannery was always an exciting time. It was not unusual for them to get loose and the owners would chase them all over the dock and boardwalks. It is said that some of the wags at the cannery or from the steamboat crew would let them loose on purpose just for the entertainment. Sunday was slaughter day and the squeal of pigs was commonplace on that day of leisure.

The Chinese cook in the whitemen's messhouse was also a fixture of most canneries. He would have his own quarters in or next to the messhouse and, in most instances, would spend his leisure time with his compatriots in the China House. But oddly, in some cases, he did not associate with the plant workers—a case of *intra*-racial bias.

The ethnic Japanese also occupied a separate part of the cannery village.

In most plants that had Japanese fishermen—and most did—they themselves wanted to be separate from the Indian and white fishermen. Typically they would have their own floats and netracks and probably the better housing because they maintained their temporary homes in top condition.

The Japanese fishermen took part, almost exclusively, in the gillnet and troll fisheries. As a group they were known for their industriousness, cleanliness and attention to quality. As in any group, these characteristics did not always hold, but on average, they did.

Their wives and daughters worked in the cannery. They shared the hand-filling with the Indian women and worked on the patching lines and in the canloft and packing rooms. At some plants, Japanese girls would be hired in Vancouver to work in the plant and they would be housed in a separate bunkhouse, with a cook/matron paid by the company. The thinking was that they preferred food different from the white girls.

Anti-Asian bias was general and strong in the early part of the 20th century. Many whites took pride in it. For example, the owners of the Nanaimo Fish and Bait Company in 1912 "hold strong views on the question of Oriental labour, and although the fishing industry is one in which Japanese are almost exclusively employed, the employees of the Nanaimo Fish and Bait Company Ltd. are all white men."

Paradoxically, many of the herring salteries, even in Nanaimo, came to be owned and operated by Japanese, who employed white fishermen to man the fishing boats.

Other sources also hint at the notion that the Japanese were becoming dominant in the fisheries. In 1912, the Chief Inspector of Fisheries for the Department of Marine and Fisheries was writing to Henry Doyle about "boat rating" in District #2, the far-flung north coast fishing area. "At the moment, the actual fishing operations are to a very large extent in the hands of a foreign element and which, I think you will agree, is a condition of affairs that should not be encouraged and that any changes leading up to additional interest in this industry by white fishermen are most desirable and necessary in the general development of the Province."

In his biography of Mayor Gerry McGeer of Vancouver, David R. Williams writes in reference to the 1935 federal election campaign, "The B.C. Liberal party took out a full-page newspaper advertisement, in which the most prominent heading was "50,000 Orientals in B.C. ...." After noting that the CCF party urged that they be given suffrage, the advertisement declared in bold type: "A vote for any CCF candidate is a vote to give the Chinamen and the Japanese the same voting right you have. A vote for a Liberal candidate is a vote against Oriental enfranchisement." It seems astonishing now that as recently as 1935, British subjects of Chinese or Japanese origin should be denied the franchise, but legislative discrimination against Orientals in that area and others (for example, the prohibition against renting foreshore leases from the Crown) continued for some years thereafter.

This kind of xenophobia was not shared by the cannery operators; at least not insofar as the supply of cannery labour was concerned. H.O. Bell-Irving records a meeting with the Chinese ambassador in 1896, when Bell-Irving was President of the Vancouver Board of Trade. He told the ambassador that there were 12,000 Chinese in B.C. and only 1,500 to 2,000 "Japs" and that China should have a consulate in Vancouver. In his journal, Bell-Irving records a conversation which gives a revealing insight into one side of that very pressing issue: "He (Li Hung Chang) said we had a large and undeveloped country—they had a surplus population—we should be of mutual benefit to one another. I said the shiftless would always agitate against Chinese labour, but those who had the best interests of the country at heart thought it would be undesirable to impose any further restrictions on Chinese. That the present Dominion government was in favour of free trade and no action toward further restrictions was to be feared from them. That this new country wanted capital and labour and judicious application of both. He said we should use our influence against this anti-Chinese agitation. I said, when it became a live question, we should be prepared to act.

"I said I could testify to the very satisfactory nature of business relations with the countrymen of his Excellency."

H.O. Bell-Irving was one of the first to recognize the superior abilities of Japanese fishermen. In 1893, he met with the Japanese consul, a Mr. Kito, and, according to his journal, "asked him where I could lay my hands on a number of men at short notice. Kito said he could furnish 130 fishermen, 3 days notice and 200 more, a little longer notice." Apparently, Bell-Irving was not concerned about the "yellow peril" fear which was already gripping the local population, including white fishermen. Japanese fishermen began arriving in B.C. in numbers, shortly after.

Some insight into the relationship of the Chinese contractor can also be gleaned from Bell-Irving's records. In 1895, the first season for his Good Hope cannery in Rivers Inlet, he was complaining about the Chinese foreman: "Good Hope wants another foreman for the Chinese crew—this one has no authority." The next year, he was considering an application from a contractor to supply the labour for one of the Anglo-B.C. plants: "Has never done any cannery work but *controls plenty of experienced cannery hands and foremen.*"

The expulsion of the Japanese from the B.C. coast after Pearl Harbour had a profound effect on the salmon canning industry. Few would argue that the seizure and subsequent disposal of their assets, and especially fishboats and other vessels, was justified or just. But there is still divided opinion on the rightness of their transport from the coast and internment.

Japanese immigrants began to arrive in B.C. in numbers in 1893 or 1894. They quickly established themselves as capable and industrious fishermen. They also aroused the resentment of both Native Indian and white fishermen who saw their growing numbers as a threat to their livelihood. In 1907 alone, 4,000 Japanese entered British Columbia. Over the next few decades this resentment grew and often resulted in personal violence and damage to the Japanese fishermen's boats and gear. Even the fishermen's union was opposed to them.

The Japanese fishermen were recruited by Japanese "bosses". In 1904, they were petitioning the Fraser River Canners Association for a commission on the supply of fishermen. They argued that "It is over 10 years since we Japanese first came to the banks of the Fraser River," that "others were called back to Japan to serve in the Army," and that they "have been gathering men for the different canning companies," and that "these men (who) are entirely strangers to us."

Apparently, at that time, fishermen did not need to be citizens. In 1922, Henry Doyle notes that the "Japanese had taken over the Fraser River fishery."

Chinese immigrants were charged a head tax by the federal government from 1885 to 1923 and this effectively limited the numbers entering Canada. In 1923, the Canadian government enacted the Chinese Exclusion Act, which prohibited further immigration of Chinese (with some exceptions for close family members). At the same time, the numbers of Japanese entering B.C. grew. In response to the pressures from various sectors of the B.C. community, Ottawa made an agreement with the Japanese government to limit the number of new entrants to 400 per year. That same year, the government made a 40 percent reduction in "oriental licences" for fishing.

The tensions continued through the Great Depression and were exacerbated by the conditions that developed from it. During the 1930s there were public accusations that Japanese military officers were living on the coast as fishermen. This prompted a policy debate in government which led to intelligence officers and the Royal Canadian Mounted Police putting a watch on residents of Japanese background.

One veteran of the fishing industry whose father was fishery officer at Tofino recalls, as a boy in the 1930s, "The RCMP used to come into Tofino, always late at night, 10 o'clock or later, and come and get my father up and out of bed, and then they would go around to each and every Japanese house and check their credentials. Once they picked up a chap who, I think, was a

Lieutenant Commander in the Japanese Naval Reserve. He was a fisherman out of Tofino. What happened after that, I don't know. It was things like this that led to the feeling that there may have been some collusion along the road."

Another remembers, "Before Pearl Harbour, some of these Japanese on the coast were running around in Japanese army uniforms in Rivers Inlet. They had Japanese army hats. And there was a guy at Goose Bay—he was a Japanese leader—who sent his family back to Japan a month before Pearl Harbour and he disappeared about a week before Pearl Harbour.

"I know they were measuring places. I had a good friend there (in Rivers Inlet). He was born here, a Canadian, his father was born here, a Canadian and his father, my friend's grandfather was also a Canadian. So there were three generations of Canadians. And when this stuff was going on, he showed up with a uniform and cap on. I talked to him and he was almost belligerent. We were no longer friends and Canada meant nothing to him."

At the same time, teenage boys from Japanese families in the Lower Mainland were leaving high school to go to Japan to train in the Japanese airforce.

Jessie Graham at Duncanby Landing in Rivers Inlet tells the story about how she was running the store, "And people would come in—they didn't do like you do now and pick things up themselves. They would say, 'Give me a loaf of bread, etc.,' and we'd go and get it for them. One day these Japanese men came in and one jumped up on the counter and over on the other side and got something. I said 'You don't need to do that, just tell me what you want and I'll get it for you.' And this fellow made some remarks and he said, 'Well, we'll be taking the place over pretty soon anyway.'"

Jessie recalled that the Japanese fishermen "came in and measured everything at Duncanby. They measured the depth, probably to see what ships they could get in there and they measured the fuel tanks and everything."

Bones Bay Cannery had a fishpacker that they chartered each year from the Cowichan salt herring company, owned and operated by Japanese. When the cannery manager and his family went for an outing, they usually used this vessel. The boys on the crew were favourites of the family. But in the summer of 1941, their whole attitude toward the family changed and they said to Mrs. Dorman, "You boss lady this year but we be boss next year."

And the Dorman family recalls, "The Japanese boats were built in a different fashion. They were all shallow draft, very beamy, they had huge holds, they carried 200 gallons of diesel fuel and 500 gallons of water. The boats they had prior to that, that they used to strap together to travel to Rivers Inlet or Knights Inlet, were much smaller. All of a sudden, they went to these wide boats."

So there were strange things taking place with all the rumours that such things generate, and an undercurrent of suspicion, all against the background of Japanese aggression in China and Korea in the 1930s. This grew to near panic after Pearl Harbour in December 1941, and the lightning thrust of Japanese armies through Hong Kong, Malaya, Singapore and the Philippines. The occupation of some of the Aleutian Islands, the attempted shelling of the Estevan Lighthouse and the sinking of the Fort Camosun at the entrance to Juan de Fuca Strait, brought the Pacific war to the front door of B.C. and Canada.

Air Raid Precaution (ARP) teams were formed in every community, blackouts were the order of the day (or rather the night), and all able-bodies, including children, were trained in putting out fires because of the expected potential for incendiary bombs from aircraft and from balloons carried on the jetstream (although that name was not yet in general use). Every community was equipped with air raid sirens and drills were practised regularly. Training took place for militia and teenagers for guerilla fighting in the mountains and hills in case of invasion. The Fishermen's Navy (RCNFR) was mobilized to patrol the 7,000 miles of B.C. coastal waters. Coastal steamers were armed with guns and required to report any unusual activity on their runs.

So the expulsion of the Japanese was part of a much greater preparedness strategy that had to be organized and carried out in a very short time. The first evacuation was of male "enemy aliens" from "sensitive areas" and began as early as January 14, 1942. This included Germans and Italians who were not Canadian, and some 1,700 Japanese men who were sent to Alberta to road construction camps. On February 24, 1942, the order was given to remove *all persons* of Japanese ancestry from a 100-mile coastal strip and from the Trail area (the smelter being considered of strategic importance). Most were not allowed to return until 1949. Many did, and resumed their place in the fishing industry in what in time became much more tolerant conditions.

During the early fishermen's strikes, Japanese fishermen were often independently minded and less likely than their white counterparts to join in collective action. This made them targets for intimidation—damage to gear, rifle shots at the boats, and even physical beatings.

After World War II, in 1947, the 1923 Chinese Exclusion Act was repealed and Canadian citizenship and enfranchisement was granted to all, regardless of race. Many of the Japanese fishermen returned to the coast (many did not), and to the fishing industry. They were welcomed by the canneries and eventually by the fishermen's organizations as well.

The racial segregation at the canneries continued, partly because the races themselves insisted on it, and partly because it had become an institutionalized feature of the cannery village. With the closure of the upcoast plants, this anachronism has disappeared and racial factors no longer play a significant role in the industry.

Chapter 4

THE OUTLYING PLANTS

The upcoast fisheries in total were as important as those of the Fraser River. This chapter identifies the many canneries and plants that were located outside the Fraser River and Burrard Inlet. At one time, around the turn of the century, there were 51 canneries operating on the Fraser and in Burrard Inlet. Between 1877 and 1987, a total of 122 canneries were built in the out-lying areas. It was in these plants that the unique cannery culture, arose, thrived and died, all in that span of about 110 years. They, and the people who lived their lives in them, responding to the seasons and the generosity or stinginess of nature, are part of this province's history.

THE SKEENA RIVER
The Skeena is the second most important salmon river in B.C. It is famous for the quality of its sockeye, which is second to none in the world. Its principal source is Babine Lake, the spawning area and nursery for most of the Skeena sockeye. It is supported by its main tributary, the Bulkley River. Inverness cannery was the first to be built on the Skeena River. It opened in 1877. The canneries were mostly located within the tidal estuary of the river. By 1901, when the B.C. Packers Association was being organized, 11 canneries were operating: North Pacific, British American, Cunningham, Standard, Aberdeen, Herman's, Carlisle, Inverness, Balmoral, Ladysmith and Claxton.

The whole area had been named Port Essington by Captain Vancouver in 1793. And that was the name given by Robert Cunningham to the village he established at the confluence of the Skeena and Ecstall rivers in 1872. Port Essington became the main town on the north coast and was the centre of the fishing industry for many years. There were no fewer than three canneries built within the townsite itself and many others within sight of it. Port Essington was the supply centre and the cultural centre for the north coast and for the inland settlements as well, until the Grand Trunk Pacific Railway (GTP) established Prince Rupert in 1906 (incorporated in 1910), and linked it with the British Columbia interior and the east with the completion of the railway in 1914. (It is worth noting that the GTP had considered Quatsino Sound on Vancouver Island as their western terminus before Kaien Island was chosen. How different would have been the development of the two areas, had this been the case.)

Each year, the missionaries at Port Simpson followed their charges to the Skeena for the fishing season and established a summer hospital at Port Essington, which operated each season until Prince Rupert's hospital opened in 1910. Port Essington's last cannery closed in 1936, but the town continued its long decline until its old enemy, fire, dealt the final blow in 1965.

The first processors were interested primarily in the large redspring salmon that were native to the Skeena system. Early salteries for this species led to canning of redsprings. But very soon, the abundant and prime Skeena sockeye took over. In time, the cannery operations were concentrated on the Inverness Slough on the mainline of the GTP and in Prince Rupert itself. The south shore canneries were closed, one by one. Even so, Carlisle survived until 1950. Today, there are no operating canneries on the river and all the canning is done in Prince Rupert.

Transportation was not the only deciding factor in this movement. The availability of a dependable labour force living at home was a key factor. The out of town canneries had all been required to supply and maintain accommodation for their employees at the plant—an ever-increasing cost of doing business. As government imposed higher and higher standards for this accommodation, the increased costs could not be ignored.

Aberdeen: also known as the Windsor cannery was built by Robert Draney in **1878** for the Windsor Canning Co., Ltd., of London, England. In 1889, it was sold to B.C. Canning Co. It was the second Skeena cannery and was located on the north bank of the Skeena, opposite Port Essington. In 1895, it was destroyed by fire and rebuilt that year. It burned down again in 1902 and was not rebuilt. The company replaced it in 1903 with a new cannery on Smith Island called the Oceanic. Aberdeen had a telegraph office which served much of the river, including Port Essington.

Alexandria: was built in **1904** by the Alexandria Canning Co. It was located at the junction of the Ecstall and Skeena Rivers, opposite Port Essington. It was named for a daughter of Alexander Ewen, who must have had an interest in the company. In 1906, it was bought by Kelly and Burnett, in 1908 by George Cripps. In 1909, ownership passed to Grenville Packing Co., and later the same year to Clarence Marpole. Still later the same year, he sold to Kelly, Marpole Canning Co. They sold in 1910 to B.C. Packers Association. In 1909, it became known as Alexandra cannery, no doubt in honour of Queen Alexandra. It ceased canning in 1915 and was abandoned in 1936.

Babcock Fisheries: In **1950**, William Babcock bought a small fresh fish operation on the Prince Rupert waterfront from Bacon Fisheries (Jim Bacon), and added a cold storage and a small cannery. Babcock sold the plant to N.B. Cook in 1972. They were in receivership in 1974 and the next year, Bingham Fisheries Ltd. bought the plant. In 1976, it was sold to Queen Charlotte Fisheries Ltd., and in 1977 J.S. McMillan Fisheries Ltd. became the owners. They expanded the plant in 1982. In 1993, J.S. McMillan acquired the Prince Rupert Fishermen's Co-op plant and closed the former Babcock facility.

Balmoral: built in **1886** by Messrs. H.C. Beeton, J.H. Turner, R.S. Byrnes and M. Cuthburt, who also owned Inverness cannery. Balmoral was located next to the Alexandra site on the opposite bank of the Ecstall from Port Essington. It was sold to B.C. Packers Association in 1902. A cold storage was added around 1910 and mild cure operations were in place. In 1921, B.C. Fishing & Packing Co. acquired the plant and it became part of the B.C. Packers Ltd. organization in 1928. It was closed in 1934 and dismantled in 1936.

British-American: was built in **1883** by the British American Packing Company (Gus Holmes) at Port Essington. It was also known as the Boston cannery, but was usually referred to as the B.A. Cannery. This was one of the main acquisitions of the Anglo-B.C. Packing Company amalgamation when it was formed by H.O. Bell-Irving in 1890. It was destroyed by fire in 1923. The company did not rebuild, but instead, bought the Skeena River Commercial cannery from R.V. Winch and Company, which they renamed the British American. It operated until 1936.

Carlisle: was built by John Carthew in **1895**. The first equipment came from Price's cannery in Gardner Inlet, which he had bought in 1894. In 1896, he sold to the Carlisle Canning & Packing Company (Okel and Morris of Victoria). Located on the south bank of the River, downstream from Port Essington, it was sold in 1906 to Dawson and Buttimer who changed their name to Kildala Packing Company the same year. The plant included can-making equipment which supplied both Kildala and Manitou canneries with cans. In 1925, it was purchased by The Canadian Fishing Company Ltd., who operated it continuously until 1950 when Oceanside cannery was built in Prince Rupert.

Cassiar: built in **1903** by the Cassiar Packing Co., Ltd. on the Skeena River slough. The principals were Messrs. D.M. Moore, Cy Peck, Alfred Wallace, G. Ball, Geo. Morrow, O. Brown, Henry Doyle and J.S. Scott. Control was bought in 1910 by John Macmillan, son-in-law of Alexander Ewen and father of Ewen Macmillan, who managed the plant for many years. Ownership remained in

The Outlying Plants 33

Balmoral

Carlisle

Cassiar

the Macmillan family as long as the plant operated and until it was sold to Ocean Fisheries Ltd. in 1983. In 1973 a minority share in the company was sold to Marubeni Company of Japan.

Claxton: was built in **1892** by Royal Canadian Packing Co., owned by Messrs. Claxton, Dalby, Carthew and Robertson. It was located on the south bank of the river, downstream from Carlisle. The site also included a sawmill. In 1898, it was purchased by Victoria Canning Co. In 1900, it was purchased by John Wallace and in 1901, by Wallace Bros. Packing Co., which had been formed by John Wallace and his brother Peter. A cold storage plant was added in 1900. Wallace Fisheries Ltd. was incorporated in December 1910 by A.D. McRae and bought Claxton from Peter Wallace, who remained president of the new company. (The brothers had had a falling out and John Wallace left the organization and in 1905 built Arrandale, and in 1911, Butedale on his own.) Claxton came into the B.C. Fishing & Packing Co. ownership in 1926 in the merger with Wallace Fisheries Ltd., and to B.C. Packers Ltd. in 1928. The cold storage was destroyed by fire in 1934 and was not rebuilt. The cannery was closed in 1945 and was used as a seine loft until 1949. In 1950, it was dismantled.

Cunningham's: built by Robert Cunningham at Port Essington in **1883**. He had established the village when he opened a trading post there in 1872. A cold storage plant was added in1892. Also known as the Skeena Cannery, it was part of the B.C. Packers Association amalgamation in 1902. It was closed by them in 1928 at the time of the reorganization, which became B.C. Packers Ltd. It was abandoned in 1937.

Claxton

Dominion: was built in **1906** at the top of Smith Island by Malcolm, Cannon and Company. In 1909 it was purchased by B.C. Packers Association. The last year of canning was 1927, and B.C. Packers Ltd. closed it in 1928.

Haysport: a cold storage was built here in 1912, during the construction of the Grand Trunk Pacific Railway, by Maritime Fisheries Ltd., Messrs. Sir Thomas Lipton, C.W. Milne, D. Sandison, and A.Weir. It was closed before the cannery was built in **1919** by the same company who also owned a cannery at Alliford Bay on the Queen Charlotte Islands. Haysport was sold to Canadian Fishing Co., Ltd. in1929. It was dismantled in 1938 after the fishing boundary was moved downstream, leaving the cannery too far upriver from the fishing grounds.

Inverness: built in **1877** at Woodcock's Landing, on what came to be called Inverness Slough, by Northwest Fishing (or Commercial) Company out of San Francisco and Victoria. At first it canned only redspring salmon, but in 1879 it began canning sockeye. In 1880 it was acquired by Turner, Beeton & Co. of Victoria. This was the first cannery built on the Skeena, just seven years after the first plant on the Fraser. In 1893, it was destroyed by fire and was rebuilt that year. J.H. Todd and Sons Ltd. purchased the plant from Turner, Beeton & Co. in 1901. In early 1920, the plant was again destroyed by fire and it was rebuilt in time to can that summer. In 1943, the netloft burned to the ground and was rebuilt for the next season. The cannery was closed in 1950. It operated as a camp and was acquired by B.C. Packers and Canadian Fishing Co. jointly in 1954. They closed it the following year. In 1973, another fire took the cannery and its buildings. It was not rebuilt.

Ladysmith: was built in **1901** by John Turnbull on a small island at the mouth of the Ecstall River, adjacent to Port Essington (also known as Village Island). In 1904, it was taken over by Ladysmith Canning Co. (Peter Herman), who operated it until 1906, after which it was closed.

Metlakatla: was built by Reverend William Duncan and his flock in **1882** at the Metlakatla village, outside what is now Prince Rupert harbour. It operated until 1901, when fire destroyed many of the main buildings of the village. Duncan, after a dispute with the church powers-that-be, had moved in 1887, with most of his flock, to Annette Island in Alaska, where he established New Metlakatla.

North Pacific: was opened in **1889** by North Pacific Canning Company Ltd. on the Inverness Slough. The principals were Messrs. A.R. Johnston, J.E. Jinkins, J.A. Carthew, and A.G. McCandless. It was purchased by Anglo-B.C. Packing Company when it was formed in 1890, and was operated by that company continuously until 1968. A cold storage plant was added in 1910, and in 1917 Anglo-B.C. expanded the cannery and established a can making

North Pacific

plant there which operated until 1937. It supplied cans to many other plants on the Nass and Skeena and in Rivers and Knights Inlets. A reduction plant was built in 1955. In 1969, North Pacific came into the possession of the Canadian Fishing Company, who operated it for the 1972 season, following the destruction by fire of their Oceanside cannery in Prince Rupert. When B.C. Packers took over the northern assets of Canfisco in 1980, they became the owners of North Pacific. They closed it in 1981. The plant has been preserved as an historical site and museum by the Port Edward Historical Society.

Oceanic: built by B.C. Canning Co. in **1903** to replace the Aberdeen cannery which had been destroyed by fire in 1902. B.C. Fishing & Packing Co. purchased it in 1924. In 1929, B.C. Packers Ltd. closed the operation. In 1932, they sold the plant to Ocean Canneries Ltd. They operated it until it burned in 1934. In 1935, they sold the property to Canfisco, who operated it as a camp until 1950.

Oceanside: built in **1950** and opened in 1951 by The Canadian Fishing Company. This modern cannery, located on the Prince Rupert Ocean dock, replaced Carlisle and Butedale canneries. The first cannery had been built there in 1940 by Nelson Brothers Fisheries Ltd., who operated it for two seasons before being dispossessed by the U.S. Army in 1942. Nelson Brothers built a new cannery at Port Edward and the U.S. Army used the whole of the dock for warehouses and transshipping to Alaska. The U.S. interests relinquished it after the war. In 1972, a disastrous fire destroyed Oceanside and it was rebuilt at a new site in Prince Rupert harbour. It was also to replace the company's Atlin Fisheries and Northern Fishermen's Cold Storage plants at Cow Bay. When B.C. Packers acquired the northern assets of Canfisco in 1980, this plant was included. The two companies used it jointly until 1999, when a rejuvenated Canfisco acquired the assets of B.C. Packers.

Oceanic

Oceanside fire

Porcher Island

Porcher Island: built in **1929** by Chatham Sound Packing Co., owned by Brand & Co. of England. It was located in Humpback Bay on Porcher Island, near the mouth of the Skeena. It was a victim of the big canned salmon pack of 1930, and the market problems of the Depression. In 1933, Canfisco leased the plant but didn't operate it. In 1934, they bought it and used it thereafter as a gillnet camp. After the closure of Carlisle in 1950, Porcher became the company's principal gillnet base for the northern area. In 1969, this role was transferred to North Pacific when the Company acquired the northern assets of Anglo-B.C. Packing Co.

Port Edward: built in **1913** by Port Edward Fisheries Ltd., but was not opened until 1918. It was located on the Port Edward townsite, which had been planned as an industrial park by the Grand Trunk Pacific Railway. In 1918, the cannery was acquired by Northern B.C. Fisheries Ltd., an amalgamation of the R.V. Winch and Henry Doyle properties. In 1924, it was transferred to Queen Charlotte Fisheries Ltd. (also R.V. Winch). As a result of the spoilage of most of the Namu pack of 1923, Northern B.C. Fisheries, which also owned Namu, went broke and in 1925, Skeena River Packing Company, a subsidiary of Pacific American Fisheries of Bellingham, bought Port Edward cannery. In 1930, B.C. Packers Ltd. traded its George & Baker Salmon Canning Co. cannery at Point Roberts, Washington, for the Port Edward cannery which still belonged to Skeena River Packing Co. It was closed in 1931 and remained idle until a reduction plant was installed in 1937. The reduction plant processed the fish offal from all the Skeena River canners who had been required by the Department of Fisheries to cease disposing of their waste in the river. In 1938,

Port Edward—first cannery

it was expanded for herring reduction. In **1942,** Nelson Brothers Fisheries, displaced from the Ocean Dock in Prince Rupert by the U.S. Army, built their big cannery at Port Edward. They opened in 1943 and operated it until 1981, when the parent company, B.C. Packers Ltd., moved their operations to the new Oceanside cannery. In 1947, the B.C. Packers reduction plant was sold to Nelson Brothers Fisheries.

Prince Rupert Fishermen's Cooperative: The Co-op was formed in 1931 and operated for many years at their Fairview plant in Prince Rupert, but principally as a fresh and frozen operation. Their canned product was custom canned for them, mostly by Cassiar cannery. In **1962,** they added a small cannery to their plant. The complex was acquired by J.S. McMillan Fisheries when the Co-op entered bankruptcy in 1993.

Royal Fisheries: was primarily a fresh and frozen plant, established on the Prince Rupert waterfront by Dr. Arthur Gallaugher. He installed a small cannery in **1959** and canned salmon that year and the next. He operated the plant until 1962. It was subsequently acquired by Ocean Fisheries who operate it as a fresh and frozen facility.

Seal Cove: opened in **1926** in Prince Rupert harbour as a clam cannery by Somerville Canning Company (Francis Millerd). In 1927 it passed to Millerd Packing Co., who intended to can salmon as well. Francis Millerd had a provincial salmon canning licence, but not a federal one, and the federal government closed him down. This led to the famous Somerville or Millerd case that was taken through all the courts to the Privy Council in London, which determined that the federal parliament did not have jurisdiction to license salmon canneries. In 1943, Francis Millerd & Co. again opened the Seal Cove cannery and B.C. Packers canned there in 1952. It was closed after the 1953 season.

Skeena River Commercial: built about **1898** at Port Essington, as the Anglo-Alliance cannery, by Peter Herman. After he drowned in 1906, his financial backers seized his properties for non-payment on mortgages and put the cannery up for sale. It was bought by Henry Doyle as Skeena River Commercial Company, which renamed the cannery. The property included a store and hotel. R.V. Winch was also involved financially and in 1916, he and Doyle formed Northern B.C. Fisheries Ltd. Skeena River Commercial was taken over by the new company who operated it until 1923. Anglo-B.C. Packing Co. leased it and then bought it to replace the British American cannery which had been destroyed by fire. They renamed it British American and operated it until 1936, after which they concentrated all their operations at North Pacific.

Standard: built in **1890** by John Carthew for Messrs. R.P. Rithet, J.A. Laidlaw and John Irving (son of William Irving, founder of Canadian Pacific Navigation Co.). Located on the mainland six miles south of Claxton, opposite Kennedy Island. In 1892, it was sold to Victoria Canning Co., of which Rithet, Laidlaw and Thomas Ladner were the principals. It was acquired by B.C. Packers Association in 1902, along with Victoria Canning Company's other plants. It ceased canning in 1904. In 1914 it was acquired by B.C. Fishing & Packing Co. and in 1928, by B.C. Packers Ltd. It was used as a camp by B.C. Packers until it was closed in 1942.

Sunnyside

Sunnyside: built in **1916** by Gosse-Millerd Packing Co. It was located on the Inverness Slough. In 1921, the company was purchased by Gosse-Millerd Ltd., in 1926 by Gosse Packing Co. Ltd., and in 1928 by B.C. Packers Ltd. In 1950, the plant was rebuilt and upgraded and the company's northern operations concentrated there. Its last canning season was 1968. It was demolished in 1986.

Tuck's Inlet: built in **1913** by Canadian Fish and Cold Storage Co., Ltd. Located in Tuck Inlet, near Prince Rupert. B.C. Packers Association operated it in 1918 and 1919, after which Canadian Fish and Cold Storage again operated it until 1924. In 1925, it was operated by Somerville Canning Co., in 1926 and 1927, by Millerd Packing Co. and in 1928, by B.C. Packers Ltd., who then closed it. In 1931, it was bought by Millerd Packing Co. It was purchased by Nelson Brothers Fisheries in 1937 and a reduction plant was added. It was closed by them when they built their cannery on the Ocean Dock in Prince Rupert in 1940.

Mrs. Sarah Morrisson,
netwoman,
Carlisle, circa 1947

North Pacific native village

North Pacific

Sailboats – Skeena Slough

Sunnyside – waiting for the train

The Glory Hole

Lunch Break – Cassiar

The Outlying Plants 45

Port Essington, 1945

Carlisle

Birthday party – Carlisle

Claxton

NASS RIVER

Building of canneries on the Nass River followed hard on the heels of those on the Skeena. The Nass is a smaller producer but nevertheless, an important one, particularly of high quality sockeye. The Nass salmon were always subject to a degree of interception by Alaskan fishermen, and this has been an extremely serious problem since the Noyes Island fishery was developed by them after World War II.

As transport of fresh fish improved, the Nass River plants were closed and the catch processed in the Skeena River plants.

Arrandale: built in **1905** by John Wallace on the southeast shore near the mouth of the Nass River. He had bought the Pacific Northern cannery in Observatory Inlet and moved the machinery to his new plant. In 1911, he sold the cannery to Anglo-B.C. Packing Co., who operated it until 1942. Thereafter, it was used by Anglo-B.C. Packing Co. as a gillnet camp until it was abandoned in the late 1950s.

Barnard Cove: built in **1927** by Millerd Packing Co., Ltd. and acquired by the new B.C. Packers Ltd. in 1928, shortly after that company was formed by the merger between B.C. Fishing & Packing Co., Ltd. and Gosse Packing Co., Ltd. Later that year, it was sold to Canadian Fishing Co.

Cascade: built in **1889** at Echo Cove in Iceberg Bay by Cascade Packing Co.—Messrs. R.P. Rithet, J.A. Laidlaw, D.R. Harris and M. Strouse, two of whom, Rithet and Laidlaw, built the Standard cannery near the mouth of the

Arrandale

Skeena in 1890. In 1892, the partners, along with Thomas Ladner, formed Victoria Canning Co., which took over ownership. Cascade was closed in 1893 and in 1902, B.C. Packers Association became the owners, succeeded in 1910 by B.C. Fishing & Packing Co. They operated until Millerd Packing Co. became the owner in 1934 and the plant was closed.

Douglas: built in **1882** by Douglas Packing Co. and abandoned after 1884. Later became the site of the Somerville cannery.

Kumeon: built in **1918** in Steamer Passage on Portland Canal near Khutseymateen Inlet by Portland Fisheries (Northern B.C. Fisheries). In 1921, it was closed. In 1925, it was leased by Canadian Fishing Co., who purchased it in 1926.

Mill Bay

Mill Bay: an early cannery was built in **1879** by Henry Croasdaile on the Nass, upriver from Kincolith, on the site of a sawmill which dated from 1877. In 1888 it was purchased by Messrs. Findlay, Durham and Brodie of the B.C. Canning Co., at which time a new cannery was built. In 1893, it was sold to Federation Brand Salmon Canning Co., who also bought Nass Harbour cannery across the river. It was sold to Kincolith Packing Co. (Henry Doyle) in 1908. In 1911, a cold storage was added using electricity from water power. It was one of the first plants to install can making machinery. In 1916, it passed to Northern B.C. Fisheries Ltd., which had been formed by Henry Doyle and R.V. Winch. In 1925, it was purchased by Wallace Fisheries. In 1926, it became the property of B.C. Fishing & Packing Co. when they bought out Wallace Fisheries by share transfer. B.C. Packers Ltd. closed the cannery in 1937, but continued to operate it as a camp until 1959.

Nass Harbour: built in **1888** opposite Mill Bay, at Iceberg Bay, by A.J.

McLellan, utilizing equipment from the Nass River cannery. B.C. Canning Co. of England (Federation Brand) bought the property in 1893. In 1904, it was leased and then purchased by Canadian Canning Co., Ltd., who sold it to Evans, Coleman & Evans in 1911. In 1912, it was purchased by B.C. Packers Association. When B.C. Packers Ltd. was formed in 1928, this cannery was closed. It was abandoned in 1934.

Nass River: built in **1881** by Henry Croasdaile at Fishery Bay on the north shore of the Nass above Mill Bay. It was closed in 1884 and in 1888, it was moved to Nass Harbour by A.J. McLellan.

Pacific Northern: opened in **1903** by the British Columbia Canning Co. on Observatory Inlet. In 1905 it was sold to John Wallace who, in 1906, moved the machinery to his new site on the Nass River at Arrandale.

Portland: built in **1907** by M. Desbrisay. Located on Pearse Canal, through which the boundary between B.C. and Alaska runs. It operated for only one season.

Port Nelson: built in **1905** near Arrandale cannery by Port Nelson Canning & Salting Co. on the site of a former salmon saltery. It was managed by Henry Doyle. In 1911, it was sold to Anglo-B.C. Packing Co., along with Arrandale.

Port Simpson: opened in **1975** at Port Simpson by the Pacific North Coast Native Cooperative, financed by the federal and provincial governments. It was closed after the 1988 season. Guy Williams, one time president of the Native Brotherhood of B.C. and later Senator, described the venture as the "biggest white elephant Indian Affairs had ever created."

Somerville: built in **1918** by Western Salmon Packers Ltd. (Evans, Coleman & Evans) on the site of the Douglas Packing Co. cannery which had been closed in 1884. In 1924, Francis Millerd formed Somerville Cannery Co. and acquired this cannery which he had leased in 1923. In 1926, it was sold to Wallace Fisheries and then the site passed to B.C. Fishing & Packing Co. with the merger, and in 1928, to B.C. Packers Ltd. Francis Millerd named his cannery in Seal Cove Somerville cannery in 1927. That plant was the subject of the federal jurisdiction litigation which followed.

Wales Island: built in **1902** on Pearse Canal by an American company, Wales Island Packing Co. The boundary between B.C. and Alaska was still in dispute and the company believed their site was in Alaska. It was closed when the boundary settlement was reached and in 1911, M. DesBrisay & Co. rebuilt it and opened in 1912. DesBrisay had been operating a cannery in Hidden Inlet, nearby, which turned out to be in the U.S. He had been granted a licence in 1910 to build and operate a cannery in Work Canal. Instead, he found it desirable to purchase Wales Island cannery and his Work Canal licence was transferred there. He was not permitted, however, to fish in Observatory Inlet or the Nass River, "to guard the operations of the Naas River canners." The cannery was permitted traps in 1925 and 1926, because traps were permitted on the Alaska side of the border.

In 1926, The Canadian Fishing Co., Ltd. bought Wales Island cannery. It was closed in 1942 and 1943 and opened again in 1944. After the 1949 season, it was closed for the last time and this was the end of canning on the Nass until the Port Simpson cannery was built in 1975. Canfisco used Wales Island as a gillnet camp until 1957 and abandoned the property in 1983.

QUEEN CHARLOTTE ISLANDS

The Islands do not have sockeye streams and the canneries there were built for the processing of fall salmon—pinks, chums and cohoes. Some had reduction plants for the processing of the abundant herring and as well, dungeness crab and razor clams provided the basis for an industry for many years.

In some cases the operations were combined with those on the mainland. For example, the Margaret Bay operation was for sockeye only and the manager and key personnel went from there to Lagoon Bay for the fall fishery. Similarly with Boswell and Shannon Bay.

The ability to transport fresh fish for long distances led to the closure of the Queen Charlotte Island salmon plants and the processing of the catch on the mainland. Camps were established to service the seine boats and the salmon trolling fleet operating on the west, north and east coast of the Islands.

Alliford Bay: opened in **1912** by B.C. Fisheries Ltd. Included a cannery, cold storage and reduction plant. It operated through 1914, but the reduction plant was not used because they intended to reduce all species which the government would not allow. B.C. Fisheries Ltd. went into liquidation in 1914. In 1915, the plant was acquired by Maritime Fisheries Ltd., who operated it until 1927. In 1938, B.C. Packers bought the plant machinery and transferred it to Pacofi, which they were rebuilding. The property and remaining buildings were sold to the federal government for the Flying Boat Station, which opened in 1939.

Ferguson Bay: Somerville Cannery Co. (Francis Millerd), built this cannery in Masset Inlet in **1922**. The floating cannery, Laurel Whelan was anchored there when processing Masset Inlet pinks. In 1927, Ferguson Bay became the property of Francis Millerd's new company, Millerd Packing Co. In 1928, the new B.C. Packers Ltd. acquired Millerd Packing Co. and this cannery. They closed it in 1929.

Henslung Bay: built in **1919** in Parry Pass by Eugene Simpson and Hume

Babington. This was the cannery they had moved from Lockeport. The location was poor and the plant operated for only one year. It was moved that winter to Naden Harbour as the partners' new crab cannery.

Jedway: built in **1926** on the east coast of Moresby Island by Somerville Cannery Co. It was acquired by B.C. Packers Ltd. in 1928 with the acquisition of Millerd Packing Co. It was closed in 1929.

Lagoon Bay: built in **1918** by Western Salmon Packers Ltd. in Selwyn Inlet on the east coast of Moresby Island. In 1923, it was sold to The Canadian Fishing Co., Ltd.

Langara: built by Langara Fishing & Packing Co. at Masset in **1924**. The company was headed by Eugene Simpson and Hume Babington, with financing from Everett Packing Co., which also owned Nootka Packing Co. It processed both salmon and crabs. The owners built the clam cannery at Tow Hill the same year, and were able to operate practically year round on salmon, crabs and clams. The Langara cannery was acquired by Nootka Packing Co. in 1930 and was operated by them until 1938.

Lockeport: built in **1918** by Lockeport Canning Co. in Klunkwoi Bay on the east coast of Moresby Island (Eugene Simpson was one of the partners). It operated for one season and then went into liquidation. Canfisco leased it in 1923 and purchased it in 1927. It was closed in the 1940s.

Masset: built by Masset Canners Ltd. (John Dybhavn and Olaf Hanson) in **1927**. They sold it to Nelson Brothers Fisheries in 1938. Nelsons operated

Lagoon Bay

Langara

Masset

for one season. In 1940, they leased it to Sam Simpson, who operated it until 1950, when he built a new crab and clam cannery at New Masset.

Naden Harbour: built by Wallace Fisheries in **1911** in Naden Harbour. After the whaling station was built nearby, the salmon fishery failed and in 1919, the plant was moved to Watun on the east side of Masset Inlet. Eugene Simpson and Hume Babington built their first crab cannery at the Naden Harbour site in the winter of 1919/20.

Pacofi: built by Pacific Coast Fisheries Ltd. in **1910** and acquired by Standard Fisheries Ltd., which was incorporated that year to purchase it. Located in Selwyn Inlet. The principal was C.A. von Alvensleben, who had emigrated to B.C. from Germany in 1904 and was an established businessman in Vancouver. He built a reduction plant, cold storage and ice plant and processed trawl fish, but operated for only one season. In 1913, Standard Fisheries was still the owner but they were shut down by government because they were processing halibut in the reduction plant.

Standard Fisheries Ltd. had two halibut schooners that operated into Prince Rupert and Vancouver where the company had wharves. They also had a steam trawler, which was the first to use an otter trawl in the B.C. fisheries. In 1916, Ocean Products Co., Ltd. became the owner, but they did not operate. In 1917, it was purchased by International Chemical Co. Ltd., who installed equipment to extract potash and iodine from the kelp beds in Cumshewa Inlet. Subsequently, there were several ownership changes until 1927, when T. Matsuyama Co., Ltd. operated a salmon saltery there. B.C. Packers bought it in 1938, demolished the buildings and rebuilt a modern plant consisting of a cannery for seine pinks and chums and a reduction plant for herring. During this process, B.C. Packers discovered an underground concrete structure that had evidently been intended as a submarine base—a mystery that remains unresolved. B.C. Packers bought the canning machinery from the Alliford Bay cannery and installed that in the new Pacofi plant. In 1943, the cannery and reduction plant were destroyed by fire. In 1945, they added a liver oil plant on the former reduction plant site. In 1949, the plant was closed permanently.

Queen Charlotte Canners: the Langara Fishing & Packing Co. cannery at Masset was taken over by Sam Simpson of Queen Charlotte Canners Ltd. in 1940. It succeeded their crab cannery that his father had established in Naden Harbour in 1919, and which had run intermittently since. In 1950, they moved the crab and clam cannery to a new plant in New Masset. In 1960, they added a salmon cannery. In 1965, the company was sold to their sales agents, McCallum Sales Ltd. In 1966, Nelson Brothers became the owners of McCallum Sales Ltd. and as a result, of Queen Charlotte Canners. The salmon operation was closed, but the crab and clam operations continued. The plant was destroyed by fire in 1971 and was rebuilt the following year as a cooking and freezing plant for crabs and a troll fish operation. Canning ceased at that time.

Shannon Bay: built in **1926** by Gosse Packing Co. in Masset Inlet. The cannery operated on alternate years on the Masset Inlet pinks. It became a B.C. Packers plant in the 1928 merger. It was closed from 1931 to 1935 and refurbished and reopened in 1936. It was closed for good after the 1940 season.

South Bay: built in **1926** by B.C. Fishing & Packing Co. on Moresby Island in Skidegate Inlet. In 1929, the cold storage plant which was located on a scow was lost in a gale in Hecate Strait when it was being moved from South Bay to Walker Lake cannery. It was eventually salvaged. B.C. Packers closed the South Bay plant in 1931 and abandoned the property in 1932.

54 Cannery Village—Company Town

Queen Charlotte Canners – New Masset

Watun: established in **1919** by Wallace Fisheries Ltd. when they moved their Naden Harbour plant to this location on the east side of Masset Inlet. It was acquired by B.C. Fishing & Packing when they bought the Wallace company in 1926. B.C. Packers Ltd. closed the plant in 1931.

Lagoon Bay – Canadian Rover at dock

The Outlying Plants 55

Lockeport

British Columbia Airways at Lagoon Bay, 1930

Mechanical Clam Digger – The Great Experiment, 1971

Lagoon Bay

RIVERS INLET

Although it produced runs of all five Pacific salmon species, Rivers Inlet was known for its consistent runs of sockeye and its large redsprings. The beginning of salmon canning here coincided with that on the Skeena and Nass Rivers in the late 1800s. It was always a gillnet operation, although there was some minor trolling carried out. At the peak of the season each year, there would be upwards of 1,000 boats fishing in the Inlet. The Rivers Inlet runs have declined to the point where there is no longer a commercial fishery in the Inlet. This tragedy is attributed to abusive logging practices in the Owikeno Lake watershed, the nursery of the sockeye, and to overfishing in the Inlet by the commercial fishermen themselves, due to discontinuation of Fishery guardians by the Department of Fisheries and Oceans. While there are many creeks and rivers emptying into Rivers Inlet, and even more into Owikeno Lake, this was not the origin of the name. Captain Vancouver's expedition named it for a British aristocrat, Baron Rivers.

As on the Skeena River, missionaries would follow the Indian fishermen to Rivers Inlet for the fishing season. Dr. A.E. Bolton, the missionary doctor at

Beaver

Port Simpson, established the first small summer hospital on Rivers Inlet at the Wannuck cannery in 1897. The Bella Bella hospital was established in 1902 by Dr. R.W. Large, who had taken over the mission there in 1898. The Rivers Inlet hospital was destroyed by fire in 1904 and a new and bigger hospital was built by Dr. Large at the Green's cannery site in 1905/06. This served the Inlet for many years until it was closed in 1950 and was replaced by a Red Cross outpost station at Wadhams cannery, called the Darby Medical Centre.

In the early days, the Bella Bella hospital was closed for the sockeye season and the staff moved to Rivers Inlet. As the demands grew at Bella Bella, medical students were hired for the summer for the main hospital. Dr. George Darby, who would become an institution in his own right at Bella Bella and district and at Rivers Inlet, arrived in the Inlet as a medical student in 1912. He took over the Bella Bella and Rivers Inlet hospitals in 1914. A most extraordinary man, he would serve the central coast until his retirement in 1959.

Transportation technology made possible the closure of the Rivers Inlet canneries and the processing of the catch in the larger centres. The last cannery, Goose Bay, ceased canning in 1957.

Beaver: built in **1906** by J.H. Todd & Sons. Located on the north side of the Inlet on a site purchased by Mark Gosse in 1896. Todd's canned there until 1950 and subsequently used it as a gillnet camp until it was permanently closed. The missionary doctor at the hospital usually held Sunday services at Beaver cannery.

Brunswick: built in **1897** by Brunswick Canning Co., Messrs. George Dawson, Alfred Buttimer and George Wilson, who later incorporated Kildala Packing Co. Located on the north side of the Inlet near the Wannuck cannery. It was sold to B.C. Packers Association in 1902 as part of that amalgamation and passed to B.C. Fishing & Packing Co. in 1914 and to B.C. Packers in 1928. It canned until 1930 and then was used as a camp for Wadhams until 1942. It was demolished in1945.

Good Hope: built by Anglo-B.C. Packing Co. in **1895**. Located on the south side of the Inlet. It operated continuously until 1950, when it ceased canning and was used as a camp. When Anglo-B.C. sold its northern assets to Canfisco in 1968, they retained this property and converted it into a sportsfishing resort—the first on Rivers Inlet.

Goose Bay: built in **1926** by Frank Inrig and Alex Rutherford as Standard Packing Co. Frank Inrig had been the long-time manager at Wadhams. The first plant was built at the head of the bay which is near the mouth of Rivers Inlet. It was ready in time to can fish in 1926. But the pilings became infested by toredos, so the next year the plant was moved further towards the

The Outlying Plants 59

Brunswick

Good Hope

Goose Bay

Kildala

mouth of the bay. In 1928, they sold the cannery to Canadian Fishing Co., Ltd., who operated it continuously until 1957. It was the last of the Rivers Inlet canneries to process fish. It was subsequently sold and converted to a sports fishing resort.

Green's: built in **1897**. Also known as Vancouver cannery, it was about a quarter mile from Brunswick cannery and across the bay from Wannuck cannery. In 1902, it became part of the B.C. Packers Association amalgamation. The Rivers Inlet hospital was built there in 1905 by the Mehodist Church, on land donated by the Company and survived the cannery itself. The hospital was operated by the Bella Bella hospital and most of its staff moved there each year for the fishing season.

Kildala: built in **1906** by Dawson & Buttimer with Dan Groves as manager. In 1908, they changed their name to Kildala Packing Co. In 1925, Canadian Fishing Co. purchased Kildala Packing Co. and thus acquired Kildala, Carlisle and Manitou. It ceased canning in the 1940s and was operated as a gillnet camp until 1960.

Moses Inlet: opened in **1932**, by Frank Inrig. He had sold his Goose Bay cannery to Canadian Fishing Co. in 1928 and had continued as manager there until this time. His first choice for a site was Duncanby Landing but the water supply was insufficient. He built the Moses Inlet plant about three miles inside the inlet. A group of Japanese families who had a sawmill at Green's cannery moved with their mill to Moses Inlet and cut the timbers for the new cannery, houses and other buildings. Later they built boats at that location. Moses Inlet

Moses Inlet

operated just three seasons and then closed, a victim of the Great Depression.

McTavish: built in **1918** across from Kildala, by McTavish Fisheries (G.S. McTavish had been manager at Rivers Inlet from 1892 to 1897, at Aberdeen on the Skeena in 1897 and 1899, and at Rivers Inlet and Victoria canneries from 1899 to 1913). In 1920, it was sold to Gosse-Millerd Packing Co. The company name was changed to Gosse-Millerd Ltd. that year and in 1923, they closed the cannery. It came into possession of B.C. Packers Ltd. through the mergers and in 1932, was sold to Anglo-B.C. Packing Co.

Provincial: built in **1917** in Schooner Pass by William Todd and Robert Johnson who was J.H. Todds long time Manager on the Skeena at Inverness. He also had overall responsibility for Beaver and Klemtu. J.H. Todd was thought to have financed Provincial.

Rivers Inlet (RIC): built in **1882** by Robert Draney and Thomas Shotbolt (Shotbolt, Hart & Co., Victoria merchants). Draney had been a blacksmith at Inverness cannery when it was built in 1877. In 1888, they sold out to B.C. Canning Co., owners of the Victoria cannery, nearby. RIC was the first salmon cannery built in Rivers Inlet and was located at the head of the Inlet at the mouth of the Wannock River. The Victoria sawmill was operated in conjunction with the cannery until 1922. In 1924, RIC was purchased by B.C. Fishing & Packing Co., and in 1928 became the property of B.C. Packers Ltd. It canned until 1933, then was used as a camp for Wadhams. B.C. Packers sold the site in 1964 to Western Tug Ltd.

Strathcona: built in **1906** by Strathcona Packing Co., immediately south of Good Hope. In 1911, it was purchased by Wallace Fisheries. (John Macmillan had wanted to buy it and create Cassiar and Strathcona Packing Co., but his partners would not agree. He arranged the purchase for Wallace Fisheries.) In 1926, B.C. Fishing & Packing Co. acquired Wallace Fisheries, including Strathcona. B.C. Packers closed the plant in 1928 and dismantled it in 1934.

Victoria: built in **1883** by B.C. Canning Co. of England at the mouth of the Wannock River across from RIC on the site of a sawmill.

Wadhams: built by E.A. Wadhams in **1897**. He had sold his Fraser River cannery to Anglo-B.C. Packing Co. in 1890. It was taken over by B.C. Packers Association in 1902, in 1914 by B.C. Fishing & Packing Co., and in 1928 by B.C. Packers Ltd. In 1916, can-making equipment was installed. In 1942, fire destroyed the netloft and office building. They were replaced, but the plant ceased canning and was operated as a camp.

Wannuck: (sometimes Wannock or Whonnock), built in **1884** by Wannock Packing Co., Messrs. A. McNeill, W. McDowell, and S. McDowell. It was located at Wannock Cove, on the north shore of the Inlet, west of Moses Inlet. It was acquired by Victoria Canning Co. (R.P. Rithet, Thomas Ladner and partners) in 1892 and became part of the B.C. Packers Association merger in 1902. In 1926, it was acquired by B.C. Fishing & Packing Co., with R.P. Rithet Co. as agents. In 1928, it was included in the B.C. Packers Ltd. merger. It was abandoned in 1934. It was the site of the first summer hospital on the Inlet.

Wadhams

Bella Bella boats at Rivers Inlet, 1899 – Steamer Oscar

Haidas at Wadhams, 1905

Dawson's Landing

Wadhams

The Outlying Plants 65

Netracks at Goose Bay

Goose Bay Beauties

A day off at Goose Bay

Cardena at Goose Bay

SMITH'S INLET

Smiths Inlet is almost exclusively a sockeye producer. Almost all the spawning occurs in the streams of Long Lake and Wyclees Lagoon. The canning season there was only a few weeks each year, and once these fish could be transported to Rivers Inlet and Namu, the canneries were closed. They continued as servicing centres for the fleets, however, for some years.

Boswell: built by Gosse Packing Co. in **1926**. It was located on the north shore of Smiths Inlet. B.C. Packers Ltd. took possession with the merger of B.C. Fishing & Packing with Gosse Packing Co. in 1928. They leased the plant to Anglo-B.C. Packing from 1928 through 1931. B.C. Packers operated it from 1932, through 1936. It was subsequently used as a camp until the mid-1950s.

Leroy Bay: built in **1929** by Kingcome Packers Ltd., who had a plant at Charles Creek in Kingcome Inlet. It was located at the south side of the entrance to Smiths Inlet. It burned in 1937 and was not rebuilt. The site was later used by Nelson Brothers Fisheries as the seasonal location of their K5 camp.

Margaret Bay: built in **1916** by Robert Chambers of Western Packers Ltd. It was located on the mainland facing the mouth of Smith Sound. In 1923, Canadian Fishing Co. bought the plant from Western Packers along with Butedale and Shushartie. It canned until 1945 and was then operated as a gillnet camp until 1959, when it was closed.

Smith's Inlet: built in **1883** by Quashella Packing Co., Messrs. R.P. Rithet and J.A. Laidlaw. They were granted exclusive drag-seine fishing rights on "Quascila" Creek in 1884, in the path of the sockeye migrating to Wyclees

Margaret Bay

Lagoon and Long Lake—Smith's Inlet's sockeye producer. The cannery operated only one year and in 1885, the machinery was transferred to Wannuck cannery in Rivers Inlet and all the Smith's Inlet catch was canned there through 1901. The property and fishing rights were transferred by Rithet and Laidlaw to their Victoria Canning Co. In 1902, B.C. Packers Association (BCPA) bought Victoria Canning Co., including the cannery property and the foreshore rights in Wyclees Lagoon, expecting also the exclusive drag-seine licence to continue. But late in 1901, the government had granted this instead to Wm. Hickey Canning Co., Ltd. (W. Hickey and R. Kelly. Kelly was provincial Liberal leader at the time). Hickey and Kelly did not get the foreshore use, nor were others precluded from gillnetting in Queshella Lake (no one gillnetted in the open waters of Smith's Inlet in those days). BCPA, of course, protested long and loud but to no avail. Nevertheless, they rebuilt the cannery in 1902, and fished 35 gillnets in Queshella Lake.

Queshella Lake, Queshella Creek and Wyclees Lagoon were all the same body of water. It is a tidal lagoon but, in 1903, the Dominion Fisheries ruled it was a fresh water lake and except for the drag seine, no further fishing was permitted. This was "to protect Mr. Kelly in his privilege." Henry Doyle, then general manager of BCPA, charged the fishery officer with unfairness and partiality, and this resulted in protracted legal dealings.

In 1912, the drag seine licence and cannery were purchased by Wallace Fisheries. In the meantime, Japanese fishermen had begun fishing seines at the head of the Inlet. After the First World War, in 1919, gillnet fishermen, opposed to exclusive rights, forced the Japanese fishermen out of the Inlet with shotguns and burned their seines and the drag seines. Wallace Fisheries replaced the drag seines, but the government cancelled the drag seine licence. In 1926, Wallace Fisheries was sold to B.C. Fishing & Packing Co., who thus acquired the Smith's Inlet cannery. The cannery was closed in 1931 and demolished in 1938.

WEST COAST OF VANCOUVER ISLAND

The west coast plants were established primarily for reduction of the pilchard and herring resources. Some were salmon canneries as well, however, utilizing the sockeye runs of Alberni Inlet and Nitinat Lake and the chum and cohoe salmon that returned to the many small streams flowing westward to the ocean. In some years, the Fraser sockeye and pinks passed relatively close to the west coast on their homeward migration, but the net fishery was seldom able to intercept them, and these species were not attracted to the trollers' lures of the day. In 1954, the Department of Fisheries opened the Juan de Fuca Strait to large seiners in a bid to force the Americans into including the Fraser pink salmon runs in the International Pacific Fisheries protocol. This was a successful fishery and these catches were transported to the mainland canneries.

By 1927, there were some 26 pilchard reduction plants operating between Barkley Sound and Kyuquot. In 1940, pilchard fishing had moved outside and the very small plants with small vessels had closed, leaving only 10 plants operating. The pilchards disappeared after 1945, and for awhile the reduction plants processed herring, but the west coast catches came to be transported to the mainland plants. Only Port Albion, near Ucluelet, continued into the late 1950s.

Most of the west coast canneries were short-lived and the dominant salmon operation was for troll-caught cohoe and springs. To service this fleet, a system of troll camps was established, and the salmon transported to fresh fish or freezing facilities, primarily in Victoria and on the mainland.

Plants with canning capacity participated in the great canned herring program in the Second World War, to provide food for the troops overseas and the British people and at one point, to the Russian people. The product was not appetizing and the market disappeared immediately after the War.

Capt. Heating had a herring saltery on Sydney Inlet and brought young women from Aberdeen to process the catch with the Scotch cure. The saltery was destroyed by a storm in 1920. In the 1930s, there were a number of chum salmon salteries on Esperanza Inlet. They were owned and operated by Japanese and supplied by Indian and white fishermen. The market was Japan, often by way of China.

As of the early 1930s, the only hospitals on the whole of the West Coast of the Island, were at Port Alberni and Port Alice, with a First Aid station at Ceepeecee. Later, the residents of Tofino built a hospital in their town.

Bamfield: built in **1919** by Bamfield Fisheries Ltd.

Caledonia: built in **1928** in Kyuquot Sound by Anglo-B.C. Packing Co., along with a pilchard reduction plant. It operated only a few years.

Ceepeecee: built in **1926** as a reduction plant by Canadian Packing Corporation, a subsidiary of California Packing Corporation. It was located on Esperanza Inlet. In 1934, the company offered the operation to Richie Nelson who had been doing some work for them, so it became the property of Nelson Brothers Fisheries. They added the cannery that year. Its main business was pilchard reduction and later herring reduction. The plant was destroyed by fire in the 1950s.

Clayoquot Sound: Clayoquot Fishing & Packing Co. was established in **1895** by Messrs. Earle and Magnesen, who built a one-line cannery at the mouth of the Kennedy River. It was also known as Kenfalls cannery. Clayoquot

Sound Canning Co. took over in 1902 and operated into the 1940s.

Ecoole: built in **1916** by Messrs. Butterfield, Mackie and Basterrechea (B. Gregory) as a herring saltery and for fresh herring and salmon and Scotch cure. It was located near Rainy Bay in Barkley Sound. It was sold to Northern Packing Co. in 1926, and a ten ton reduction plant was installed. The company was reorganized as Northern Chief Packers Ltd. in 1924. In 1937, B.C. Packers purchased the plant. In 1942, it was sold to Nelson Brothers Fisheries and after the pilchard failure in 1946, it was dismantled.

Hecate: built in **1926** by Gosse Packing Co., in combination with the reduction plant. It was located in Hecate Channel on Nootka Island across from Ceepeecee. The cannery operated only in the first year—1926. The reduction plant was sold to B.C. Packers Ltd. in 1928. It was closed down from 1931 to 1935, after which it was modernized and reopened. It was closed in the late 1940s and demolished in 1954.

Kildonan/Uchucklesit: in **1903**, Alberni Packing Co., Ltd., (C. Tiernan and Capt. D. MacDonald) built Uchucklesit cannery in Alberni Inlet near its entrance to Barkley Sound. Wallace Bros. Packing Co. bought the plant in 1909 and renamed it Kildonan. In 1911, ownership passed to Wallace Fisheries Ltd. In 1913, they added the cold storage plant and in 1925, the reduction plant. B.C. Fishing and Packing Co. bought the plant in 1926, and in 1928 it was transferred to B.C. Packers Ltd. In 1936, equipment for herring and pilchard canning was added. Canning of albacore tuna was begun in 1939. The cannery closed in 1946 and the rest of the plant, in 1959. In 1965, the property was sold.

Kildonan, 1913

Koprino: built by Canadian Fishing Co. in **1927**. It was located on Quatsino Sound. In 1927, they added the reduction plant for pilchards.

Nitinat: built in **1917** by Lummi Bay Packing Co. Before the cannery was built, C. Tiernan, who had been a partner in the Uchucklesit plant, obtained exclusive fishing rights for Nitinat Lake, but lost some boats on the bar and gave up the rights. In 1924, the cannery was acquired by Nitinat Packers Ltd. and was purchased by Gosse Packing Co. in 1927. In 1928 it became part of the B.C. Packers Ltd. assets. B.C. Packers Ltd. closed the plant in 1931, and it was abandoned in 1934. In 1918, a tragedy took place when the fishpacker, Renfrew, was wrecked crossing the Nitinat bar. It was carrying 26 cannery employees from the steamboat stop at Clo-oose to the cannery and thirteen were drowned.

Nootka: built at Friendly Cove in **1917** by Nootka Packing Co. W.R. Lord Sr. had established a salmon saltery there and encouraged the Everett Packing Co. to register a B.C. company to build a salmon cannery there. This was the first of several plants for Nootka Bamfield Packing Co. Later they added a pilchard reduction plant. In 1945, the last season before the pilchards disappeared from the B.C. coast, The Canadian Fishing Co. purchased Nootka Packing Co. (1937) Ltd. While the investment in the plants was a losing proposition, Canfisco acquired a first-rate seine fleet and company president, Sidney Rosenberg, who became president of Canadian Fishing Company in 1954.

Port Alberni: built in **1929** by Francis Millerd Co. for chum salmon. In 1930, the B.C. Fishermen's Cooperative Association (formerly Sointula Cooperative), purchased the plant. Francis Millerd stayed on as manager of the Co-op's plants.

Port Renfrew: built in **1918** by Defiance Packing Co.

Quatsino: Wallace Fisheries constructed a plant here in **1911**. It was transferred to B.C. Fishing & Packing Co. in 1926 and to B.C. Packers in 1928. It was closed in 1931 and abandoned in 1934.

In **1924**, Francis Millerd of Somerville Canning Co. stationed his floating cannery, Laurel Whalen at this site for fall fishing. Floating canneries were made illegal by the Provincial government in 1933.

San Mateo: built in **1918** by Gosse-Millerd Packing Co. It was located opposite Kildonan in Barkley Sound. The plant was built for canning herring. It came into the possession of B.C. Packers in 1928 and was closed that year. It was abandoned in 1936.

Tofino: opened in **1962** by Tofino Packing Co. (Andy Tulloch). It was sold to Canadian Fishing Co., Ltd. in 1976 and to B.C. Packers in 1980.

CAPE CAUTION, SOUTH

There were many salmon streams between Victoria and Cape Caution, both on the Vancouver Island side and in the mainland inlets. They attracted a host of small canneries in the early days as the industry moved out from the Fraser River base. But the fisheries were not concentrated in any one area like the Skeena River or Rivers Inlet. So most canneries had a small resource base.

With powered boats, the fishermen moved out of the inlets and stream mouths, to more open water, in the Gulf of Georgia and in Johnstone and Queen Charlotte Straits, so that the main canning centres became Alert Bay, Bones Bay and Glendale Cove. In their turn, these too succumbed to the advances in fresh fish transportation.

The Johnstone Strait fishery proved to be very successful, especially in those years when the Fraser River sockeye approached the river by that route, rather than through Juan de Fuca Strait, where the catches had to be shared equally with U.S. fishermen. But it was blamed for the demise of the salmon runs in Bute, Toba and Loughborough Inlets. The criticism was that the Johnstone Strait fishery did not distinguish the runs to those inlets from those of the Fraser with which they were mixed.

Alert Bay: built in **1881** by Stephen Spencer and T. Earle on the site of a salmon saltery erected in 1862 by Messrs. Mack and Neill. This became the Alert Bay Canning Co. In 1902, the plant was acquired by the B.C. Packers Association. They also received a grant of exclusive fishing rights for the Nimpkish River and were required to maintain a hatchery there. In 1908, they built a box factory. This and the cannery were taken over by B.C. Fishing & Packing Co. in 1914 and by B.C. Packers Ltd. in 1928. It was closed down in 1933, but was rebuilt and reopened for the 1940 and 1941 seasons, and then closed permanently. A herring reduction plant was installed in 1939 and expanded in 1941. Herring canning also commenced in 1941.

Bones Bay: built in **1928** in Clio Channel on Cracroft Island by The Canadian Fishing Co. The Company closed down Shushartie and transferred the machinery and equipment to the new cannery. In 1943, it was expanded and modernized. 1951 was the last year of canning and it was then used as a camp for Canfisco's fishing fleet.

Bute Inlet: built in **1890** by C.G. Hobson and C.S. Windsor. It operated only for the one season.

Charles Creek: built in **1914** by Gilford Fish Co. on Kingcome Inlet. In 1915, it was purchased by William Hickey of Preston Packing Co., and by 1921, he was the principal owner. He changed the name to Wm. Hickey & Son, and then to Kingcome Packers Ltd.

Alert Bay

Bones Bay

Deep Bay: built by Deep Bay Packing Co. at Bowser. In 1937, it was destroyed by fire and was not replaced. B.C. Packers bought the property in 1940 and operated a dogfish liver plant.

Empire: built in **1905** at Esquimalt by J.H. Todd & Sons. This became their main plant. For 60 years the Sooke traps owned by Todd's were the only salmon traps in British Columbia.

Glendale

Glendale: in **1907**, Capt. Richard E. Gosse built a cannery at Sargeaunt Pass at the mouth of Knight Inlet near Minstrel Island. In 1910, he moved the plant to Glendale Cove in Knight Inlet proper at the mouth of a pink salmon stream. In 1911, he sold the Glendale cannery to Anglo-B.C. Packing Co. Anglo-B.C. operated the plant continuously until 1946. The company then moved their gillnet and seine facilities to Alert Bay. In 1954, Glendale was dismantled.

Great Northern: built in **1900** by Great Northern Canning Co. in West Vancouver. In 1924, it was owned by T.W.B. London, who partnered with Francis Millerd in the Laurel Whalen floating cannery venture. In 1935, Francis Millerd & Co. acquired the Great Northern cannery. In 1938, they installed herring canning equipment, which they used through the war years. They operated the salmon cannery continuously until 1967, when they sold the site to the federal government's Fisheries Research Board.

Jervis Inlet: opened in **1912** by Jervis Inlet Canning Co. (Windsor and Percival). It burned in 1914 and was not rebuilt.

Lasqueti: built in **1916** by Gulf Islands Fishing & Canning Co. at False Bay. The owner also owned San Juan Canning Co. of Friday Harbour.

Nanaimo: built in **1914** by Nanaimo Canning Co. In 1926, it was sold to The Canadian Fishing Co., Ltd. (Ted Quisenberry was part owner). The first vacuum closing machine was installed here in 1925. (The Nanaimo Fish and Bait Co., Ltd. had a herring operation in Nanaimo from about 1897 and processed herring for halibut bait and by dry salting for markets in the Orient.)

Oakland: built in **1960** in the former J.H. Todd headquarters in Victoria

Quathiaski

by Oakland Industries Ltd., Bill Hillborn, proprietor. Later he built a new cannery at Laurel Point in Victoria, but financial difficulties forced its sale to Marubeni Co. in 1977.

Puntledge: built in **1918** at Courtenay by Puntledge Canning Co. It operated only one season.

Quathiaski: opened in **1904** as the Pidcock cannery in Quathiaski Cove on Quadra Island by Pidcock Bros. & Co. In 1906, they sold it to T.E. Atkins, who sold it in 1908 to Quathiaski Packing Co., who changed the name to Quathiaski cannery. In 1909, the plant was destroyed by fire and was rebuilt. In 1912, it was transferred to Quathiaski Canning Co. (W.E. Anderson and W.H. Malkin). In 1938, it was purchased by B.C. Packers Ltd. In 1941, the plant again burned to the ground and was not rebuilt, although a large netloft was erected and the site was operated as a camp from then on.

Redonda: built around **1935** by Francis Millerd & Co. at Redonda Bay on Redonda Island. It was closed in 1942 and re-opened in 1946 and closed again in 1948.

Saanich: built in 1905 as a clam cannery by Saanich Canning Co. In 1908, began canning fruit. It started salmon canning in **1926**, but only canned for two seasons and ceased salmon canning after 1927.

Seafood Products: built in **1965** at Port Hardy, by Seafood Products Ltd., owned by the Van Snellenberg family. They had been in the fish business since 1925, when they specialized in mild cure products. They did their first canning on Cordova Street in Vancouver in 1951. This cannery had a unique line which produced a four pound salmon and tuna pack for Jack Elsey's institutional trade. In 1959, they built a modern cannery on Commissioner Street.

Shushartie: built in **1914** by Goletas Fish Co. in Shushartie Bay on Goletas Channel at the northeast tip of Vancouver Island. Western Packers Ltd. bought the plant in 1917 (along with Butedale). In 1923, it was one of three plants bought by Canadian Fishing Co. from Western Packers (Butedale and Margaret Bay). In 1928, Canfisco closed the cannery and transferred the machinery to their new cannery at Bones Bay.

Sointula: built in **1924** by Somerville Cannery Co. (F. Millerd) at Sointula on Malcolm Island. It passed to Millerd Packing Co. in 1927 and to B.C. Packers Ltd. in 1928. B.C. Packers closed the plant in 1929 and sold it for a machine shop in 1935.

Victoria: opened in **1913** by Victoria Canning Co. near the city of Victoria.

CAPE CAUTION, NORTH

This sector of the coast was dominated by Rivers and Smiths Inlets and by the Skeena and Nass Rivers. However, like the more southerly coast, there were many salmon producing streams outside those dominant areas, and the industry entrepreneurs were quick to erect facilities to utilize them.

Outside Prince Rupert and the Steveston/Burrard Inlet area, there were three plants which developed into multi-purpose, year round operations and all three—Butedale, Klemtu and Namu—were located on this part of the coast. Each had a village of more or less permanent residents (see Chapter 5).

Bella Bella: In 1905, some Japanese erected a small cannery on Denny Island, across from Bella Bella where they salted chum salmon and canned clams and abalone for the Japanese market. In **1912**, East Bella Bella Packing Co. Ltd. (Robert Kelly) built a modern cannery on the site. In 1915, it was bought by Gosse-Millerd Packing Co. The plant burned down in 1923 and

Bella Bella

was rebuilt the next year. In 1928, it became the property of B.C. Packers Ltd. who closed it down in 1931. The main buildings were dismantled in 1938/39, but the store and fishing station continued.

Bella Bella is a permanent Indian village which originally grew up around the HBC Fort McLaughlin in McLaughlin Bay (established in 1833). The first Methodist church mission in Bella Bella was established by William H. Pierce in 1880. The first medical missionary, Dr. J.A. Jackson, arrived in 1897 and found the village congested and unsanitary. It was decided to move the village to a better site, about two miles north, the location of the present village. Dr. R.W. Large took over the mission in 1898, and supervised the completion of the move. He took charge of the hospital in Rivers Inlet and in 1902, opened the first hospital in Bella Bella. From then on, the Rivers Inlet hospital was operated as a branch of the Bella Bella hospital.

Bella Coola: built in **1900** as Clayton cannery by John Clayton and Tom Draney of Clayton Canning Co. Tom Draney was a cousin of Robert Draney. In 1902, it was purchased by B.C. Packers Association. In 1928, it became the property of B.C. Packers Ltd. In 1929, the cannery burned and was reconstructed for 1930. It operated continuously until 1936, when it was closed down and was then operated as a camp.

John Clayton had arrived in Bella Coola in 1878 over the pack trail from the Cariboo gold fields. He went to work for the Hudson's Bay Company, which had built a trading post there in 1858. He bought considerable land in the area. He built a trading post of his own and in 1883, leased the HBC fort. He bought all of HBC's property in the valley in 1885. He was the dominant settler when the first Norwegian colonists came in 1894.

Butedale: built in **1911** by John Wallace, formerly of Wallace Bros. Fisheries. The location was on Princess Royal Island in Princess Royal Channel. In 1917, it was sold to Western Salmon Packers Ltd., who sold it to Canadian Fishing Co. in 1923. A large cold storage was added in 1925. In 1940, the company enlarged both the cannery and the reduction plant. In 1950 the cannery roof collapsed from the exceptionally heavy snowfall. The cannery was not reopened and would have been closed in any case, with the opening of the Oceanside cannery at Prince Rupert. In 1959, the reduction plant collapsed into the bay. A new reduction plant was built the next year and operated for two seasons before being closed. Canfisco subsequently sold Butedale to sports fishing interests.

Captain Cove: built in **1926** at Captain Cove on the northwest coast of Pitt Island by Captain Cove Canning Co. It was sold the same year to Gosse Packing Co., who operated it for the 1926 and 1927 seasons. It became the property of B.C. Packers Ltd. in 1928, and was closed down for good.

Butedale

China Hat: built in **1900** by Toms, Morris and Fraser. It was part of the amalgamation that resulted in B.C. Packers Association in 1902. In 1903, it was closed. Morris became a cannery manager for J.H. Todd & Sons and, much later, persuaded them to build Klemtu on the site.

Kimsquit: built in **1901** by Robert Draney of Namu Canning Co. It was located five miles from the head of Dean Channel. In 1912, it was purchased by Henry Doyle, along with Namu. He electrified the plant with water power. In 1915, R.V. Winch acquired 52 percent of the company. In 1916, Winch and Doyle formed Northern B.C. Fisheries and took full control. In 1924, the cannery was purchased by Gosse-Millerd Ltd. and in 1928, by B.C. Packers Ltd. It was closed down in 1935, and operated as a camp until 1938, when the buildings were dismantled.

Klemtu: built in **1927** by Klemtu Canning Co., Ltd. The company was associated with the Todd family, but was separate from J.H. Todd & Sons. The cannery was located on Swindle Island near Finlayson Channel on the Indian reservation of Klemtu. In 1930, the plant was closed and in 1934, was reopened by J.H. Todd & Sons. In 1941, they decided to upgrade the plant and hired Lewis Hogan to manage it. He upgraded the cannery, built a cold storage plant and ice plant, a groundfish operation (run by Jack McMillan), and a clam cannery. In 1954, Canadian Fishing Co. and B.C. Packers jointly purchased the J.H. Todd company, including Klemtu. In 1969, the assets of the company

Kimsquit

were divided between the two owning firms, and J.H. Todd & Sons became a subsidiary of Canfisco. Klemtu became the property of B.C. Packers, who closed it that year. The plant has now been demolished. Klemtu, Butedale and Namu were for many years substantial year round operations on the north coast, with modern production facilities, fleet maintenance facilities and large villages.

Lowe Inlet: built in **1890** by Lowe Inlet Packing Co. (Robert Cunningham and John Rood), a subsidiary of Victoria Canning Co. It was located on the mainland side of Grenville Channel. It was purchased by B.C. Packers Association in 1902, by B.C. Fishing & Packing Co. in 1914 and by B.C. Packers Ltd. in 1928. It was closed after the 1930 season and dismantled in 1937.

Manitou: built in **1907** by Dawson & Buttimer. It was located on the opposite shore of Dean Channel from Kimsquit, about five miles from the head. In 1925, Canadian Fishing Co. acquired the plant when they bought Kildala Packing Co. The plant was closed shortly after and dismantled, the lumber and timbers being used at Tallheo.

Millbanke: built in **1966** at Shearwater on Denny Island, opposite Bella Bella, by Millbanke Fisheries Ltd. (Jack Elsey). In 1975, the Central Native Fishermen's Coop (CNFC) was formed and purchased the assets of the company. The CNFC upgraded and expanded the plant in 1981. They soon ran into financial difficulties with soaring interest rates, as did other fishery enterprises, and the plant closed shortly after.

Namu: erected in **1893** by Robert Draney of Namu Canning Co. He was the former owner of RIC in Rivers Inlet. The property was given to him by

John Clayton of Bella Coola, with the agreement that Robert Draney would not build a cannery at Bella Coola. In 1909, a sawmill was erected to produce boxes and lumber. Many of the canneries built in the area, including Rivers Inlet, used lumber and timbers from this mill. In 1911, a new cannery was built and the existing one added to the mill. In 1912, the plant was sold to Henry Doyle, Daniel Drysdale and Donald Moore, who changed the company name to Draney Fisheries Ltd. and rebuilt the cannery. In 1915, R.V. Winch bought a 52 percent interest in the company and in 1916, Northern B.C. Fisheries Ltd., owned by Winch and Doyle, took full control. In 1923, this company went broke after most of Namu's pack was spoiled, and Namu and Kimsquit were bought by Gosse-Millerd Ltd. In 1926, it was transferred to Gosse Packing Co. Ltd. In that year, the sawmill and the original cannery were converted to the large netloft which was the familiar Namu landmark, and a new cannery built. In 1928, Namu became the property of B.C. Packers Ltd. The reduction plant was added in 1936 and enlarged in 1937, and again in 1938. In 1940, the cold storage and ice plant were constructed and in 1946, the cannery itself was rebuilt. There was also a modern ship repair yard. In December 1961, fire destroyed the plant. It was rebuilt in 1962 and opened in 1963. In 1970, the cannery was closed and the cold storage continued to be operated until 1988. B.C. Packers sold the site in 1991.

Price's: built in **1890** in Gardner Inlet by Price's Salmon Canning and Preserving Co., Messrs. H.M. Price and P. and W. Coats. Closed in 1893. John Carthew bought it in 1894 and transferred the equipment to Carlisle, which

Namu

he built in 1895.

Princess Royal: built in **1900** on China Hat Island in Finlayson Channel, by Princess Royal Packing Co. (Messrs. Toms, Morris and Fraser).

Tallheo: built in **1917** as the Nieumiamus cannery by B.F. Jacobsen of Bella Coola. It was located in North Bentinck Arm of Burke Channel, opposite Bella Coola. R.V. Winch was involved in the financing and he transferred it to Northern B.C. Fisheries Ltd. and renamed it Tallheo. In 1925, it was leased to The Canadian Fishing Co. and in 1926, sold to them. It canned until 1951, after which it was used as a gillnet camp. Finally, the property was sold to a Bella Coola resident who planned to convert it to a resort.

Walker Lake: built in **1927** by B.C. Fishing & Packing Co. on Johnson Channel, about ten miles from Ocean Falls. This plant and South Bay represented B.C. Fishing & Packing Co.'s late entry into the "cheap fish" sector of salmon canning. It included a cold storage which at first was located on a barge that had been transferred from South Bay on the Queen Charlotte Islands. In 1928, it became the property of B.C. Packers Ltd. In 1929, the cannery and cold storage were destroyed by fire. The cannery was not rebuilt, but a new cold storage was built in 1930. In 1939, this was dismantled and the operation moved to Namu.

The Floaters: Floating canneries would seem to make good sense where many plants existed to harvest very local runs that were available to the fishery for a very short period each season. Considerable investment was required to provide the means of canning, including a full crew for literally, just a few

Tallheo

Walker Lake

weeks. And the costs did not cease with the end of the season. Maintenance and security were on-going matters the year round. In some cases the cannery crew could be moved from plant to plant, where the runs did not occur at the same time. But the shore installations remained with all their fixed costs.

The floating cannery could be moved—machinery, crew and all—from place to place and in theory at least, would save the canner considerable costs. Moreover, cannery maintenance could be done in the winter in the major centres where prime facilities were available.

There were four vessels outfitted for floating canneries, but their operations were short-lived. These were the *Laurel Whalen*, the *Chilliwack I*, *Princess Beatrice* and the *Princess Ena*.

Francis Millerd, after separating from Gosse-Millerd Co. organized the Somerville Cannery Company Ltd. In 1924, he acquired the five-master *Laurel Whalen*, which had run into mechanical problems in Hawaii. He had it towed to Vancouver and converted into a floating cannery with a one-pound tall line. It first operated in Masset Inlet on the pink run of that year and packed 41,000 cases, a huge pack in the circumstances. Later in the season, it was moved to Quatsino Inlet to can the fall run of chum salmon.

In 1926, Gosse Packing Co. purchased the *Chilliwack I* from Union Steamships and converted her to a floater.

The next conversion was the *Princess Beatrice*, purchased from Canadian Pacific Steamships in January 1929 by Capt. B.L. Johnson & Associates. He removed the engines and boilers and sold the hull to Independent Packers Ltd., which was organized that April by T.G. Macmillan, N.S. Rogers and C.C. Bell. It operated in Rivers Inlet that season and later at New Westminster. B.C. Packers Ltd. purchased the company in 1930 and removed all the cannery equipment from the *Beatrice*.

Finally, Canadian Pacific Steamships sold the *Princess Ena* to Francis Millerd in 1933. He outfitted her for canning, but by the time she was ready, the province had outlawed floating canneries and she was never used in this way. Ownership reverted to Canadian Pacific and the vessel ended her days on the mud flat in Coal Harbour, Vancouver.

The fate of the floating canneries is a fascinating case of fishing industry politics. In the 1920s, both the federal and provincial governments issued licences for canneries. Somerville Cannery Co. had provincial licences for the *Laurel Whalen* and the cannery in Seal Cove. The operation of the *Laurel Whalen*, at times within sight of shore facilities of the larger companies—for example, her station in Masset Inlet was close to B.C. Fishing and Packing Co.'s Shannon Bay cannery—created indignation on their part. So in 1927, they appealed to the federal Minister of Fisheries to deny licences for floating plants. The Minister responded by ruling that Millerd could have a licence for salting salmon and for canning clams, but not for canning salmon.

Francis Millerd and his lawyers argued that the licensing of processing facilities was a provincial right and *ultra vires* the federal government. The federal government charged Somerville Cannery Co. with operating salmon canneries without federal permission. The lower court agreed with Francis Millerd and the government appealed the decision. The case went to the Supreme Court of B.C., the Supreme Court of Canada and finally to the Privy Council in London which, at that time, was the final court of appeal for Canada. At each stage, the original decision was upheld and, in 1929, licensing of fish plants became the sole jurisdiction of the province. Francis Millerd had won his case and established an important matter of constitutional law. But the process cost him dearly, financially, and he had to sell his plants to B.C. Packers Ltd., shortly after the merger with Gosse Packing Co.

Political influence was still being used and predictably, the province was convinced to require that floating canneries be limited to one location only, which, of course, obviated the advantage they were intended to have. Then in 1933, just as Francis Millerd was preparing his new floater, the *Princess Ena*, the province outlawed floating canneries altogether.

Ironically, B.C. Packers had a cold storage plant on a scow at the cannery which they had built in 1926 in South Bay, Queen Charlotte Islands. It was lost in Hecate Strait in 1929 as it was being towed to the Walker Lake cannery on Johnson Channel. It ended up on the rocks, but was salvaged and eventually repaired in Prince Rupert and finally made it to Walker Lake before fire destroyed that plant in December.

Chapter 5

THE MULTI-PURPOSE PLANTS

Most of the outlying plants were seasonal operations, some operating for only a few weeks each year. The costs associated with gearing up for such a short period of production were often enormous. And there was never any certainty as to the volume of catch that a cannery would be called upon to process. Under-utilization of capital assets and of key personnel, who had to be kept on the payroll if they were to be available in the canning season, was always a curse of the fishing industry. Prudent operators, of course, were always on the lookout for ways to mitigate these concerns. This gave rise to the multi-purpose, multi-season fish processing plants. There were not many of them that succeeded in achieving economic viability. But those that did created a unique industrial and social milieu in very isolated places.

The evolution of the multi-purpose plants took place primarily in the Steveston/Burrard Inlet area and in the Prince Rupert/Port Edward area. These plants typically included the cannery (salmon, tuna, herring, crabs, clams); reduction plant (herring, offal); cold storage; ice making; curing; in some cases, prepared products; and in later years, fish roe production. In the upcoast areas, some plants had two or more of these functions, but were still seasonal operations. There were three that achieved year round operating status: Butedale, Klemtu and Namu.

Butedale was The Canadian Fishing Company's north coast showplace plant. It was built in 1911, by John Wallace after he and his brother Peter, had dissolved their partnership, Wallace Brothers Fisheries. The location was exceptional because of an unlimited supply of fresh water from the seven mile lake above the plant, and an unlimited supply of electric power available to be generated from the same source. It was situated about 100 miles south of Prince Rupert in the Inside Passage, on Princess Royal Channel on Princess

Butedale

Royal Island. It thus had access to the productive salmon net fisheries and troll fishery which surrounded the plant, the halibut longline fishery of Hecate Strait and the Queen Charlotte Islands (and even further afield), and the north coast herring fisheries.

John Wallace sold the plant to Western Salmon Packers Ltd. in 1917, and they in turn sold it to The Canadian Fishing Co., Ltd. in 1923. The large cold storage plant was added in 1925 and it was completely modernized in 1936/37. In 1940, the cannery and the reduction plant were enlarged.

While the location had many advantages, it also had a serious flaw that would eventually prove fatal. That was the lack of good solid ground on which to build the plant. The foreshore was very steep and was not ideal for driving pilings. In fact, the plant was literally tied to the shore with cables to maintain its stability. The area was also subject to huge snowfalls, and as a result of one such winter the cannery roof collapsed under the weight. This coincided with the opening of Canfisco's Oceanside plant in 1951, so the cannery was not rebuilt. But even more serious for Butedale was the collapse of the reduction plant in 1959. Apparently, water coming off the side of the mountain behind the plant, had eroded the underwater sill on which the pilings were driven. No one knows how long this had been underway. But one evening in November, the reduction plant began to come apart and fall into the bay. Bob Lindsay, who was the head bookkeeper at the time, describes the event.

"We were working late in the office and a fellow came running in and said, 'Where's the First Aidman?' We said he was up in the bunkhouse, so away he went and as he was going out the door, he says, 'Oh, by the way, part of your dock just fell down.'

"So we ran out the door and ran over—there were two walkways there, one along where the boiler room was and the other to the weigh station. Well, we stood there for a few minutes and we couldn't see anything happening. And we just started to turn away and these planks went ping, ping and nails went flying out. Gradually, they all came out and then the pilings started going and then it started going in the reduction plant. The front of the plant was starting to fall and the marine leg fell off the front of the building. Then the building started tilting and here come the dryers. They were 50 or 60 feet long and they flew out of there and disappeared down in the water.

"And the plant kept going—more and more and more was collapsing. Across from the plant was the carpenter shop, the electrical shop and upstairs was where we had our movie equipment. People were in and out of those shops and there were outboard motors in there, just inside the door of the shops and the next thing you know, it jumped and it took the whole dock out and it took the shops out with it. The whole thing floated away. If you had been inside the building, you were gone. If you were standing just outside the door you would be alright. The outboard motors were on dollies. All they had to do was pull them out the door, but they never thought it was going to

Butedale – remains of reduction plant

jump. So everything went into the chuck. And in the morning, all the pilings, hundreds of them were gone. All that was sitting in the middle of the bay was the top of the rec hall.

"Underneath the plant there was a stream coming down. We had had torrential rains and I think what happened was that there could have been some trees fallen up the hill and dammed the creek, and all of a sudden had given way and the water came roaring down. Over the years, the creek had eroded the shelf and with this, it started to go. It took all that out and it also took out the drain where the boiler was. We had 2,400 barrels of bunker C which all drained out during the night. We never saw a trace of it in the bay.

"In the morning, we had divers come down from Rupert and they went down and they said there was just little bits of stuff sticking up through the sand that came down. You couldn't see the dryers and all that piling disappeared."

The plant was rebuilt, but it only operated for two more years or so, when the herring fishery for reduction purposes gave way to the herring roe fishery. The cold storage plant also operated for a few more years, and then it too was closed and the company's operations moved to the new Oceanside plant in Prince Rupert in 1973.

During its heyday, Butedale was a thriving operation and a thriving community. Like all upcoast plants it had its China House and its Indian village. Butedale was associated primarily with the Kitimaat Indians. Some were from Hartley Bay as well, but that band was associated more with Klemtu.

The Department of Fisheries officer for the north coast was based at Butedale. For many years the man in charge was Cliff Levelton, who was born in Bella Coola and rose to become the second in command of the Department of Fisheries in Ottawa.

Butedale took much of its character from its dynamic manager, Billy Malcolm, who was in charge from 1945 until the end of the operations, with a short hiatus when he was also managing the Oceanside cannery.

Billy Malcolm began his career with B.C. Packers as the storekeeper at San Mateo in 1928. He rose through the ranks and into the sales department and worked there throughout the war years.

In 1945, he left B.C. Packers and became manager of Butedale for Canfisco. He built Butedale into a model operation and energetically pursued the production targets that he set for himself to justify the company's investment in this relatively remote location. Billy Malcolm developed the disease of alcoholism, which was so common in the remote canneries and logging camps. But he was one of the exceptions who managed to overcome it and he became a life-long abstainer and member of Alcoholics Anonymous. Not only that, he provided employment for many talented and capable people who were not as able as he to cope with their drinking problem. He provided the atmosphere at Butedale for these people to avoid the temptation. Not everyone was successful at that all the time, and from time to time there were falls from the wagon. But Billy Malcolm was a lifesaver for many members of AA.

The isolation of Butedale was not for everybody, but to some it was a beautiful place to live and work. Bob Lindsay is one of those and his experience is worth recording. Bob had his first taste of the cannery life in 1943 at Claxton, when he and some high school buddies were recruited to help fill the gap in labour ranks created by the exiling of the Japanese to the interior of the province in 1942. Later, he joined the Army and then joined Canadian Fishing Co. as a bookkeeper in 1952. In February 1955, after seasons at Rivers Inlet and Tallheo, he was sent to Butedale with his bride. The theory was that in the upcoast plants there was an opportunity to save money because housing was provided and there was little to spend money on. Here is how Bob describes life in Butedale.

"Butedale in those days comprised a reduction plant and a large cold storage but no cannery. The snow had smashed the roof in some years earlier. It had a large store that did a real good business. There was an Indian village attached to the plant. They stayed year round, quite a few hundred people.

"Behind the reduction plant, there was the machine shop, electrical shop and carpenter shop. And above that there was our rec hall, where we played bingo, had whist drives and on Friday and Saturday nights we had movies and the office staff would show the movies.

"We usually took in over a million pounds of halibut every year. We had a large ice-making plant. Fishermen thought we had the best ice on the coast. We would make it all in the fall and then it would mature over the winter months and then by February, the boats would be stopping on their way to the Bering Sea. They would deliver their catch to us, too. They were required to tie up for eight days after delivery. So if they went to Vancouver, they would be that much further from the grounds when their lay-up started. So they would sell to us. We were paying a competitive price, too. But we did that for all species.

"Butedale was a beautiful spot, actually. It had a nice waterfall beside the plant which was fed by a seven mile lake. We had a large pipeline coming down from the lake, running our power plant. People got along fairly well. We had a First Aid man there all the time. He spent a lot of time over at the Indian village looking after people. We had a radio man who was also the night watchman.

"In those days the herring started in September and went until February, and then you got ready for the halibut boats and the salmon trollers. And there was always painting going on. Mr. Malcolm made sure that any spare time that people had was used in keeping the place looking good. The houses were painted, the buildings were painted, everything was kept up to scratch and in really good shape.

"The salmon season lasted for quite awhile. There was a big fishery in Whale Channel. Lots of weekends, we would have 50 or 60 seine boats in there, getting groceries and repairs, etc. Not all of them were Canfisco boats—Butedale was considered a service centre for all boats fishing in the area. They did a real big business in that store. The butcher would just cut—that was all he had time to do, and somebody else would do the wrapping and weighing and everything else.

"It's a shame things like that couldn't last forever.

"There was one fellow died up there and when they went in to clean up his place, they found all these wet sacks on the floor. And they lifted the wet sacks and they were covering halibut heads that he had been saving. I never saw such a sight.

"One night I was working late in the office and my wife phoned me and said, 'There's a bear on our verandah!' So I ran up the hill and I said, 'Where is it?' She said, 'It just left.' She didn't know what to do, so she was putting honey on buns and throwing them out the door. It wasn't that big a bear, but when he stood up he was five or six feet tall. The guy next door wanted to wrestle it! But the poor bear, he came back the next night to the wrong house and he was shot.

"We had a wolf that they shot down by the dock one time. And he was just skin and bones.

"One thing that sort of put us off—a bunch of people came up from St. Louis who had an okay from the government in Ottawa to take a Kermode bear off the Island. They had permission to shoot one and take it back to St. Louis for their museum and stuff it and stick it up there. The first year, they stayed at Butedale and they went out and later, they told us they were just ready to shoot at one when somebody started up an outboard motor and the bear was gone. The second year, they came back and got one. They are very rare.

"Butedale had lots of snow and lots of rain. One year, it rained so much, Billy Malcolm called in a steamer and took all the women and children off the hill and sent them to Rupert because he was afraid the dam might break. Of course, he left all the men in their houses.

"I had a boat at Butedale. We used to go down to Altenhash Inlet. It was so peaceful out there and we'd get these big springs, and late in August there were two coho streams where you'd get nine or nineteen pound coho. They'd come out of the water and flash their tail at you. Right in the bay at Butedale you could get big salmon.

"Pete Seifert and I built a houseboat for the lake. It was 16 feet long and 6 feet wide. We had a cabin and a stove for it and we bought an outboard motor. We hauled it up to the lake by the pipeline with the help of a bunch of other guys. The trout up there were fantastic."

Peter Seifert went to Butedale in 1953 for four years, and he has fond memories, too. "We used to have quite a few parties. Christmas and New Year's Eve, we had a big party and Billy could be just as funny being sober as us being drunk. It was always fun and that was what I liked about Butedale. Billy was always the actor at social events. At New Year's he was the old year going out, dressed up as an old man with the scythe. And at midnight, the lights would go off and when they came on, here he comes with the diapers on as the New Year. The Browns would make a big dinner for the whole crowd, everyone who was in the townsite at the time.

"There were three boats came in. The two Union Steamship boats, *Camosun* and *Chilcotin* and the C.P.R.'s *Princess Louise*. So we were well in touch with Vancouver and Prince Rupert, because they would stop both going north and on the way back. They'd pick up salmon and herring meal. The tourists would say how nice it was there—that we'd get paid to be there and they would have to pay to visit.

Party time

"We had a big office, a post office, a little school and the rec hall. We had a huge bunkhouse and a big messhouse. There were about 12 homes on the hill where the employees lived with their families. Then there was the big powerhouse and the lake and the dam.

'We had a few gillnetters of our own—some Natives from Kitimaat. We had quite a few seiners and about four or five boats from Bella Bella, and we had the Cliftons from Hartley Bay.

"There were a lot of good Norwegian seine fishermen there and they were all good strong drinkers. That was part of their life and part of their heritage. But at that time, there was a lot of drinking. Alcohol was sort of number one in the whole industry. The herring seiners were mostly Norwegian; they were the originals in the herring reduction fishery.

"One year, we had the biggest runs of herring at the bottom of Queen Charlotte Islands and the boats brought in fish to us and plugged us. And Billy didn't want any herring going to Vancouver; he wanted it at Butedale even if we had to put it in the houses. At that very time he was rushed to the hospital in Prince Rupert because of his ulcers which were very bad. He left us the job of keeping it going. He kept in contact with me while he was in the hospital, telling me when I got on the conference calls to tell them we can handle all of the fish we get. But we were completely plugged. We had barges of herring and anything we could put it in so we could show we weren't overloaded. But somebody looked after us fools and the herring quit in the Queen Charlottes just at the right time. We put through one of the biggest yields the company had ever had anywhere. The next year, the reduction plant fell in the chuck."

Butedale was on the circuit for the Native basketball league. Teams from Kitimaat and other villages would play a regular circuit, which included Prince Rupert, and were often the north coast champions.

Klemtu was J.H. Todd & Sons' north coast entrepot. It was unusual in that it was located on the Klemtu Indian Reserve. The adjacent village was the main source of labour for the plant. It was located on Swindle Island in a narrow protected passage behind China Hat Island, which separated it from Finlayson Channel. Klemtu cannery had a varied history. It was built in 1927 by Klemtu Canning Co., one of the Todd group of companies. It was closed at the end of 1930 and did not reopen until 1934.

In 1941, the company decided to expand the plant and was fortunate in being able to hire Lew Hogan to manage the operation. He rebuilt the cannery and added a large, modern cold storage and ice plant. He also built a small reduction plant for the processing of offal, but never went into the herring

Klemtu

reduction business. The cold storage brought them business from the halibut fishermen and salmon trollers and they established live herring bait ponds for the halibut boats. Jack McMillan, who later founded J.S. McMillan Fisheries Ltd., was in charge of the fresh and frozen operation and even established groundfish processing—unusual at that time. As well as salmon, the cannery processed herring and abalone and clams. So Klemtu became a multi-purpose, year round operation.

Besides the Klemtu Natives, there were Indians from other northern villages as well—Kitimaat, for example and some of the Cliftons from Hartley Bay. Lew Hogan, Jr. affirms that Louis Clifton was the best fisherman Klemtu had. In fact, the Clifton family were known throughout the coast as outstanding people. Most of the Klemtu men went to Rivers Inlet for the sockeye gillnetting season and in the fall would return and crew the company's 16 seine boats.

Lew Hogan was drowned in 1948, on a trip to Hartley Bay to arrange for clam diggers. The operation carried on and in 1954, J.H. Todd & Sons was bought by B.C. Packers and Canadian Fishing Co. together. A few years later, a huge processing error resulted in a significant part of the salmon pack being undercooked and spoiled. This was a blow to Klemtu and to Todds. In 1969, the partnership dissolved and B.C. Packers became the owners of Klemtu. The plant was closed shortly afterward and ownership was transferred to the Klemtu band. It was subsequently removed.

The plant, of course, was of huge economic significance to the Native people of Klemtu and the region.

In the summer season, at its peak, **Namu** was the largest community between Port Hardy and Prince Rupert, except for Ocean Falls and Bella Coola. It is located in Namu Bay on Fitzhugh Sound on the Inside Passage route. The first plant was built there in 1893 by fishing industry pioneer, Robert Draney, as Namu Canning Co. In 1909, he built a large sawmill which was the source of timbers and lumber for many of the early canneries in the central area of the coast. The site was one of those happy combinations of a deep water, protected harbour, with a reliable year round source of quality fresh water, located central to major fishing grounds.

In 1911, a new cannery was built and the existing one was used to expand the sawmill. Eventually the mill was closed and the building became the netloft, which, with NAMU painted in large letters on its roof, was a landmark on the coast for many years. Robert Draney sold the establishment in 1912, to Henry Doyle and his associates, who changed the name of the company to Draney Fisheries Ltd. In 1915, R.V. Winch bought a 52 percent interest in the company and the following year, took full control. In the same way, he acquired the Kimsquit cannery, which had been built by Draney in 1901. In 1918, R.V. Winch and Henry Doyle incorporated Northern B.C. Fisheries Ltd. to amalgamate their various canneries, which at that time, were Namu, Kimsquit, Tallheo, Skeena River Commercial and Mill Bay. Henry Doyle was vice president of the company.

In 1923, Northern B.C. Fisheries was in financial difficulty, and when the bulk of the Namu pack was ruined because of undercooking, the Royal Bank cut off financing and the company went under. Gosse-Millerd Packing Co., Ltd. bought Namu and Kimsquit in 1924. In 1926, it was transferred to Gosse Packing Co. Ltd., which in that year became a subsidiary of B.C. Fishing & Packing Co. In 1928, Namu became the property of B.C. Packers Ltd.

B.C. Packers made Namu their central coast headquarters. In 1936, they built a herring reduction plant which they enlarged in 1937 and again in 1938. In 1940, the cold storage and ice plant were constructed and in 1946, the cannery was rebuilt and modernized. Between 1946 and 1949, the residences, bunkhouses and Indian village were reconstructed and the recreation hall and school built.

The cannery at that time had five lines (plus two hand packing lines)— one of the largest on the coast—and could can 4,800 cases of salmon in an eight-hour shift.

In the winter of 1961, Christmas week, the cannery and cold storage were destroyed by fire. It was rebuilt in 1962, and although it had one fewer lines than the old plant, was probably the most modern fish processing plant on the coast at that time. But that season, which was a record pink salmon run in

The new Namu plant

the area, the salmon had to be transported to Klemtu, Sunnyside, Port Edward and Imperial. This was made possible by the introduction of refrigerated seawater which was just coming into general use.

For a few years before the fire, the plant was equipped with Birdseye freezers and produced some groundfish fillets.

The plant would have a payroll of between 400 and 500 at peak times. Many of the employees came from Bella Bella and Bella Coola and Kitimaat, and even from as far away as the Nass River, as well as from the Vancouver area. There were many Vancouver residents who financed their university education by working at Namu in the summers.

There was a large Indian village, the population of which could reach 1,500 in the summer. There were four bunkhouses and houses for Japanese fishermen and their families, many of whom also worked in the plant. Some of these lived at Namu year round.

Eric Kramer, who was personnel manager and later plant manager, spent ten years there. He was responsible as well, for the townsite and all the facilities. He has recollections, of course, of good as well as bad times with the residents and employees. He recalls that "there was usually a dance every week and sometimes you had to adjust the time of the dance or the movies so we could get finished canning.

"There used to be a big bloodbath when the Alert Bay gang (seine boats) showed up on their first weekend. They'd have come all the way across the Sound and it wasn't usual to see that many boats go over into the central area as it is today. Today they go anywhere, but then it was quite a voyage. They'd either bring the booze with them or go up to Ocean Falls and get it and have a party at Namu. There was animosity between some of the different bands.

"In most Indian villages, there were some families that may be more successful than others. They're good fishermen and good boat operators and good businessmen and they do very well. That was the case in Bella Bella and there were some leading people came from there.

"Dr. Darby used to travel on the William H. Pierce. He'd go down to Rivers Inlet in the summer. He'd stop at Namu going down and again coming back. In later years, he'd have an intern or another doctor. He might leave the younger doctor at Bella Bella and he'd make the trip to Rivers. He did that every week during the fishing season."

There was a two-room school with two teachers on a year round basis. There was a large messhall, a café, a bowling alley and a gymnasium for basketball games and dances. There was a modern store with a staff of 10 which served the community and the many fishermen who made Namu their base, or who stopped in on their northbound or southbound trips.

There was a ship repair yard and a machine shop with shipwrights, electricians, machinists, mechanics and welders. There was a standby boat, the *Namu*, equipped as a hospital boat, which would transport people who needed hospital attention to Bella Bella.

The new plant operated full out until 1981, but the refrigerated seawater phenomenon spelled its doom and that year, the Company sold the plant and the townsite.

Milton "Mac" MacLean built most of B.C. Packers' reduction plants and in 1946, he became manager at Namu, succeeding A.E. Moorehouse, who had had a "squabble" with Bob Walker, the president. Mac related, "Namu is one of the nicest memories I have."

He tells how the recreation hall was built. "I heard they were going to tear down the old cannery on the Skeena (Claxton). There were a lot of people at Namu in the season with their families and I thought I'd like to build a recreation hall. And I daren't ask for new lumber or anything. But I had the gang around on the scow and I went up with the scow and the old *Nishga*, which we used as a towboat and I took this gang with me and we tore the cannery down and loaded it on the scow. Then we built the recreation hall."

Mac was well loved and respected by all the fishermen and employees. He loved to tell stories and some of his favourites were about the people who lived in Namu's Indian village.

"At Namu we had an interning doctor as First Aid attendant. He told me about a girl who came over to the First Aid shack. She said, 'My mother is awful sick and she's got to see a doctor.' So Phil grabs his bag and follows the girl down to the village. And the door's closed and he knocks on the door and this big guy comes to the door and Phil says, 'I'm the doctor and I'm here to see your mother.' He says, 'She's too sick to see anybody,' and he slammed the door on Phil.

"When the season was about to start, you'd let the word out at Bella Bella and they'd start coming down. They would be coming in all day and packing their stuff in. And invariably there'd be a knock on the door about nine or ten o'clock at night. And there'd be an Indian saying, 'I want a light bulb.' I'd say, 'For Christ sake, you were in here all afternoon, why didn't you get your light bulb from the store?' 'It's just getting dark now!' was the answer.

"One of the girls with kids came this night to the door. 'You gotta come quick; Charlie's got a rifle and he's going to shoot my sister.' So I get some clothes on and go down and this drunken guy is there with a gun alright, and he's yelling his head off and half the time you don't know what he's saying. And I says, 'Give me that gun'. He says, 'No, that's my protection.' I said, 'For God's sake,' and I took the gun away from him. He says, 'You take my protection away from me.' I says, 'Protection from who?' He says, 'From her!'

"I'll never forget the time Norman Nelson came in with the Masset bunch. They had that fleet over there. The trouble is he stopped at Ocean Falls and loaded up with liquor. I don't know why the hell he didn't stay in Ocean Falls; I guess he was afraid to. But he brought them all down and unloaded them at Namu, then he got the hell out of there. They were standing around and then they got over into our village and then the fights started. One of them came up to the house and got me. 'There's a hell of a fight going on at so and so's house.' The sidewalk went along there and then up to the houses. He told me which house and he said, 'He's going to kill us all,' and a lot of BS like that. So I ran down there and I just turned to go up this sidewalk to the house when the door flew open and here's this big Queen Charlottes guy and I always remember he had a bottle of whisky stuck in his belt. He looked at me, he didn't know who the hell I was, I was just white and I could see he was thinking he was in good shape and he was going to fix this white son of a bitch. He came down the slope swinging, 'I'll fight you, you son of a bitch.' So I just stood aside and just leaned back over the rail. And he went past me and that sidewalk was a real slope and he went right through the rail and knocked himself out. But he wasn't hurt.

"This is a real sad story. This was one of the coldest nights we had at Namu—it got below zero (F). The Union steamship was due in and everybody, of course, was down to the Union steamship. One couple left some kids locked up in the house. They all had wood stoves and the kids set the house on fire. By the time we got there, we couldn't do a thing about it and we had no water because everything was frozen up including the water lines. The kids burned to death. We couldn't do anything that night; we consoled the family and we took them into our house in the guest room we had there. They had lost three kids. Norman Campbell was my storekeeper and I said, 'Norman, I've got the family at the house and I'm going to bring them down to the store about eight in the morning as soon as we get them breakfast. They've lost everything—no blankets or anything. You stop and figure out what they might need and be ready for them.' So they had breakfast and I said, 'Now you go down to the store and Mr. Campbell will give you anything you need.' So after a bit, I thought I'd better go down and help Norman out. So I walked in the door and here they're all just inside the door—this is where the ice cream counter was—and Norman's away down at the hardware end. I said, 'Go down where Mr. Campbell is and he'll get you what you need.' 'Yes, but we want some pop first.' As long as it was free they were going to have a treat."

Not all Mac's stories were about the Indians. "When I built the reduction plant at Namu, we got that real cold winter. And we drew all our water from the lake. Finally the pipeline froze up. I had anticipated this and I had taken a couple of small oil tanks out of the plant and filled them with fresh water and I put a circulating system on the one diesel we had for lights. We ran a week or so while this cold weather was on, just on this circulating water. Something happened—this lad I had watching it, he said, 'God, we've run out of water, we'll have to shut the diesel down.' The only lights we could see in the place were at the Moorehouse's. I went in there and she had a bridge game going. I said, 'Mrs. Moorehouse, you better put some lamps or candles on, we're going to have to shut the diesel down.' She says, 'You'll shut it down when I tell you!' Needless to say, she and I were never friends after that.

"I've always looked back on Namu as just one big family. The companionship there was good and the feeling was of a close community. I still run into people who worked there and I haven't run into anybody who's had a bad feeling about Namu."

Art Miller would concur. Art grew up at Bella Bella and Namu and learned his fisheries and marine expertise there. He credited his years at Namu as his training ground for his whole career.

Chapter 6

THE CAUSES OF DECLINE OF THE OUTLYING PLANTS

The phenomenal growth in the number of salmon canneries in the early part of the 20th century was a result, on the one hand, of a burgeoning growth in the market for canned salmon, particularly in the U.K. and British Empire countries, and on the other, the need to locate production facilities as close as possible to the source of the raw fish.

The early export market had been established by brokers in San Francisco and, to a lesser extent in Victoria. In some ways, in Britain, it was based on the British taste for fresh salmon, which more and more was becoming a scarce commodity in their own country. Canned salmon filled a need which already existed when the North American product became available.

Men like Henry Bell-Irving had the connections and the know-how to bypass some of the middlemen who had built the distribution chain to their advantage, and made it possible for B.C. canners to gain a greater share of the market value. This made the small cannery with short seasons economically viable and the entrepreneurs rushed in.

The American producers were the first in the British market, but the Canadians took it over as the Americans built up their own domestic market. Later, as Puget Sound and Alaska came on stream, the Americans came again to dominate the British market. But by that time, the market demand itself had increased dramatically. Later still, the Japanese and Russians entered the canned salmon export markets and because of their low-cost fishing operations using traps, were able to do considerable damage to the B.C. producers' earnings.

The early canneries were capital intensive only in terms of the buildings, boats and nets. Mechanization was virtually absent and every part of the production process was done by hand labour. Generally, the outlying canneries were located in unpopulated areas, so it was necessary to provide accommodation and services for the labour force, both fishermen and cannery crews. The cannery village, with all its separate parts, was a cost of doing business, and though it persisted for many decades, it had in its very existence, the seeds of its own destruction.

The two great objectives for cannery operators from the beginning were: 1) to find labour-saving measures which would permit reductions in the size of the crew or increases in the capacity of the plant, and 2) to find the means of transporting raw fish longer distances without losing quality, so as to permit the concentration of processing facilities and the extension of the season for those larger plants.

These two processes were on-going and continuous. They manifested themselves in both small ways and in some very dramatic ways.

Can making: In the early days, all the cans were made by hand. The bodies and the ends were actually cut out of tin plate with shears and soldered together. Each season, the Chinese crew would arrive at the cannery well before fishing started and make the stockpile of cans necessary for the upcoming pack. The first innovation was the press which stamped the ends—a big labour saver and a big improvement in consistency. Then came the automatic soldering machine, which soldered the side seams of the bodies.

Factory-made cans were introduced fairly early. Henry Bell-Irving organized the Automatic Can Company in New Westminster in 1897. He followed this with a can-making plant at North Pacific cannery, which provided cans for Anglo-B.C.'s northern plants and for those of other companies. B.C. Packers installed a can making line at Wadhams and supplied many of its own plants for many years. Eventually this all gave way to the mass-produced can of American Can Company and Continental Can Company. American Can came to own the modern canning machinery and gained a virtual monopoly on the production of cans.

The invention of the double seam eliminated the need for soldering. While it was invented in 1906, it did not come into use by B.C. salmon canners until 1913. The collapsed can body was a great innovation in that it reduced freight costs for shipping empty cans to the canneries from the factory in Vancouver. Most upcoast canneries came to have reform lines which reshaped the bodies and attached the CANADA end prior to filling. In time, this process also declined and the cans were shipped ready for filling. It ended entirely with the introduction of the one-piece seamless can, which is now the norm in the industry.

The Marine Leg: Unloading the raw fish from the boat or scow to the cannery was a labour intensive and time-consuming task. The single-tined fish pugh was the instrument and each fish had to be speared individually through the head and pitched to the dock. Balmoral cannery was using a waterwheel in 1894 for unloading, but the first innovation in common use was the brailer and winch. Power was provided by steam in the early days and this limited the use of the brailer. The larger vessels had their own winch capability and were able to brail their loads themselves to the cannery dock and gutshed.

When electricity became available (by water power in some cases and by diesel generators in most), the marine leg became the method of choice. This ingenious invention was an elevator which was placed in the hold of the vessel where unloaders pitched the fish onto the leg. It carried the fish to the cannery "gutshed" by a continuous belt with slats or buckets attached at intervals. The marine leg in its various forms and brailing continued for many years until the conversion of fish packers to refrigerated seawater resulted in the pumping of fish to the processing plant.

The Iron Chink: This was the first significant mechanization of the canning process and, along with the vacuum closing machine and refrigerated seawater, remains one of the most significant in the history of salmon canning. Prior to its introduction, all the cannery fish were dressed or butchered by hand. The head and tail were removed, the belly slit open and the entrails and "kidney" removed. The Iron Chink was invented by Smith Bros. in 1903. Its use became universal in very short order and it has remained an integral part of the canning process ever since. It immediately made a big dent in the number of workers. It does all the work of the hand butcher, and at remarkable speeds.

Hand butchering was done primarily by Chinese men and hence the unfortunate name of this ingenious machine. Today it is more commonly referred to as the Iron Butcher, but the original name still appears on the machine itself.

The filling machine: The automatic filling machine—first the 4-spindle filler and then the high speed filling machine in use today—enabled a quantum leap in the capacity of a plant. In the early canneries, all the cans were filled by hand—primarily by Indian women and later by Japanese women as well. The job was at once demanding and monotonous, but the workers developed remarkable dexterity and skill. Pay was by piecework and the good fillers could make impressive earnings. The automatic filling machine eliminated most of these jobs. But while it was fast, the quality and appearance of its pack was inferior to the hand-filled product. And while improvements were made in the machine, hand-filling continued where superior quality was required, and for the 1/4 pound cans, which defied good machine filling for many years. (The first 1/4 pound filling machine was devised by Tom Van

Snellenberg of Canfisco in the 1960s.)

The vacuum closing machine: This was one of the all-time most important improvements in the canning process from the point of view, both of cost of production and of safety of the product. It eliminated the double cook and the "punch and solder" of the can tops. Along with the double seam can, it reduced the number of rejects and improved the integrity of canned salmon for the consumer.

Prior to the introduction of the vacuum machine, the exhaust box system was used to create the vacuum which is essential to preservation of the product in the can. Henry Doyle gives this terse description: "After salmon is cleaned, it is passed into a brine for 20 minutes (improves flavour), or dry salt is added to the can. From clincher to the exhaust box on a continuous chain with steam heat of 200 degrees for 14 minutes. This pre-heats the fish to 150 degrees which is sufficient to expel the air from the can and create a vacuum. Then to the closing machine which hermetically seals the cans. Then to the washing machine to remove dirt and grease. Then to cooler trays and to retorts—15 to 18 lbs. of steam pressure, 238 to 248 degrees temperature for 1 hour and 15 mins. for talls and 1 hour, 30 mins. for 1/2s. Then maybe to lye tank (weak solution). After cooling, to lacquer machine."

Peter Matthews adds a little more detail: "They used to have steam boxes to seal the cans. They would be heated to the boiling point, but not cooked, and the cans cooling down would create the vacuum. Then to the retorts for cooking. Then they would wheel them all out and wash them in a big kettle of lye. There would be two men washing them off with a stiff brush and then there would be one man with a little hammer and he would tap each can to see if the vacuum held or if it was a leak. And then the cans were lacquered and piled in the warehouse."

The Bussey System: This invention automated the loading of retort cars and made possible the automatic casing machine, both of which eliminated much of the labour at the tail end of the cannery.

Others: The automatic weighing machine, which doesn't actually weigh the can but can be set to detect and reject underweight cans from the line, made possible the high-speed filling line.

Prior to the towmotor, just about everything except the raw fish was moved by two-wheeled steamer trucks. This included all the freight off-loaded from the steamboat and all the freight, including case goods, loaded onto the freighter. Every cannery would have hundreds of these indispensable dollies.

The labelling machine tackled one of the most difficult automation challenges, not just in the salmon canneries but in every can labelling situation. At first, every can label was attached by hand with glue—a terribly labour-intensive and costly process. The challenge was to devise a machine which would separate the labels from the stack, have them meet the can at the proper time and deposit the glue at the right time, the right place and in the right amount, all at high speed. There were many attempts before a reliable labeller was developed.

All of these innovations and mechanizations made possible the reduction in the number of workers required and the increase in the capacity of any given plant. As the cost of labour increased, primarily through collective bargaining with the rise of the Union movement, the pace of mechanization accelerated. And so did the pace of consolidation and concentration of processing facilities. The capital outlay to mechanize a cannery, whose source of raw material was available for only a few weeks, was prohibitive. That, along with the rising cost of preparing the plant for a short season, the cost of direct labour and the cost of the skilled employees, who were essential to the maintenance and operations of the machines, hastened the closing of the many plants which had been built to utilize a particular run of salmon.

But this rationalization could not have occurred without improvements in the transportation of fish. Probably no mass-produced product is more perishable than fish, and salmon, even in prime sea run condition is no exception.

The earliest plants had no means of delaying the deterioration, not even the ability to make ice. Believe it or not, Glendale cannery, for example, never did have ice-making capacity. It was not unusual for fishermen to take ice from the nearby glacier, which at one time actually met tidewater.

So, great efforts were made to improve the capacity and speed of the packer boats and to find practical means of refrigeration for carrying raw fish longer distances.

The first tender boats were the steam tugs that towed the sailboats to the fishing grounds. Each cannery had its small collector boats, powered by gasoline engines, and scows, that collected the fish from the boats and delivered them to the cannery at least once a day. The introduction of the diesel engine made it possible to deliver fish in good condition over longer distances, without ice. But icing of fish as a commonplace was not far behind.

Probably the first cold storage plant upcoast was at the Cunningham cannery in Port Essington. But this was designed for mild curing rather than for freezing and ice making. Similarly with the cold storage plant built by Wallace Fisheries at Claxton. The first true cold storage with sharp freezing capability was at Canadian Fish and Cold Storage in Seal Cove in 1910. This was quickly followed by Home Plant in Vancouver, Northern Fishermen's Cold Storage in Rupert harbour, Butedale and Namu. These plants were built to provide ice for the distant water halibut fleet and to freeze and store their catch. So with the availability of an ice supply, the industry embarked on a building spree of large diesel powered packers which would carry ice to the fishing grounds and collect the raw salmon from the seine boats and gillnet collectors at strategic locations. This made it possible to transport salmon to processing plants at central locations and spelt doom for the small, short season cannery.

Steveston and Vancouver had always been the centre of processing in the south and the plants there were expanded and consolidated and diversified. Similarly, Prince Rupert became the main centre in the north and Butedale, Namu and Klemtu were enlarged and diversified to serve as the main depots in the Central area. Nelson Brothers, the late comers of the "big four", never did have a processing plant in the central coast, relying on their packer fleet to speed their catch to St. Mungo or Paramount in the south and Port Edward in the north.

Many of the smaller canneries persisted, however, into the 1930s and 1940s as this transportation revolution evolved. But as they ceased processing, they became servicing operations for the fishing fleet or were simply abandoned along with their villages and infrastructure. The last single-purpose salmon cannery to operate north of Cape Caution (outside the Skeena River), Canfisco's Goose Bay, ceased processing in 1957. (The exceptions were the plants of niche operators like Millbanke Fisheries at Bella Bella, Seafood Products at Port Hardy and Tofino Packers on the west coast of Vancouver Island.)

With the introduction and perfection of the refrigerated seawater system, the remaining upcoast canneries were doomed. Butedale was the first of the last to go. The cannery roof caved in under an exceptionally heavy snow load in the winter of 1950. The reduction plant collapsed into the bay in 1959, and while it was rebuilt, it operated only for a few years. The cold storage plant continued also, but it too was eventually closed.

Klemtu became the property of Canadian Fishing Co. and B.C. Packers when they bought J.H. Todd & Sons in 1954. They didn't need the plant for their own operations and a disastrous under-cook of a large part of one year's pack hastened the decision to close the plant.

Namu suffered a devastating fire in December 1961. The plant was rebuilt as a condition of the insurance policy, but in the interim, B.C. Packers had found that they were able to get along without it, and the cannery canned its last salmon in 1970.

Refrigerated seawater was the brainchild of Stuart Roach and John Harrison of the Technological Station of the Fisheries Research Board. They did their initial research at Millerd's Great Northern Cannery in West Vancouver. The practical trials were made on vessels of several of the fishing companies and after much trial and error, the system was perfected. The effect on the B.C. fishing industry was revolutionary. Once the vessels were converted, it was possible to carry fish at temperatures just above the freezing point of the fish and deliver them to the processing plant, hundreds of miles away, virtually in rigor and untouched by human hands. The fate of the upcoast cannery was sealed and processing is now concentrated in multi-purpose plants in Prince Rupert and Vancouver. Even Steveston, the historic epicentre of the Fraser River salmon industry, no longer cans any salmon.

The locating of canneries near the salmon streams was motivated in large part by the need to assure the quality of the product. It is curious, therefore, that modern quality assurance regulations also played a significant role in the closure of some of the upcoast canneries and their villages.

The early canners were not well-versed in sanitation. They knew that the salmon must be canned as soon as possible after being caught, but they relied heavily on the sterilization of the product by the steam cooking process and the steam cleaning of the plant and equipment. So the canneries had wooden floors and open ceilings which often harboured bats and birds. Metal surfaces and equipment were usually galvanized steel and sanitation for personnel was crude at best. The fish guts and cannery water went through the floor into the sea or river below, and while this was food for other wildlife, it often accumulated to a rotting, stinking mess.

The cannery villages used outdoor privies positioned over the water and relied on the daily flushing action of tides to carry away the refuse.

These conditions eventually caught the attention of regulators who mandated that all canneries must have concrete floors, closed ceilings, stainless steel equipment and the means of disposing of offal from the plant. While admirable in their intent, these regulations were costly to comply with and these good intentions hastened the demise of many of the canneries and their villages and the employment which had become the mainstay of many upcoast people.

The same was true of cannery housing. These seasonal houses were deemed to be inadequate by certain bureaucrats who demanded systematic upgrading. To the marginal cannery the cost of doing so, added to the cost of providing and maintaining the housing in the first place, was decisive. So the villages were dismantled and the employment of the people who had occupied them for generations was gone.

The modern canneries in major urban settings have ready labour supply without the need to provide the housing and services that the isolated canneries had provided.

It is anomalous that the Skeena River canneries bucked the trend as long as they did. The Grand Trunk Pacific Railway linked Prince Rupert with the up-river Indian villages which provided much of the cannery labour in 1910, and with the rest of Canada in 1914. This took the centre of gravity away from Port Essington which was the base for upriver steamboat travel, and put the south shore canneries at a disadvantage to those located on the Inverness Slough which was now on the new rail line. Yet canning continued in Port Essington until 1934 and at Claxton until 1945 and at Carlisle until 1950.

Port Edward, North Pacific and Cassiar, all of which had cannery villages, operated into the 1970s and 1980s in spite of the existence of the road from Prince Rupert as far as Cassiar.

So the decline of the upcoast canneries was the result of the built-in inefficiencies of single purpose, short season plants; the costly infrastructure that the cannery townsite required; the mechanization of the canning process; government regulations aimed at food safety; and the development of fast refrigerated transportation of the raw fish.

Early can factory

Vacuum sealer

Belts and wheels

Feeding the Iron Chink

Pretty slimers

The patching line

Reform machines

Chapter 7

THE GREAT AMALGAMATIONS

Over the decades, the salmon canning industry has had a pattern of growth, overcapacity, mergers, buy-outs, bankruptcies and amalgamations. Since 1870, there have been over 175 canneries built on the B.C. coast outside the metropolitan areas, and as many as 95 of these have operated in a given season. Some of these were fly-by-night operations, where some enterprising citizens threw up a shed and a retort in some likely spot and canned for one or two seasons and then abandoned the site. There was a cycle of over-expansion and overcapitalization followed by either forced or voluntary retrenchment. Many canneries fell victim to fire and were never rebuilt. Some of these must be viewed as 'suspicious', as the underwriters would say, but fire was part of the periodic rationalization process.

Amalgamation was the preferred method. And there were a few major ones that changed the face of the industry in a lasting way.

The first of these was the formation of the Anglo-British Columbia Packing Co., Ltd. in December of 1890. Henry Bell-Irving "got some scales on him," through his import-export company, Bell-Irving and Paterson. They represented some of the canners in wholesaling their packs in the United Kingdom. In 1889, Bell-Irving had chartered the *Titania*, owned by the Hudson's Bay Company in England to bring out a shipload of various materials, including tinplate for the canneries; whiskey and other spirits for which the partners were the exclusive distributors in B.C.; and other goods for the import-export company's customers. On the return journey, the ship carried a full load of canned salmon to London and Liverpool. This was the first direct shipment of salmon to the U.K., rather than via the usual route through agents in San Francisco. That same year, he acquired an interest in the Garry Point cannery at the mouth of the Fraser River and it took him no time to realize that there were too many canneries there and elsewhere on the coast and that inefficiency threatened the viability of the salmon industry.

He devised a strategy whereby he raised capital in Britain from his relatives and his and their influential acquaintances. Willing cannery owners would sell their plants to Anglo-B.C. in exchange for shares in the new company and some cash.

Many, if not most of the canners of the day were approached and the result was that nine plants came into the amalgamation and became the property of Anglo-B.C. Packing Co. The total cost was 68,400 GBP or $330,000. The total capacity was 180,000 cases and the average pack for the preceding 4 seasons was 120,000 cases.

The nine plants were seven of the seventeen then operating on the Fraser River—Garry Point, Britannia, British American (Fraser), Canoe Pass, Wadhams (Fraser), Phoenix (M.M. English), B.C. Packing Co.—and two of the seven plants on the Skeena—British American at Port Essington, and North Pacific.

J.H. Todd offered his canneries to Bell-Irving for $50,000 each, but this was refused. However, the two parties agreed to work amicably together regarding supplies for the Skeena and shipments of canned salmon.

In its first year, the company produced about one quarter of the canned salmon in the province. Its Fraser River production that year was processed in just one plant and the others were left idle. There was an immediate improvement in the cost picture of the combined plants.

In 1892, Anglo-B.C. purchased Arrandale on the Nass and Dumfries on the Fraser. In 1895, they built Good Hope cannery in Rivers Inlet. Glendale in Knights Inlet was purchased from Capt. Gosse in 1911 and this "team" of canneries was to remain with the company throughout most of its existence. The company was incorporated in England and was listed on the London stock exchange. But its shares were held in relatively few hands. Its head office was also in London.

By 1902, there were seventy-two canneries licensed to operate on the B.C. coast. Forty-eight of these were located on the Fraser River! After the success of the Anglo-B.C. amalgamation, a New York brokerage firm, Delafield, McGovern & Co., who at that time owned the Cloverleaf Brand, made a proposal for a combination of Fraser River canneries. This did not bear fruit. But in 1902, Henry Doyle and Aemelius Jarvis, who had met for the first time the previous year, put their heads together and saw the potential for rationalization of the salmon canning business. Doyle, who was president of the family fishing supply firm, had the fishing industry experience and Jarvis, an investment banker from Toronto, had access to financing. Henry Doyle also happened to be the son-in-law of Marshall English, who had sold his Phoenix cannery to Anglo-B.C. in 1890.

1901 had seen a huge pack of salmon and many of the canners were faced with the need to finance carryovers of canned salmon. To this was added the problem of much of the pack arriving in the U.K. in poor condition. That, coupled with the obvious over-capacity, was a built-in incentive for an amalgamation effort.

After Doyle and Jarvis had discussions with cannery owners and their banks, Jarvis organized a syndicate of businessmen in eastern Canada and formed a new company which would acquire certain of the plants. It was organized under New Jersey State laws and was known as The British Columbia Packers Association of New Jersey. Although it was called an association, it was a corporation with both preferred shares and common shares. The date of incorporation was April 8, 1902.

Doyle and Jarvis acquired options on the properties to be purchased and these they sold to the company in May, 1902.

The main prizes in the acquisition were Alexander Ewen's Ewen & Co. and Thomas Ladner and R.P. Rithet's Victoria Canning Co. Altogether, 42 canneries and cold storage plants became the property of B.C. Packers Association.

They were:

Fraser River:

Alliance	Anglo	American Atlas
Acme	Albion	Bon Accord Cold Storage
Brunswick No.1 & 2	Canadian Pacific	Celtic
Cleeve Cold Storage	Colonial	Currie McWilliams & Fowler
Delta	Dinsmore Island	Ewen & Co.
Empire	Federation	Fishermen's
Greenwood	Harlock	J.R. Hume & Co
Imperial	London	Pacific Coast
Provincial	Terra Nova	Wellington
Westham Island	Westminster (Columbia Cold Storage)	

Skeena River:

Balmoral	Cunningham	Standard

Nass River:
Cascade

Rivers Inlet:

Brunswick No.3	Vancouver (Green's)	Wadhams
RIC		

Smiths Inlet:
Quashela

Cape Caution, North:

Bella Coola	Lowe Inlet	Princess Royal (China Hat)

Cape Caution, South:
Alert Bay

The organizers had intended to amalgamate all the packers on the coast, but there were still 30 plants not included in the amalgamation including those of Anglo-B.C. and J.H. Todd.

They were:
Fraser River:

Beaver	British Columbia	British American
Britannia American	Canoe Pass	Dease Island
English Bay	Great Northern	Gulf of Georgia
Industrial	National	Phoenix
Richmond	St. Mungo	Scottish Canadian
Star	Vancouver (F.R.)	Wadhams

Skeena River:

British American	Carlisle	Claxton
Inverness	Ladysmith	North Pacific
Skeena	Commercial	Windsor (Aberdeen)

Nass River:
Federation Brand (Nass Harbour)
Rivers Inlet:
Good Hope   Victoria
Cape Caution, North:
Namu   Kimsquit
West Coast of Vancouver Island:
Clayquot

Alexander Ewen became the first president of B.C. Packers Association and Henry Doyle, the general manager. As a foreign incorporated company, the Association was not permitted to own or operate boats in Canada. So, at the end of 1902, Packers Steamship Co., Ltd. was incorporated in British Columbia as a subsidiary of B.C. Packers Association.

In 1910, the Association changed its incorporation to the province of British Columbia. This was done through a provincial bill called the British Columbia Packers Association Act. In 1914, the company sought a Dominion charter and formed British Columbia Fishing & Packing Co., Ltd. Share transfers were arranged and in 1920, the new company purchased the B.C. Packers Association.

In 1916, B.C. Fishing & Packing Co. was considered ultra-conservative under its president, William Barker who had succeeded Doyle in 1904. When the B.C. Packers Association was formed in 1902, they had 54 percent of the canning industry. By 1916, their share of pack had decreased to 19½ percent!

Nevertheless, the amalgamation continued as the company acquired the Dominion and Alexandra canneries on the Skeena and the Nass Harbour cannery on the Nass River. In 1926, it purchased Wallace Fisheries Ltd. and its subsidiary Wallace Diesel Ships Ltd.

Wallace Fisheries Ltd. had been formed in December 1910 when A.D. McCrae bought out the Wallace Brothers Fisheries Ltd. from Peter and John Wallace. At that time, they owned Claxton and Kildonan canneries. Under

McCrae's leadership, Wallace Fisheries continued to expand until its sale to B.C. Fishing & Packing Company. That sale brought into the company the seven Wallace properties: Claxton on the Skeena; Kildonan in Barkley Sound; Mill Bay and Somerville on the Nass River; Smith's Inlet cannery; Strathcona in Rivers Inlet; and Watun in Masset Inlet.

In 1927, the company built South Bay on the Queen Charlotte Islands and Walker Lake on Johnson Channel, near Ocean Falls.

In 1928, both B.C. Fishing & Packing Co. and Gosse Packing Co. were feeling extreme financial strain and their principals decided to merge. This they did by incorporating a new company, British Columbia Packers Ltd. Within weeks, B.C. Packers acquired Millerd Packing Co. Ltd., which had been formed in 1927 by Francis Millerd as a successor to his Somerville Cannery Co., which he had formed in 1924 after his split with Capt. Gosse and the demise of Gosse-Millerd Packing Co. Ltd. The merger with Gosse Packing Co. brought 13 canneries and 3 reduction plants into B.C. Packers Ltd. The acquisition of Millerd Packing Co. brought in 9 more canneries and 2 salmon salteries.

The Gosse plants were: Canadian Canning Co.'s three Fraser River plants; Bella Bella; Captain Cove on Pitt Island; Hecate on Vancouver Island's west coast; Namu on Fitzhugh Sound; Kimsquit on Dean Channel; Matilda Creek reduction plant on Vancouver Island's west coast (jointly owned with Gibson Bros.); McTavish in Rivers Inlet; Nitinat; San Mateo in Barkley Sound; Shannon Bay in Masset Inlet; and Sunnyside on the Skeena.

The Millerd properties were: Barnard Cove on the Nass; Ferguson Bay in Masset Inlet; Jedway on the Queen Charlottes; Seal Cove at Prince Rupert; Somerville on the Nass; Sointula on Malcolm Island; Tucks Inlet near Prince Rupert; plus salteries at Port Alberni and at Finn Bay in Rivers Inlet; plus two floating canneries, the *Laurel Whelan* and the *Chilliwack*.

In that year of amalgamation, the new company permanently closed the following canneries: Captain Cove; Cunningham in Port Essington; Dominion and Strathcona in Rivers Inlet; Kimsquit; Nass Harbour; San Mateo; and Terra Nova on the Fraser.

British Columbia Packers Ltd. thus became the dominant company in the industry, a position it held until its final demise in 1999.

From 1928 to 1931, B.C. Packers leased Boswell in Smiths Inlet to Anglo-B.C. Packing Co. and sold Barnard Cove on the Nass to Canadian Fishing Co. in 1928. In 1929, they closed Oceanic, Ferguson Bay, Jedway and Sointula canneries. In 1930, the Point Roberts cannery was exchanged for Port Edward on the Skeena. In 1931, B.C. Packers closed Brunswick, Ewen and Vancouver canneries on the Fraser; Brunswick in Rivers Inlet; Smith's Inlet cannery; Bella Bella; South Bay and Watun on the Queen Charlottes; Nitinat; Quatsino and Matilda Creek reduction plant on the west coast of Vancouver Island; and Port Edward cannery. In 1932, they sold Oceanic on the Skeena to Robert C.

Gosse and McTavish in Rivers Inlet to Anglo-B.C. In 1934, they closed Balmoral on the Skeena and Lowe Inlet and lost the Claxton cold storage to fire. In 1936, they closed Boswell in Smiths Inlet and Bella Coola.

In 1937, B.C. Packers closed Mill Bay cannery on the Nass (it continued as a camp), and purchased Ecoole in Barkley Sound. The reduction plant at Port Edward was built. In 1938, they acquired Quathiaski cannery (which burned in 1941), and built the cannery and reduction plant at Pacofi on the Queen Charlotte Islands. In 1939, they bought Edmunds & Walker in Vancouver and installed a reduction plant at Alert Bay. 1940 was an active year for expansion. Alert Bay cannery was rebuilt, a new cold storage was erected at Namu, and B. Gregory & Co. at Port Alberni was purchased.

In 1941, Victoria Cold Storage was purchased and so was Nelson Brothers Fisheries Ltd. The latter was done in secret and only a very few of the senior executives were in the know. The strategy was to continue to operate the two companies separately and to keep the ownership secret. The senior executives of B.C. Packers and Nelson Brothers Fisheries met regularly and frequently, but the management of Nelson Brothers was left to the Nelsons.

In 1942, Wadhams cannery burned and was not rebuilt, but a new larger netloft was erected. Ecoole was sold to Nelson Brothers. In 1945, a liver oil plant was installed at Pacofi and the company bought Canadian Fish and Cold Storage at Seal Cove in Prince Rupert Harbour. In 1946, B.W. Brown & Son of Victoria and Fraser Fish Co. and Monk & Co. of New Westminster were acquired.

In 1949, Pacofi was closed and demolished and in 1950 Claxton was dismantled. The same fate befell Hecate in 1954. The same year, B.C. Packers and Canfisco became joint owners of J.H. Todd & Sons—a partnership that lasted until 1969 when the assets were divided among the two companies.

In 1964, George Weston Ltd. became the dominant shareholder of B.C. Packers when they acquired the shares of the H.R. MacMillan and Gordon Farrell estates. B.C. Packers was in financial difficulty, due to an expansion binge which saw them build the large new fresh fish and cold storage plant at Steveston, herring plants and groundfish plants on the Atlantic coast, a shrimp operation in Texas and so on. Westons changed the top management and in 1969, Dick Nelson became CEO. At the same time, it was finally revealed that B.C. Packers owned Nelson Brothers Fisheries and as a result, the two companies were integrated.

By 1984, Westons owned all the shares and the company became a wholly owned subsidiary. As it turned out this was the beginning of the end for B.C. Packers Ltd. Westons, with all their experience and expertise in grocery retailing, were not equal to understanding the unique features of the B.C. fishing industry and the special expertise it requires to operate it successfully.

In 1959, B.C. Packers sold the RIC site in Rivers Inlet. In December 1961, Namu cannery and cold storage were destroyed by fire. The plant was rebuilt in 1962.

From this point on, plant closures continued as operations were consolidated at Imperial on the Fraser and at Sunnyside/Port Edward. When Canadian Fishing Co.'s parent company, New England Fish Co. experienced serious financial difficulties in the late 1970s, B.C. Packers acquired Canfisco's northern assets, including the new Oceanside cannery at Prince Rupert and North Pacific on the Skeena. This was followed shortly after with a joint canning arrangement, whereby Oceanside would can for both companies in the north and Canfisco's Home Plant in Vancouver would can for both in the south. The cannery at Imperial was closed in 1993, and the last herring was processed there in 1997. Sunnyside closed in 1968 and Namu in 1970. The Namu cold storage operated until 1988. The company then undertook to develop its large real estate holdings in Steveston. The ultimate irony occurred when George Weston Ltd. decided to sell the assets of B.C. Packers entirely and in the event, sold them in 1999, to The Canadian Fishing Co. Ltd., which had become part of the Jimmy Pattison corporate empire.

The third great amalgamation was the entry of The Canadian Fishing Co., Ltd. into the salmon canning business. It wasn't an amalgamation aimed at improving the efficiency of the industry or at eliminating unprofitable plants. It was a case of the company deciding to expand its operations and to become a major factor in salmon processing and the effect was that of an amalgamation.

Canfisco had been formed in 1905 to engage in the halibut fishery. Its main customer was New England Fish Company of Boston, who were major factors in the east coast halibut industry. In the meantime, New England Fish Co. was well established in Washington State. In 1894, they established a receiving station in Vancouver and chartered Union Steamships' *Capilano* and outfitted her for halibut fishing under Capt. Absolem Freeman. In 1909, Canfisco was sold to the New England Fish Co. to provide them with a Canadian centre for halibut and salmon operations and Al Hager took over management of the company. This was the genesis of the long distance halibut fleet of dory fishing steamers.

In 1910, the company built the large cold storage and ice making plant at the foot of Gore Avenue in Vancouver. In 1912, they bought out Atlin Fisheries on the Prince Rupert waterfront for handling fresh salmon and halibut which was shipped fresh to the eastern U.S. once the Grand Trunk Pacific was completed in 1914. (The first successful shipment of fresh halibut to the Atlantic coast was made by New England Fish Company from Vancouver to Boston, in bond, via the CPR in 1893.) In October, 1910, Canfisco shipped the first trainload of frozen halibut from Vancouver to the east coast.

The Home Plant cannery was built at Gore Avenue in 1918 and this was Canfisco's entry into salmon canning. But it wasn't until 1923 that they made a substantial investment in outlying canneries. In that year, they bought Butedale, Shushartie and Margaret Bay from Western Packers Ltd. and Lagoon

Bay in Masset Inlet from Northern B.C. Fisheries Ltd. In 1925, they leased the Tallheo plant of Northern B.C. Fisheries in Burke Channel, and Kumeon on the Nass. And they made a major purchase in taking over Kildala Packing Co. and its canneries, Carlisle on the Skeena, Kildala in Rivers Inlet and Manitou at the head of Dean Channel.

In 1926, they bought Tallheo and Kumeon from Northern B.C. Fisheries and the Nanaimo cannery from Nanaimo Canners and Packers. That same year, they bought the Gulf of Georgia cannery in Steveston and Wales Island cannery on Pearse Channel, from M. Desbrisay & Co. In 1927, they built a new plant at Koprino on the west coast of Vancouver Island and purchased Lockeport on the Queen Charlottes. In 1928, they closed Shushartie on Goletas Channel and moved the machinery to a new cannery at Bones Bay in Johnstone Strait. That same year they purchased Goose Bay cannery from Alex Inrig's Standard Packing Co.

1929 brought Maritime Fisheries' Haysport cannery on the Skeena into the company. This plant had the advantage of being on the Grand Trunk Pacific Railway, but when the Fisheries Department moved the fishing boundary downstream, the plant had the disadvantage of being outside the Skeena fishing area. It was dismantled in 1938.

In 1933, they leased the Porcher Island cannery of Chatham Sound Packing Co. and purchased it in 1934. Canfisco never canned there, but used the plant as a fishing station and, after the closure of Carlisle and Oceanic in 1950, it became their main gillnet station in the north. A facility for building and repairing gillnet boats was built there in 1951.

In 1935, Robert C. Gosse of Ocean Salmon Canneries Ltd. sold them the Oceanic site. The cannery having burned the year before, Oceanic was used as a fishing station. In 1940, a major expansion took place in the cannery and reduction plant at Butedale. In 1943, Bones Bay cannery was remodelled and employee facilities improved.

In 1945, Canfisco made a big move with the purchase of Nootka Packing Co. Ltd., which gave them important pilchard and herring reduction plant capacity and salmon canning on the west coast of Vancouver Island. This purchase also included a large fleet of modern seine boats. That same year, they acquired Northern Fishermen's Cold Storage on the Prince Rupert waterfront. The plant had been built adjacent to Atlin Fisheries in 1934 and the company had leased freezing and cold storage space there.

In 1950, Carlisle cannery was closed down and the Oceanside cannery on the Ocean dock in Prince Rupert opened in 1951.

In 1954, B.C. Packers and Canfisco became joint owners of J.H. Todd & Sons Ltd.

In 1962, Canfisco purchased the Glenrose cannery of Johnson Fishing & Packing Co. on the Fraser. In 1969, both Anglo-B.C. and Todds closed their doors. Canfisco became the owners of Anglo-B.C.'s North Pacific and Phoenix canneries. The partnership of B.C. Packers and Canfisco in Todds came to an end and the assets were divided between the two parents. Canfisco retained the Todd name and continued to operate the company as a subsidiary for a time. The partners couldn't agree on the value of Todd's Sooke trap properties and those were placed in a new company which remained in joint ownership.

In January 1970, Northern Fishermen's Cold Storage was destroyed by fire and in June 1972, the same fate overcame the Oceanside cannery. North Pacific was reopened for that season and the company rebuilt Oceanside on the former drydock property inside the harbour in time for the 1973 season. In 1976, Tofino Fisheries cannery, which had been opened in1962 at Tofino, was purchased.

In the late 1970s, Canfisco's parent company, New England Fish Co. in Seattle, got into financial difficulty, as a result of which, Canfisco, its most important subsidiary, had to divest itself of some of its assets. About 40 percent of these were sold to B.C. Packers Ltd.: Oceanside and Atlin in Prince Rupert; North Pacific on the Skeena (including 122 gillnet boats); Tofino; Phoenix in Steveston; Britannia Shipyards at Steveston; and the 50 percent ownership of the Sooke site.

New England Fish went into bankruptcy in 1980, and the trustee sought a buyer for the balance of the Canfisco facilities. In 1984, the Pattison group became the new owners.

Canfisco and B.C. Packers formed a joint canning subsidiary and concentrated their southern canning operations at Home Plant (Imperial was closed), and their northern canning operations at New Oceanside (then owned by B.C. Packers).

Ironically, Canfisco became the sole survivor of the big four—the ultimate amalgamation! Anglo-B.C. Packing Co. was gone and when George Weston decided to sell the operating assets of B.C. Packers Ltd. in 1999, The Canadian Fishing Co. became the buyer. B.C. Packers, along with Nelson Brothers Fisheries, passed out of existence.

In the meantime, other realignments were taking place. J.S. McMillan Fisheries Ltd. and the Safarik family's Ocean Fisheries grew dramatically. In 1980, J.S. McMillan bought the Norpac plant on Commissioner Street in Vancouver. In 1977 they bought the Babcock Fisheries plant in Prince Rupert. The Prince Rupert Fishermen's Cooperative, arguably the most successful producing Co-op in British Columbia, if not in Canada, went into receivership and McMillans acquired their extensive multi-purpose plant at Fairview in Prince Rupert. J.S. McMillan Fisheries was incorporated by long-time groundfish man Jack McMillan in 1951. McMillan was also a leader in utilizing so-called scrap fish for mink feed when the mink farms were in full swing. And he was in the forefront of utilizing the dogfish shark resource which, besides being a threat to the salmon resource, made a palatable product when treated properly. Jack's sons carried on the business after his retirement and expanded it.

Ocean Fisheries was a long time occupant of a small space at the Campbell Avenue fish dock in Vancouver. In 1984, they bought the assets of the Cassiar Packing Co. at Cassiar on the Skeena River and at Rice Mill Road on the Fraser. Cassiar cannery was not reopened as a cannery, but was used as a fishing station. The Rice Mill Road plant had been built by Queen Charlotte Fisheries and was sold to Cassiar Packing Co. in 1978. It is still operated by Ocean Fisheries.

Chapter 8

SUPPLYING THE PLANTS

Next to the Native Indians, the first commercial fishermen in B.C. were the Hudson's Bay men at Fort Langley. They devised nets to fish in the Fraser near the fort for their own sustenance and to supplement what they were able to trade from the Native Indians on the River. Out of this grew the salting of salmon for export to the Hawaiian Islands beginning in 1837. By this time, the fort had been operating for 10 years and the relationship with the Natives had been well established. As the volume of exports grew, the Natives became the main suppliers, but acting as free agents, as they did with the furs they sold to the Hudson's Bay Company.

When canning began on the Fraser in 1870, and shortly after in the north, the canners turned to the Native Indians to supply the plants. They lived in the areas where the canneries were located, or were willing to migrate to them and they knew how to fish. The fishermen used their own boats at first—the big dugouts that were readily adapted to net fishing in the inlet waters and estuaries. The canneries supplied the nets and paid the fishermen so much per fish.

The official relationship between the fishermen and the canner was ambiguous. Were they independent suppliers or were they employees? The fisherman was paid on a piece work basis, although the cannery often paid the "boatpuller" or oarsman a daily wage. This was almost certainly an employer-employee relationship and there was no doubt that the cannery was in control.

However, changes evolved quite quickly. Company boats became the norm, although dugouts were used in some areas, almost to the turn of the century. But the double-ended "Columbia River" gillnet boat, driven by oar and sail, covered the coast in short order. These were owned by the canneries.

As time went on, some of the fishermen came to the cannery as independents, supplying their own nets. They would be paid a premium for supplying the net. A few non-Natives entered the fishery and after 1894, the

Japanese fishermen, newly arrived from Japan, became a big factor.

The number of canneries multiplied and the fleet grew accordingly. By 1898, there were 3,000 boats fishing the Fraser River and the over-capacity problem, which haunts the industry to the present, had begun.

The fishery is a common property resource and entry to it was easy and not subject to controls. The canners, eager to obtain as much of the catch as possible for their plants, made sure they had the boats and that they were manned by the best fishermen they could recruit. Most of these fishermen, having no capital of their own, were dependent on the cannery for boats and nets.

The canners came to realize that they were in a winless game if they had to continue adding more boats and fishermen to their respective fleets just to maintain their share of the catch. They invented boat limitation schemes and imposed them on themselves through quota agreements. There were several motivations. One was concern about the excessive cost of boats and gear in a fully exploited fishery. A second was concern that the earnings of the fishermen were being dissipated, and a third was concern about the ability of the runs to sustain the fishing pressure.

Conservation was becoming a concern even before the gillnetters started to move outside the river mouths and even before purse seines came into use.

In 1898, Henry Bell-Irving was advocating a total closure of the Fraser River fishery for three years to permit the sockeye runs to rehabilitate themselves. Needless to say, this was not a popular notion with the majority of the canners, but it did lead to agreements on the number of boats each cannery could fish.

The first of these was in 1902, when Anglo-B.C. Packing Co. and the new B.C. Packers Association, agreed to limit the number of boats in Rivers Inlet. The allocations were: Wadhams, 103; Brunswick, 86; Wannuck, 71; Vancouver, 67, for a total of 327 for B.C. Packers Association plants; B.C. Canning Co. at RIC, 142; and Good Hope, 95. There were other aspects to the agreement as well. The price per fish was 7 cents for those using cannery gear and 9½ cents for those with their own gear. Certain canneries had "control" of certain tribes, and this was not to be disturbed, e.g., Good Hope had control of the Bella Bellas in Rivers Inlet, and RIC, the Kitimaats. A runner was to be allowed for each tribe at $2.50 per day—a good wage at that time. Transportation was to be provided for whites and Japanese one way, and for Indians both ways. The wages in the plants for "klootchmen", 12½ cents per hour for washing fish, etc., and 30 trays for $1.00 for hand fillers (klootchman was translated simply as "woman" and at times was shortened to "klootch").

This arrangement became more formal in 1908, when the canneries in

District 2 established boat rating commissions for the Nass, Skeena and Rivers Inlet, which allocated the number of boat licences for each cannery. The government established an official one in 1910 and allocated the number of gillnet licences to each river and sub-district. No additional seine licences were granted at that time. This also meant no new canneries because boat licences were attached to existing ones.

Shortly after, the government changed this policy by agreeing to grant cannery and seine licences for pink and chum areas. They took some of the cannery gillnet licences away to be available to unattached or independent fishermen. This was the first break in the hold that the canneries had over the fishing effort.

In 1918, the government removed all restrictions on cannery licences and made fishing licences open to all Indian fishermen and to all whites who were British subjects. The Japanese were restricted to the number of licences held prior to 1918. In 1923, the number of licences for Japanese was reduced by 40 percent.

Some of the canners were anxious to use traps for harvesting salmon. There were a number of good reasons for this. Traps were common on the American side of Point Roberts and in Alaska from late in the 19th century. A well-located trap was a labour-efficient and cost-effective way to take the salmon. At least in theory, the fish could be held alive in the trap and the catch forwarded to the cannery as the plant was able to handle them, thus assuring product freshness. Also in theory, release from the trap was possible if necessary for escapement. In practice, however, if the run was heavy, the traps were emptied quickly to make room for more. The cost of production was a fraction of the cost of fishing by boats, without the messy business of dealing with fishermen, boats and nets.

Traps were the preferred method of capture in Russia and Japan and B.C. canned salmon had to compete with the lower cost product from these countries in the United Kingdom market.

Trap licences were granted in B.C.—at Wales Island, for example, because the Americans had traps nearby on their side of the international border. In 1904, B.C. Canning Co. was operating traps in the approaches to the Skeena River at Greentop Island, Rachel Island, Arthur Island in Edye Pass, and were applying for trap licences for Table Island and Lucy Island. These operated for a number of years, but efforts by other canners to obtain licences were in vain.

The chief exception was J.H. Todd & Sons, who held the Sooke trap licences by royal charter from Queen Victoria, herself. The federal government believed they were powerless to cancel them. They were the last traps to operate in

B.C. and in the end, it was competition from seiners fishing in Juan de Fuca Strait that forced the company to abandon the licences for economic reasons.

B.C. Packers Ltd. was among those keenly interested in trap licences, but they acknowledged that hardship and unemployment would result if traps proliferated. In a memorandum to the Commission of Inquiry in 1930/31, they proposed instead: "Let fishing licences be limited to that number sufficient to permit a full five days fishing." Priority would be first to those who own their own gear, then to settlers of the various coastal districts and next, to those (not already included), who had fished for the longest period.

The introduction of engines in gillnetters was a slow process in the northern areas. It was resisted by the canners for the obvious reason of the extra cost that would fall on them, but also for the more noble reason that the Indians would be disadvantaged by it. While engines were introduced in the south in 1906, and became common after 1917 with Easthope's new 2-cycle engine, it wasn't until 1924 that they were permitted in District 2—the northern coast. Then the canneries had no choice but to install engines in their gillnetters. Nevertheless, sail still remained in a few places into the 1950s.

The rental boat system was the order of the day. The company-owned gillnetters would be rented to the fishermen for a fixed amount for the season. These fishermen were still dependent on the cannery and were required to deliver all their catch to the company.

As the required investment grew with ever larger and more powerful engines and larger boats, and as upkeep became more expensive, the canners realized that a private owner would better care for his boat and nets than if the company owned them. So they began to finance their better fishermen to own their own boats and nets—and the race was on—for better, faster, bigger, more comfortable boats and in time, for more and more sophisticated navigation and fish finding/catching equipment.

One of the anomalies of the industry that has plagued cannery operators and government regulators, is that the fishermen, in their competition for the catch; in their desire to reduce some of the labour intensity of fishing; to live comfortably on the water; and in some cases, to enhance their image with their peers, have increased the cost of fishing faster than the value of the end products has increased.

As fishermen became more efficient, the pressure on the resource became of great concern. The early attempts at "boat rating" systems for the canneries had given way to the notion of the right to fish. But by the 1960s, it was evident that control was once again needed and that it had to be more drastic. The issue kept professional economists busy for years and finally, the very controversial scheme of licence limitation came into being—the so-called Davis

Supplying the Plan.

Plan. It not only froze the number of licences, it also strove to reduce the fishing effort by buying back boats and licences from those who wished to sell them. The concept was good and the plan was well conceived but it was terminated before it had reached its potential of making a significant dent in the fishing effort. One of its flaws was that the inherent value of the limited number of licences was allowed to accrue to the boat owner, rather than accruing to the resource owners—the public—as economic rent. Had the latter been done, the resource would have provided the funding needed to maintain and enhance it. Instead, another round of enhancing the catching capabilities of the remaining vessels occurred and the benefits of reducing the fleet were obviated.

The relationship between the fishermen and the processors was a special one. In law, the fishermen were contractors or individual entrepreneurs, rather than employees. But the ties with the cannery were close. Many of the fishermen considered themselves employees ("I worked for such and such a cannery," or, "I worked for Mr. so and so"). In some cases the relationship was close to bondage since the fisherman's costs were advanced at the beginning and during the season and sometimes exceeded the value of his catch.

But as the cannery people saw it, they provided services and financing to assure the "loyalty" of the fishermen so as to be assured of receiving their catch. The pre-season costs were high and repayment risky. Likewise with the in-season services which were aimed at keeping the boats on the grounds and the fishermen producing salmon. It was an infrastructure that included everything from preparation and repair of nets, to boatways, machine shops, stores and gas stations. Share of the catch was everything to the cannery manager and his employers. They saw it as a very competitive situation, especially as the mobility of the fleet grew and the temptation to sell to the often-present cash buyer was realizable.

This relationship evolved until the perceived value of services was not worthwhile to the fisherman. The cash buyer price for fish had to be met and the provision of services in return for loyalty declined.

The price of raw fish was always a matter for preoccupation of the industry's entrepreneurs. In the early days, the price of fish was set unilaterally by the cannery operators. The cannery provided the boat and net, and services to maintain them, as well as accommodation ashore for the fisherman's family. The price of fish, then, was part of a package and was based on pre-season estimates of the pack, the cost of pack and the market. Much of this was guesswork, so there had to be a margin for the unexpected.

The fishermen were controlled by the cannery, but once on the grounds, sely supervised. The good fisherman or the hard working with the ones with poor skills or those who worked less iod of payment was per fish, the price varying by species. Some of the canners in Rivers Inlet introduced bonuses to fishermen around the turn of the century. One of them started it in 1895 with a lump sum of $200 to his Bella Bella group. It was then changed to $15 per boat with nothing for the "klootchman". In 1902, B.C. Packers Association increased that to $25 per boat and $2 per "klootchman". Anglo-B.C. responded with $30 and $3, and that was met by B.C. Packers. The canners were keen to control the supply of available fishermen and at least for a time, Anglo-B.C. was successful in being the primary employer of those Bella Bella fishermen who fished in Rivers Inlet.

With the introduction of engines to the gillnetters and the increased mobility this gave the fishermen, it became clear to the canners that some sort of commonality or consistency in prices as between canneries, was needed. This became the role of the Fraser River Canners' Association, which extended its jurisdiction beyond the Fraser in 1902, and later, of the Salmon Canners Operating Committee of the Canadian Manufacturers' Association. The Committee set the prices in Vancouver and, each year, pre-season, a joint delegation would visit all the canneries and advise them what they were to pay for salmon.

Undoubtedly, there were transgressors, depending on the need to meet a market or to utilize canning capacity. But by and large these prices were honoured. Conversely, when the unexpected abundance of catch exceeded the capacity of the plants to handle it, the canners unilaterally imposed quotas or even lowered the price in anticipation of lower market returns.

But the fishermen themselves began to see the power of joint action, and "wildcat" strikes became commonplace as they sought to have a say in the pricing of fish. The first successful attempt at organizing the fishermen was the Fraser River Fishermen's Protective and Benevolent Association in 1893. Besides demanding better prices for the fishermen, the Association later advocated ridding the fishery of Japanese fishermen.

The wildcat strikes were usually local and spontaneous, with the fishermen gathering on the dock and refusing to sail or to fish until their grievance was addressed. There were broader strikes as early as 1896 on the Skeena and at Rivers Inlet. The big strike on the Fraser in 1901 and the big one in Rivers Inlet in 1936, were preceded and followed by smaller, shorter ones. It was a serious problem for the canners who had very small windows in which to take the runs and process them. Bell-Irving records state in regard to the 1936 strike: "engineered by comparatively small number of communists.

90 percent of fishermen wanted to fish." All the canneries in Rivers Inlet closed after 2½ to 3 weeks of the strike.

Various fishermens' organizations were formed, sometimes along ethnic lines, as they sought to balance the power of the buyers. Into this situation, after the Second World War, moved the United Fishermen and Allied Workers Union (UFAWU). They organized the fishermen and the payroll employees into the same organization and demanded changes. And from this, industry-wide collective bargaining was born. The Salmon Canners' Operating Committee became the Fisheries Association of B.C. in 1951, which from then on represented the processors in collective bargaining.

The organization and certification of plant workers and the crews of the fish packers (tendermen) was legitimate under labour law. The organization of the fishermen was something else. The fishermen were not employees and labour law did not apply to them. In fact, it was argued that joint action by the fishermen would be restraint of trade in contravention of the Combines Act. This led to an exemption from the Act and a definition of fishermen as "dependent contractors".

The UFAWU-minded fishermen were always a minority, so control of the fishing fleet depended on peer pressure and intimidation. This was practised openly and effectively for many years. The result was that the Union had the ability to tie up the entire fishing industry, more or less at will. While the wildcat strikes became rare, the industry tie-up became commonplace.

A strike vote was usually a given as part of the negotiations. The negotiation of the minimum price agreement coincided with the negotiation of the shoreworkers' and tendermen's contracts for maximum bargaining power. The strike vote was part of the process to bring maximum pressure on the canners. But once the strike vote was in, regardless of how it had been achieved, the union leadership were prepared to use it and did not hesitate to shut down the industry.

Brinkmanship was the order of the day and was part of the bargaining strategy on both sides. The salmon industry is not like most industrial enterprises where an interruption of production can be made up after the strike. The make or break part of the year for fishermen, shoreworkers and canners alike, is a matter of weeks or a month at the most. To miss the migration of a major salmon run through the fishery is to lose the year's production and earnings. To add to the pressure, large sums are invested in preparation for the season before the first fish is caught or processed.

With the rise of control by the UFAWU, the canners responded in kind through the Fisheries Association of B.C., and the classic adversarial situation prevailed. Brinkmanship on the part of the companies was dangerous because there was always the risk of the union leadership, proudly communist in persuasion, taking the industry out or keeping it out beyond the point of reason. There were some memorable strikes where this was demonstrated, particularly in 1963. Nevertheless, the Union was under pressure from the fishermen, if they could see their season slipping away for the sake of a bargaining tactic. This pressure was greatest, of course, from those who did not share the leadership's politics, but only tolerated strike votes for solidarity and fear of the blacklist. The canners too, were prone to get antsy as the season or the peak of the season approached. At the beginning of negotiations, they would be solid in their determination to hold the line on minimum prices at a certain point. But as time advanced and the pressure built, some would start to weaken their resolve as they calculated the cost of a higher minimum price against the loss of the whole season and the investment already made in it. It was a stare-me-down game on both sides and the stakes were huge. But this was how it worked for some 35 years.

The fishing industry is a product of the government regulators and scientists on the one hand, and the commercial risk takers on the other, including both processors and fishermen. The story of union organization in the B.C. fishery is a history in its own right. In the process of making gains and improving conditions for workers, it committed excesses which, at the same time damaged it and harmed the very people it claimed to champion. There were strong characters like Bill Rigby, Homer Stevens and Alex Gordon, imbued with post-World War II communism, in charge of the UFAWU for 30 years or more. This was at a time when communism was extremely active in the Canadian trade union movement. That activity seemed to flow from Lenin's vision of International Communism. In his pamphlet *The Infantile Disease of Leftism in Communism*, Lenin admonishes communists not to quit the trade unions. Communists must, on the contrary, infiltrate the unions. They would, to be sure, encounter every kind of obstacle. "It is necessary to know how to resist this," Lenin wrote, "to submit to all and any sacrifice, even—in case of need—to use any subterfuge, shrewdness, illegal method, deceit, the concealment of truth, anything to penetrate into trade unions, remain in them and at all costs, conduct communist activity." There was always a feeling in the 1950s and 1960s that one of the aims of the communist-dominated unions was to undermine the economic and political viability of the capitalist system. In the UFAWU, when the interests of the members and those of the Party parted, the interests of the Party appeared to prevail.

This came to a head in the great strike of 1963. The union had support for the strike in the beginning—this was usually achievable on the basis that it gave the union bargaining strength with the "operators." But as the strike wore on and the loss of the season loomed, the fishermen began to press the leaders for a settlement. The companies had made an improved offer aimed at settling the strike and the members called for a vote on it. This was refused by the union leadership and the matter ended up in court. A vote was eventually taken in spite of the leadership's position, and the strike was settled. Everyone lost in that disastrous strike but ironically, the biggest loser was the union itself. It never regained its unshakable hold on the salmon fishermen.

The characterization of the salmon price agreement with the union as a minimum price contract was its most important feature. Both sides had to make guesses about the size and timing of runs and about markets for the finished products, well ahead of the season. The Department of Fisheries and the International Pacific Salmon Fisheries Commission made their pre-season forecasts, but they too were subject to variables, natural and otherwise, that could not always be foreseen. The minimum nature of the price gave both sides some comfort. The fishermen knew that if the predicted volumes did not materialize, the competition for production would result in increased prices. The canners knew that if the minimum price was reasonable, they could afford to pay it, for whatever the best guess maximum volumes would be.

At first the minimum price was the price paid, except for outstanding highliner fishermen that each company had and rewarded, more or less secretly. But prices notwithstanding, volume was often as much a factor in fishing as price was. In the big sockeye and pink years, price was less important. If the runs were forecast to be lean, price was all-important.

It took the canners some time to catch on to how to take the sting out of the pre-season fish price contracts. But in time the bonus system came into being. In effect, this delayed the ultimate determination of the fish price until after the season. The fishermen came to know that regardless of the contract price, if markets warranted, the bonus would be forthcoming. It also allowed the canners to count on the loyalty of their fishermen to deliver all their catch to the company as this was also factored into the bonus. And finally, it reduced the power of the union to control the fishermen by making them risk losing their season for a price that probably was not real in any case.

The Native Brotherhood of B.C. was formed in Port Simpson in 1931 to speak for the Native peoples on common issues, including land claims. The Brotherhood took a strong interest in the industry collective agreements. They were not always in favour of the tactics of the UFAWU, so that sometimes they bargained jointly and at other times, negotiated separate agreements with the Fisheries Association of B.C.

The herring fishery also became the subject of collective agreements, principally regarding price. After World War II, the herring fishery was almost exclusively a seine fishery and almost exclusively for reduction purposes. There were many strikes and more than one season was lost altogether.

After the closure of the fishery for reduction herring, negotiated agreements have been produced between the processors and the union for roe herring prices.

Halibut prices were arrived at through auction at Halibut Exchange offices in Prince Rupert and Vancouver. The buyers were members of the exchange, and bid for the load of each vessel which was hailed as the boat approached port. Prices at other ports, e.g., Butedale and Namu, were based on the current prices on the exchange.

The UFAWU made a number of attempts to require the processors to negotiate prices for trawl fish. But the number of buyers was small and the trawl fishermen themselves were independent-minded and proved not to be interested in subjecting themselves to the union's bargaining strategies. So each processor and the boats which supplied him, made their own arrangements.

The processors also had contracts with the large vessel owners—the seine boat owners—regarding such things as share agreements and various conditions for crews on the vessels.

The Fishermen's Cooperatives did not negotiate agreements for fish prices. The members were the owners of the organization and its assets and they shared in the profits or losses of the enterprise.

Chapter 9

MANAGING THE RESOURCES

Canada's saltwater and anadromous fish species fall within the jurisdiction of the Government of Canada. The fishery is the only natural resource for which the federal government has responsibility and constitutional authority, all others being under the jurisdiction of the provinces. The federal government's role is huge and involves both the regulation of the fishery harvests and the protection of the resource and its habitats. For the Pacific salmon, this latter responsibility is particularly peculiar and particularly critical as the salmon's habitat reaches to streams and lakes in the interior of British Columbia many hundreds of miles from the ocean, to the river estuaries, coastal waters and the deep sea in international waters. The drainage systems of the province's salmon streams cover an awesome 70 percent of B.C.'s land area.

The federal Fisheries Act has impressive powers when it comes to protecting fisheries habitat. In spite of these powers, the loss and degradation of salmon habitat continues on a daily basis. But without those powers:
 · The Fraser and Thompson Rivers would undoubtedly have been dammed in the 1950s or 1960s for hydro power;
 · B.C.'s pulp and paper mills would not be treating their effluent chemicals before discharge into the major river and lake systems;
 · The forest industry would probably have decimated every salmon bearing stream instead of just a significant proportion of them.

It is probably safe to say that up until the early 1980s, Canada's Pacific fisheries have been the best managed in the world. Fisheries experts, from Motherwell to Whitmore to Hourston, as public servants, in their times, ran the fisheries with great success.

Canada's fisheries scientists, as a group, have been without peers in the international marine world. The Fisheries Research Board of Canada (FRB) was renowned and respected in all those circles. The huge mistake of "integrating" the FRB with the operational side of the Department of Fisheries tore the guts out of it and destroyed the *esprit* that set it apart and attracted or created world leaders in fisheries science.

This was the Pitfield years. Michael Pitfield, Clerk of the Privy Council and the head civil servant in the federal government, had the brilliant idea that "a manager is a manager is a manager." That was a watershed marking of the effectiveness and high degree of success of fisheries management in B.C. Until Pitfield, it was recognized that the resource needed professional management by fisheries professionals at all levels. But Pitfield saw the Department of Fisheries as just another department of government and top fisheries posts became a step on the ladder or training ground for development of civil servants. Pacific fisheries management has suffered from this syndrome ever since. The attitude is: if you are good at running Transport or Immigration, you can manage Fisheries—not so.

The curse of natural resource management is the intrusion of politics. Fisheries has more than its share because of the common property nature of the resource. Uniquely, the size and constitution of the fishery resource can only be determined by guesswork—scientific guesswork to be sure, but guesswork nonetheless. Trees don't move—they can be touched, counted, thinned, fed and protected from disease. Mineral deposits, including oil and gas, are stationary and exist in predictable locations.

But fish stocks are invisible for most of their life cycle, and mobile, some ranging tens or hundreds of thousands of miles in a medium which is hostile to humans. Anadromous species like salmon add a further complication, spending part of their lives in fresh water and part in salt water. With all the scientific knowledge about the species and their life cycles, with all the statistical science in use, with all the experience with individual stocks over many decades, exact knowledge of a stock's size and location is virtually impossible.

That uncertainty opens the door for politics in its rawest form—pressure on the politicians or from them, to do or not to do what is in the interests of interested parties, rather than what is in the long term interest of the stocks. With professional fisheries managers in place, Ministers, for the most part, were figureheads and their successes or failures were measured by their ability or otherwise, to convince government to adopt policies and provide resources needed to do right things.

The outstanding Ministers of Fisheries in Canada have been few. James Sinclair was, no doubt, Number 1 and Jack Davis was not far behind. Romeo Leblanc held the portfolio for a long time and happened to be Minister when the 200-mile fisheries limit came into force. But he was outstanding for reasons other than advancements achieved in his time. His populist idea that everyone (in Atlantic Canada) had the right to fish, perpetuated an overcrowded fishery with poor average returns and set the scene for the crash of the cod fishery in Canada's Atlantic waters. John Fraser would probably have qualified for the list as a competent minister if he hadn't been the victim of an internal fight with the Prime Minister's Office. John Crosbie would make the list as well, although like all east coast ministers, he had little time for the Pacific.

The Fisheries Act and Regulations provide the framework for regulating the fishing effort, which involves fishing times, types of gear, fishing areas, etc.—the so-called protection side of fisheries management. But government concern with management was not immediate in the early years of the fishery. There were licences issued, both for canneries and boats, but little attention to conservation. Patronage was part of the political system in the first half century and the local Members of Parliament had extraordinary influence in the granting of licences. (This was not confined to the fishing industry, as MPs usually had the say regarding appointments to government jobs and prerogatives in their ridings).

The first concerns with conservation came from the cannery operators. In the 1890s, some of them advocated a complete closure for three years, of the Fraser River salmon fishery which even at that time was showing the effects of too much fishing effort, including the intercepting fisheries in Washington State which had begun in earnest in 1895.

Again, it was the canners who first recognized the damage to the Quesnel River runs that was done by a dam built by mining interests at the mouth of the Quesnel River in 1898.

The first salmon hatcheries were built and operated by the canners. B.C. Packers Association built and operated the sockeye hatchery on the Nimpkish River from 1902 to 1923, albeit as a condition of the exclusive rights to the Nimpkish fishery. R.V. Winch built a sockeye hatchery at Namu in 1916 and ran it for six years. It wasn't until 1917 that government entered the hatchery game and it was the province that took on the responsibility under John Pease Babcock who had become the first provincial Commissioner of Fisheries in 1902. In that first year of his tenure, Babcock was expressing concern that Rivers Inlet was being fished out. He was instrumental in establishing the Rivers Inlet sockeye hatchery.

That there were problems with the Fraser River runs was becoming clear to everyone by 1902. In 1901, 51 canneries operated on the Fraser River and another 20 in Puget Sound. 1901 was the apex of sockeye canning on the Fraser and it could be said that it was all downhill from then until the 1950s when the International Pacific Salmon Fisheries Commission's work began to take effect. In 1908, the Bryce-Root treaty was negotiated for joint control over the salmon fishery on both sides of the border between B.C. and Washington State. It was adopted by Parliament but not by Congress, so nothing came of it. The refusal of the U.S. Congress to accept or ratify treaties negotiated by its representatives has since been a commonplace in international fisheries negotiations. Because of this, Canada terminated its adherence to that Treaty in 1914.

The next attempt at international cooperation did not occur until 1917 when the U.S. and Canada set up the Hazen-Redfield Commission to examine the salmon fishery of the Fraser River. It resulted in a convention for joint management of the Fraser sockeye fishery and resource. Parliament approved it, but again the U.S. Senate did not and the initiative died.

The Fraser runs continued to decline and in 1921 Ottawa approached the State of Washington with a view to negotiating a joint approach to rehabilitation. There was general agreement that a 5-year closure be imposed, but Washington State declined to follow through. In 1928, the two federal governments were again back at the bargaining table and a new treaty was drafted, similar to the Bryce-Root treaty of 1908. Parliament ratified it in May 1930, but the U.S. Senate did not. Canada contemplated abandoning the Fraser sockeye resource and enhancing the runs in the areas of the province that were not subject to interception by the Americans.

Talks were next opened in 1934 and resulted in the Sockeye Salmon Fisheries Convention which was formally ratified by both countries in 1937. It established the International Pacific Salmon Fisheries Commission, with A.L. Hager as its first Chairman and Dr. Loyd Royal in charge of its work.

The success of international cooperation in regard to the Fraser River sockeye resources soon drew attention to the heavy interception on the American side, of Fraser River pink salmon. Characteristically, the American fishermen and Washington State authorities were not interested in a cooperative approach and turned down Canadian overtures to have pinks included in the International Pacific Salmon Fisheries Treaty. In 1954, Fisheries Minister James Sinclair permitted Canadian seine boats to fish outside the fisheries boundary on the west coast of Vancouver Island where they were able to take the pinks before they entered U.S. waters. He had the federal government waive the customs duty on the import of fishing vessels, so that large vessels capable of fishing in the open sea could be purchased. Such vessels, redundant to the U.S. pilchard fishery, were then available in San Diego and some were imported for the purpose. Seeing the advantage of this strategy to Canadian fishermen, the Americans agreed to include pinks in the treaty.

The creation of the Salmon Commission marked a new approach to salmon conservation. Biologists and engineers were recruited, the Hell's Gate fishways were designed and built, and a determination that sockeye and pink salmon production could be enhanced through artificial spawning channels was made. The rehabilitation of the Fraser River sockeye runs, and later the enhancement of the pinks, is a world-famous tour de force in fisheries management.

It led also, to the Department of Fisheries establishing an outstanding team with similar expertise to deal with the salmon resources of the non-Fraser streams and rivers and the salmon runs on the Fraser, other than sockeye and pinks. The Skeena River Management Committee was established at that time.

The sockeye hatcheries began closing in 1934, and by the end of 1937, with the closure of the Rivers Inlet hatchery, that experiment came to an end. The Department found, however, that coho and to some extent, chinooks, could be enhanced by hatcheries and this became part of the program.

A fortuitous result of the presence of so much fisheries expertise was that the Department was well-fixed to deal with the fish versus power struggles of the 1950s and 1960s; the controversy over disposal of pulpmill wastes in the fish bearing waters; and natural disasters like the Babine slide in 1951/52 which blocked the passage of the main Skeena sockeye run, and the Chilko slide that did the same on the Chilko River in 1964.

It provided the basis of the scientific initiatives of the International North Pacific Fisheries Commission which resulted in the virtual cessation of the Japanese intercepting fisheries on the high seas, and it laid the groundwork for the acceptance by the world community through the United Nations Law of the Sea Conference, that salmon should not be fished in international waters.

The ambitious Salmon Enhancement Program, initiated in 1978 by the Department of Fisheries, built on the experience and knowledge on the Fraser River and other salmon streams. But stinting on financial resources has meant less than optimum results from this initiative. The Fisheries managers have also been beset by problems of dealing with emerging questions of First Nations rights and in the meantime, the century-old problems of U.S. intercepting fisheries have re-appeared.

The problems of controlling fishing effort arose early in the industry's history. The first efforts at control were initiated by the canners, no doubt in their self-interest of assuring that each of the canneries received its fair share of the catch. In the same way, there were numerous initiatives to have the number of canneries limited as well.

As early as 1890, the Fraser River canners were discussing "a fair distribution of boats," but they couldn't agree on what was "fair."

In 1891, Dominion Fisheries took a hesitant step at management by allocating 300 fishing licences on the Skeena—200 to the canneries and 100 reserved for "outside men."

In 1902, H.O. Bell-Irving confided to his diary an incident which demonstrates the presence of politics in fisheries management in those early years. He was interested in acquiring licences for trap fishing and had applied to the Fisheries Department to that end. He had a meeting in the old Russell Hotel in Ottawa with George Maxwell, the Liberal Member of Parliament for Burrard constituency. Maxwell is quoted as saying, "I am not going to give any man a trap licence or other licence who is not a supporter of the government and of myself."

The diary continues, "That was the most unblushing statement I had ever heard a supporter of the government make. I asked Maxwell how it came that seine licences had been refused us and given others who were in no way connected with the business.

"He said, 'You never went about it the right way. You never applied to me except once.'

"I said, 'But Mr. Maxwell, I made application to the Fishery Department in the usual way. I never looked upon you as Minister of Fisheries'.

"Maxwell said, 'You will find *I am* Minister of Fisheries within my own constituency.'!!!"

Later in the day, Dr. Templeman, the Deputy Minister is quoted: "Don't suppose I approve of all that was said."

"At 6 p.m., saw Minister of Fisheries. He knows nothing about Fisheries. I repeated Maxwell's words and asked if these views received countenance. He said, 'Well, if you were in his position, you would like to exercise patronage.'!

"'In that case,' (I said), 'It is useless my coming here or making application to the Department. I can manage the business better at the other end through Maxwell—in his own particular way—and you know how that is.'

"Then he said, 'OK, of course, I could not countenance anything of that kind in a member.'

"Morrison says Maxwell is very jealous of Templeman. Templeman assured me canners' interests would be considered in trap matters."

There wasn't much faith on the part of the canners in the Department of Fisheries' ability to manage. In 1903, Bell-Irving, in a speech to the Canadian Manufacturers' Association (CMA), said,

"At present matters are controlled by the Department at Ottawa and for years, we have suffered by their neglect and want of knowledge of the actual conditions prevailing. No clearer example could be found than the discussion that took place in the House on August 28. Salmon canners asked that the fishing (on the Fraser), be closed to allow spawning fish to ascend. The request was refused on the absurd ground that it was made for speculative purposes to influence the market. The result is an almost entire absence of spawning fish in the upper reaches which means certainty of a failure of the run in 1907.

"The Provincial government, recognizing the importance of the matter, appointed a Fishery Commissioner experienced in artificial propagation but his hands have been tied through lack of authority. Until the control of the business is removed from the domain of politics and vested in responsible parties resident in the Province, no improvement may be looked for.

"The Fraser River Canners Association represented to the Fisheries Department on April 12, 1899, that a dam at Quesnel was preventing millions of spawning fish from ascending the river. The dam still remains."

The dam was removed in 1921, but the task of restoring the sockeye runs to the Quesnel system that it had wiped out was not addressed until the Salmon Commission was in place in the 1940s.

The question of excess fishing effort was an on-going problem. It is a characteristic of common property resources—the notion that every citizen has a right to utilize those resources that belong to the Crown, regardless of economics or of returns to the people as owners. It was manifested first on the Fraser—in 1898 there were 3,000 boats fishing the river from Mission to the Sandheads—but it reached upcoast as the industry expanded in that direction. By 1930, there were 7,000 boats on the coast supplying 90 canneries.

There were many attempts at boat limitation. Again the canners were the first to grasp the nettle with agreements among themselves for the number of boats that each cannery would fish. But these were sporadic and short-lived as operators strove to put product through their plants.

The B.C. Fisheries Commission of Inquiry of 1905 and 1907, declared in its report: "Because of the serious decline in the run of sockeye to the Fraser River, greater attention is being paid by canners and fishermen to our other salmon producing rivers such as Rivers Inlet, the Skeena and Nass, and unless adequate restrictive measures limiting the fishing there are at once adopted, there is danger that these streams will become as greatly depleted as the Fraser."

In their interim report in 1905, the Commissioners unanimously recommended that "a limit be placed on the number of canneries and the number of boat licences in the district."

In 1908 the Dominion government froze the number of cannery licences. The canneries operating in District 2 (north of Cape Caution), established a boat rating commission which allocated to each cannery, the number of boats it could fish. The government replaced it with an official boat rating system in 1910. It went further and allocated the number of gillnet licences to each river and sub-district. No additional seine licences were granted. This also meant no new canneries could be established because the boat licences were attached to the existing ones. But shortly after, the government granted cannery and seining licences for pink and chum areas which were considered underfished. They also reduced the number of cannery gillnet licences and reserved others for fishermen who were not attached to a cannery. The result was that the number of canneries increased by 50 percent between 1910 and 1918, with no increase in the number of gillnet licences.

In 1918, at the end of the First World War, the government removed all restrictions on cannery licences and made fishing licences open to all white and Indian fishermen who were British subjects. Japanese were restricted to the number of licences held prior to 1918. Then in 1922, the federal government made an agreement with Japan to limit the number of Japanese immigrants to 400 per year. This included a ceiling on fishermen of 150 per year. In 1923, there was a reduction imposed on the number of licences available to Japanese fishermen, except for Japanese Canadians.

The enforcement of fishery regulations had always been a problem on the B.C. coast, especially in the huge Prince Rupert district which stretched from Cape Caution, north to the Alaska border, including the Queen Charlotte Islands. The thousands of miles of coastline could not be adequately covered by patrol boat and the protection of spawning streams was non-existent in many parts of the coast. In 1921, the Department of Fisheries contracted with the Canadian Air Force for patrols by Flying Boats. Their range and the element of surprise that went with them, made a huge difference in enforcing the regulations. It was common for fishermen to carry an extra length of net (called a "handy billy") which would be attached to the regulation size net once out of sight of the patrol boats or the "bogeymen," as they were called. And the fishery boundaries which protected the mouths of spawning streams and creeks were routinely ignored. The Flying Boats were the eye in the sky and could land right next to the violators and hand out justice on the spot.

By 1923, a temporary and seasonal base was set up at Seal Cove in Prince Rupert harbour for the aircraft. 1923 marked the first time an aircraft flew the length of the B.C. coast. An Airforce HS2L flew from Jericho, on Vancouver's English Bay, to Prince Rupert all in one day, with refuelling stops at Alert Bay and Bella Bella. In 1924, the patrols out of Seal Cove were using two HS2L Flying Boats. A boathouse on shore was used as a workshop for maintenance and for refuelling the aircraft.

The following is a description of their activities that 1924 season.

"From July 17 to September 21 F/L Earl McLeod and F/O Alan Hull and their crews, actively and effectively patrolled the Prince Rupert area in the HS2Ls, logging a total of 81 flights. The flights were made during the weekends when fishing was banned—one HS2L patrolled over the Nass and Skeena river areas in the north, while the second HS2L covered the southern area, flying either from Swanson Bay or Bella Bella. On a single weekend patrol, one of the HS2Ls logged 920 miles in 14 hours and 57 minutes, made 23 landings, and took 115 photographs between Friday morning and Sunday evening. A patrol to the Queen Charlotte Islands, a forty minute flight, completed a trip that would have required at least 15 hours by motor boat.

"With fog, rain and uncertain weather as persistent all-season obstacles, flying the HS2Ls on the northern coasts of British Columbia was not an easy job. Better facilities were needed to handle emergency repairs during the long and arduous patrols over the bleak and uninhabited coast and inland waterways.

"At the beginning of the season, to partially bridge the communications gap, the two flying boats were equipped with W.T. (radio) communication with Seal Cove. Fog and cloud often lay so close to the water that the aircraft had to fly 'on the deck,' making it impossible to lower the wireless aerial. In good flying conditions, however, they did have successful communication by both radio-telephone and Morse code."

One of these HS2Ls crashed at Klemtu in 1924. But the patrol boats continued to be the principal vehicle for enforcing regulations on the fishing grounds. Over the years, the Fisheries Department had an impressive fleet of vessels which began to be built up in the 1920s and 1930s, e.g., the *Bonilla Rock*, the *Senepa* and the *Beldis*. Then came the Post boats—55 and 60 footers—the *Chilco Post*, *Atlin Post*, *Babine Post*, *Sooke Post*, *Comox Post*, and the *Arrow Post*.

The pride of the fleet for many years were the *Laurier* and the *Howie*. They were 120 foot sister ships, built in Quebec for the RCMP in 1936 and transferred to Fisheries, Pacific Region, after the war. The *Kitimat*, *Hunter Point* and *Tanu* followed. There were, at one time, 42 patrol boats in the 35 to 60 foot range and the Department chartered many smaller vessels on a seasonal basis.

When gasoline engines began to appear on the Fraser River, they were not permitted in the northern areas. The rationale for this policy was less about concerns with conservation, than about concerns that the Indian fishermen would not be able to afford them and would thus be at a disadvantage to the white and Japanese fishermen. But the pressure mounted. Both J.H. Todd and Anglo-B.C. Packing Co. successfully opposed gas engines in District 2 from 1912 to 1922. But the 1922 Fisheries Commission of Inquiry (there were many of these over the years), recommended that the power boat restriction be removed. This recommendation was accepted by the Department and in 1924, gas-powered boats were permitted in District 2.

In 1927, in a voluntary agreement signed by 90 percent of the canners, they agreed to limit gear and operations "in the interest of conservation and economy." But the minority didn't commit and in 1929 the Dominion government granted seven new cannery licences. In 1930, licensing of canneries became the exclusive domain of the province as a result of the Privy Council decision in the Millerd case.

The fleet continued to grow over the next two decades, both in number of boats and in fishing power, but there was little action other than wringing of hands. The fleet problems were issues both of economics and conservation. In spite of ever-increasing prices to the fishermen, the average earnings were dropping as the cost of fishing out-paced the value of the raw fish. And the fishing power challenged the ability of the government managers to assure their escapements. Many economic studies were commissioned and many meetings and conferences took place. The Sol Sinclair report in 1961 brought it to a head with its recommendations for reducing the size of the salmon fleet. In 1969, the Minister of Fisheries, Jack Davis, himself an economist, brought into being the Davis Plan, which introduced limited entry to the salmon fisheries and a buy-back scheme by which boat owners could sell their boats and licences to the government, on condition that they would never again be permitted to be used in the salmon fishery.

In the intervening years, since the discontinuation of the Davis Plan in 1974, there have been periodic efforts to readdress the problem, but most of them have been opposed by one vested interest or another and the problem of overcapacity remains. The awesome fishing power that now exists in the fleet poses a huge dilemma for the fishery managers who are left with no options other than closed times and with no room for mistakes.

As the French say: *La plus ça change, la plus ça même.*

The federal authorities saw the regulation of canneries for food safety as part of their jurisdiction. As early as 1915, they were proposing a Fish and Shellfish Cannery Inspection Act. But this would not come into being until 1932.

They were also concerned about the disposal of fish offal from the canneries. The canners were less concerned about this problem—they reasoned that what had come from the water could be returned to the water and that natural processes would take care of it. No one knew much about biological oxygen demand (BOD) in the early days nor cared much about aesthetics.

While regulations were in force as early as 1895, they were seldom enforced. That year, the government went to court to seek an injunction to prevent Alexander Ewen from dumping fish offal in the Fraser River. We don't know what the court ordered, but the practice continued and was the subject of frequent lobbying by the canners to the department officials. One of the problems was that there was no economical means available for recovering and processing offal, until reduction plants were established.

Chapter 10

THE LIFELINES

For over 100 years, the coastal steamers and the salmon canneries operated in a symbiotic relationship—each depending on the other for their very existence. The Union Steamship Company was the dominant line and the most familiar to cannery crews, but it was not the first.

The Hudson's Bay Company established its coastal trading system after its amalgamation with the Northwest Company in 1821. Their first coasting vessel was the *Cadboro* (Cadboro Bay is named for this sailing vessel, not vice versa). She was introduced in 1827, the year Fort Langley was established, and served the company's fur trade until 1860. She served well but was often criticized by HBC officials. As Governor Simpson himself remarked, "The *Cadboro* is quite unfit for the Trade, there are hundreds of War Canoes on the Coast, longer and higher out of the water than she is, carrying 40 to 50 men each."

In the meantime, Fort Simpson had been opened in 1831 in Nass Harbour at the mouth of the Nass River, and in 1833, Fort McLaughlin was established near the present Bella Bella. Fort Simpson was moved to its present site (now Port Simpson), in 1834.

The first steamship on the coast was the venerable *Beaver* which arrived from England in 1836. She was the only steamship in the company's fleet until 1853 when the *Otter* arrived, also from England. The *Beaver* actually served upcoast logging camps and canneries under B.C. Towing and Transportation Co. Ltd. until she was wrecked at Prospect Point in 1888. The *Otter*, too, continued in the coastal trade until 1886.

But it was actually the Fraser River goldrush of 1858 that set up the transportation system that would be in effect when the first upcoast canneries began to operate. The Hudson's Bay vessels were pressed into service, transporting miners from Victoria to Yale. In 1859, they were joined by Capt. William Irving's British Columbia and Victoria Steam Navigation Co., changed in 1862 to the Pioneer Line which was to become the dominant steamboating company on the Fraser River. William Irving died in 1872 and was succeeded by his son, Captain John Irving who was to become a legend in his own right. The Hudson's Bay Company's fleet and the Pioneer Line were combined to form the Canadian Pacific Navigation Co., Ltd. in 1883.

The HBC brought the *Otter, Enterprise* and sidewheeler *Princess Louise* (formerly *Olympian*) into the new company and the owners of the Pioneer line, brought the *R.P. Rithet, William Irving, Western Slope* and *Reliance*. R.P. Rithet and another shareholder, Thomas Earle were prominent Victoria businessmen who would figure in the salmon canning business a little later.

In the beginning, the new company operated mainly between Victoria and New Westminster and a monthly sailing from Victoria to northern B.C. ports—Fort Wrangell, Skeena, Port Simpson, Metlakatla, Rivers Inlet, Fort Rupert and way ports.

Later that year, Joseph Boscowitz, a fur dealer, built the *Barbara Boscowitz*, a 119 foot schooner with accommodation for a few passengers and entered the "cannery trade" with a mail contract and regular sailings to Rivers Inlet, Nass and Skeena Rivers, Fort Simpson, Metlakatla and way points. In 1895, the Canadian Pacific Navigation Co. made an agreement with Boscowitz to split the traffic on the northern run.

Turner, Beeton & Co., Victoria merchants and owners of Inverness cannery, formed the People's Steam Navigation Co. in 1884 to compete with Canadian Pacific Navigation Co., but that lasted only until 1889.

The Canadian Pacific Navigation's *Otter* ceased operations in 1886 and her northern trips were taken on by the *Princess Louise* and in 1887, by the *Sardonyx*. She ran aground at Inverness cannery in 1889 and in 1890, became a total loss in the Queen Charlotte Islands on a trip from Fort Simpson to Skidegate with cannery supplies. Later that year she was replaced by the *Danube*, which became a familiar sight on the cannery run for many years. The *Danube* had an interesting sidelight in 1891, and again in 1892, when she was chartered by the Canadian government to visit the Pribilof Islands in connection with the Fur Seal dispute and arbitration. In 1894, the *Islander* also joined the northern run. She had been built for the company in 1888 and arrived in Victoria that December. She was the first of the "mini-liners" that served the B.C. coast for so many years.

Beginning in 1888, Canadian Pacific Navigation Co. commenced a service from Victoria to Alberni and Barkley Sound ports with the *Maude*. It began as a once per month sailing but quickly grew to bi-monthly, then three times per month. Even that wasn't enough for the growing business and the company purchased the *Tees* to supplement the *Maude*'s sailings. She arrived in Victoria from England in 1896, and became one of the familiar ships servicing the canneries on the west coast of Vancouver Island and northern routes. Her skipper for many years was Capt. Josiah Gosse. When the *Tees* was placed on the northern runs (including the Klondike gold rush), she was replaced on the West Coast of Vancouver Island by the *Willapa*. The *Willapa* was joined there in 1898 by the *Queen City*.

The federal government provided subsidies for mail and passenger service to northern communities. These were always a subject for heavy lobbying and political patronage. In 1892, Reverend Thomas Crosby at Port Simpson petitioned Ottawa to subsidize two steamers. But Canadian Pacific Navigation wanted only one and that was the way it remained, at least for the time being.

In 1899, Canadian Pacific Navigation Co. purchased the *Amur* for the northern routes. The *Otter*, the second of that name, and built in Victoria, made her appearance in 1900. The Canadian Pacific Railway acquired the Canadian Pacific Navigation Co. in January 1901. It was now to be operated as the B.C. Coast Service of the Canadian Pacific Railway.

In the meantime, in 1889, Canadian Pacific Navigation Co. had a new rival in the coastal service—the Union Steamship Company of British Columbia (USS Co.). And for most of the next 70 years USS Co. was the prime lifeline of the canneries and camps of the B.C. coast. The company was the first to use the Port of Vancouver as home port. It was organized primarily with the logging camps and tourist trade in mind. At that time, the 14 canneries operating upcoast were served by Canadian Pacific Navigation Co. out of Victoria.

Until 1892, USS Co. served only Nanaimo and Howe Sound routes with the steamers *Cutch* and *Skidegate*. At the end of 1891, the Company launched the *Comox* and the *Capilano* at Coal Harbour in Vancouver. These vessels had been pre-fabricated in Scotland and shipped via Cape Horn to Vancouver. The third of the trio, the *Coquitlam* was launched in April of 1892, and the USS Co. fleet was born.

The *Comox* began its upcoast service as far as Johnstone Strait in 1892, primarily to the logging camps. The *Capilano* and *Coquitlam* were chartered in 1894 to New England Fish Company as motherships for the halibut fishery.

It wasn't until 1897 that Union Steamships initiated a northern cannery run with twice-monthly sailings by the *Coquitlam* to Alert Bay, Rivers Inlet, Skeena River, Metlakatla, Port Simpson and Nass River. Many prominent Vancouver businessmen joined her on her inaugural trip, including H.O. Bell-Irving, who boarded at his new Good Hope cannery in Rivers Inlet. The *Capilano* took over this run in 1900. The *Cassiar* was launched from Wallace Shipyards in False Creek in 1901, and became the chief vessel on the logging camp run. The *Capilano* and *Coquitlam* both went on the northern run on a 10-

day scheduling.

They found it tough going in 1902 when the canning industry was experiencing the financial effects of the big 1901 pack. But by 1904, business was improved and USS Co. ordered the *Camosun* to compete with the CPR's *Princess Victoria* and Boscowitz Steamship Company's *Vadso* and *Venture*, operating out of Victoria. Commencing in 1905, the *Camosun*'s first route was Alert Bay, Bella Coola, Bella Bella, Port Essington, Skeena River canneries, Port Simpson and Nass River canneries to Stewart. There was also a service every Tuesday to Rivers Inlet and the Skeena.

The Union skippers were called "fog wizards." Navigation in the channels was by whistle echo. An echo of 11 seconds meant one mile from land. Many old timers tell of standing on the dock in heavy fog when the steamer was expected, banging pots and pans in response to the boat whistle to guide the skipper into his landing.

The *Camosun* was followed by the *Cowichan* in 1908.

At the time that the CPR purchased the Canadian Pacific Navigation Co., they were operating the *Princess Louise, Amur, Tees* and *Danube* on the northern runs, servicing all the canneries and logging camps from Alert Bay to the Nass and some calls in the Queen Charlotte Islands. The *Queen City* was making three trips a month on the west coast of Vancouver Island. The new owners almost immediately purchased the *Hating* and renamed her *Princess May* after the Duchess of York who was to become Queen Mary. The *Princess May* entered the Alaska cruise route but also served the northern canneries from time to time.

In 1903, the *Princess Beatrice* was launched at Esquimalt and she too, became a regular on the northern routes. In 1904, on one of his many trips north, Henry Bell-Irving took the *Princess Beatrice* to the Skeena via Rivers Inlet, Surf Inlet and Lowe Inlet. He apparently stayed overnight at the Lawyer Island Lighthouse, and caught the *Danube* the next day to Alaska ports.

In 1905, the *Danube* was sold (she became the *Salvor*), as was the *Princess Louise* in 1906. It is interesting that the *Transfer*, a CP Steamships paddlewheeler which operated on the Fraser between New Westminster, Ladner and Steveston, was sold by the company in 1908, and ended up, much later, as the power plant for Millerd's Redonda Bay cannery.

In 1909, with the new city of Prince Rupert being developed as the future terminus of the Grand Trunk Pacific Railway, another steamship line came into being on the B.C. coast with two floating palaces—the *Prince Rupert* and the *Prince George*. For years, the Canadian Pacific Navigation Co. had been the dominant line and had carried the lion's share of the freight and passengers on the coast. The Boscowitz line had been an early competitor, but it was the entry of Union Steamships Ltd. in 1889 that brought real competitive services to the upcoast communities. This was the beginning of the period of expansion and growth for the salmon industry and the expanded services were needed. When the CPR bought out the CPN Co., in 1901, its fleet was for the most part, tired and out of date. The CPR, over the next few years, remedied that situation as the USS Co. was improving the quality and frequency of its routes. So in 1909, the Grand Trunk Pacific's new vessels entered a thriving coastal freight and passenger trade.

They were briefly preceded by Mackenzie Brothers Steamship Company's *Rupert City* which was contracted by the GTP to provide a regular service between Vancouver and Prince Rupert. The *Prince Rupert* and the *Prince George* were sister ships and they both arrived on the coast from England in 1910. They ran an express service between Seattle, Victoria, Vancouver and Prince Rupert and Stewart. That same year, the *Prince Albert* was put in service with a mail contract between Vancouver, Prince Rupert and the Queen Charlotte Islands. (This contract had been previously held by the CPN Co.'s *Amur*.)

1910 marked the introduction of wireless radio to the coastal fleets—a milestone in communication and navigation.

The GTP purchased the *Amethyst* in 1911 and had her converted in Glasgow to the *Prince John*, which became well known on the Queen Charlotte run. Norm Hacking quotes an anonymous old-timer from 1930: "To the scattered people of the Islands, the *John* is more than a ship. She is an institution, a parent, a friend. Often they swear at her; more often they swear by her. She is as steady and as perennially welcome as the rising sun. She crawls into holes with her belly barely clear of the mangling rocks. She pounds for days into southeast seas, with chairs charging adrift in her dining room, all to bring mail and provisions and the grace of contact with the outside world to a score of lonely camps and settlements." This wonderful tribute could have been ascribed to many of the coastal steamships and in later days to those doughty "cannery" boats, the *Catala* and *Cardena*. The *Prince John* was sold to Union Steamships in 1940 and was renamed the *Cassiar*. She sailed until the early 1950s.

The *Prince Rupert* was not the first vessel of that name to figure in B.C. coast history. When the CPR was completed and transcontinental service inaugurated to Vancouver, the railway contemplated a service of its own between Vancouver and Victoria. Instead they contracted with CPN Co. to provide this service. But in 1893, they ordered the building of a fast sidewheeler for this purpose and she was launched in Scotland in 1894. She was named *Prince Rupert* and sailed from the Clyde for Vancouver in September of that year. However, the CPN Co. managed to mobilize the citizens of Victoria against the new competition to such a degree that the CPR ordered the ship back to Britain before she got past the Canary Islands. In 1895, she was placed on the run between Digby, Nova Scotia and Saint John, New Brunswick and never did see the west coast of Canada.

In 1911, Union Steamships' majority owners bought the Boscowitz Steamship Co. and thus acquired the *Vadso* and the *Venture*—both of which served the upcoast canneries. The *Venture* had been built in 1910 in Glasgow to replace the first *Venture* which had been destroyed by fire at Inverness cannery. The new *Venture* was to be in service for many years and was the perfect vessel for the intricate type of sailing that characterized Union Steamships routes.

USS Co. brought the *Chelohsin* into service after her arrival around the Horn in 1912.

In this same period, CP's Princess fleet was greatly expanded with six new vessels in two years. Of particular consequence to the fishing industry was the launching at the end of 1912 from the B.C. Marine Railway Yard in Esquimalt, of the *Princess Maquinna*. She was designed for the west coast run and took that over from the *Tees* in July of 1913. The *Tees* was back in a few months when the *Maquinna* went to the Alaska run. From 1914, for several years, the *Maquinna* served the west coast only in the summer and the Alaska run in the winters. After 1916, she was year-round on the west coast and was a fixture there until she was retired in 1954. The *Princess Maquinna* was one of the all-time best known and loved vessels on the whole of the B.C. coast.

In 1913, Union Steamships' *Chelohsin*, *Cowichan* and *Cassiar* made five sailings per week to Johnstone Strait and Kingcome Inlet. The *Comox* handled Jervis Inlet, the *Camosun* made a weekly trip to Rivers Inlet, Ocean Falls and Bella Coola and the *Venture* to the Skeena canneries and Prince Rupert. The Grand Trunk's Prince Rupert and Prince George sailed bi-weekly to Prince Rupert and further north, with the *Prince John* connecting to the Queen Charlotte Islands. The *Princess Beatrice* provided one sailing per week to the north, including Prince Rupert and called at in-between ports as traffic permitted. The west coast run was handled by the *Tees* or *Maquinna*. But clearly, Union Steamships was becoming the dominant transportation supplier to the upcoast canneries.

In 1913, mail and passenger service between Port Alberni, Bamfield and Ucluelet was inaugurated by private interests with the *M.V. Tofino* and *M.V. Roche Point*.

In 1916, the Grand Trunk Pacific Railway became insolvent and went into liquidation. It was taken over by the Canadian government. The GTP Steamship Co. continued to operate as before, for some time. But in 1917, the

Canadian Northern Pacific Railway, just completed to Vancouver, also was insolvent and in turn taken over by the government. The Canadian National Railways was formed in 1919, and the Grand Trunk Pacific became part of the new system. The Grand Trunk Pacific Steamship Co. formally became part of the CN system in 1925.

Union Steamships added the *Capilano II* and the *Chilkoot* to their fleet in 1919. The *Chilkoot* became a fixture on the northern cannery runs. But the key Skeena and Nass Rivers cannery service was provided by the *Venture* which had come to USS Co. with the purchase of the Boscowitz line. The *Venture* was ideally suited to the cannery routes and she was the model for the design of Union Steamships' next and possibly greatest acquisition, the *Cardena*. She was built on the Clyde for the company and incorporated all the best features of the *Venture* which had been built in the same yard. She was 50 feet longer than the *Venture* and was considered the best sea boat ever to sail the B.C. coast. Her name came from Cardena Bay on Kennedy Island in the Skeena, which had been named for Admiral Cardena, one of the early Spanish explorers. She was delivered in 1923 and immediately entered the upcoast service and began her long career which made her a household name and close friend of several generations of cannery people.

In the meantime, Canadian Pacific Steamships built the new *Princess Louise* at Wallace Shipyards in North Vancouver in 1921. She entered the Alaska tourist run. She handled this service for the next 40 years and, not infrequently, called at northern canneries like Butedale for loads of canned salmon.

In 1925, the *Tees* was purchased by Pacific Salvage Co. to replace the *Salvor*, the former *Danube*, of cannery fame. The *Tees* had been leased by Pacific Salvage in 1918. In 1926, Canadian Pacific purchased the freighter, *Nootka* and in 1928, fitted her with special tanks for carrying pilchard oil from the west coast reduction plants. That same year the *Princess Beatrice* had been sold to Capt. B.L. Johnson and converted to a floating salmon cannery. He sold it to Independent Packers Ltd., who sold it to B.C. Packers in 1930.

Also in 1925, CN Steamships purchased a new passenger vessel for the Queen Charlotte Island service and she became the *Prince Charles* (later sold to Union Steamships and renamed the *Camosun*, the second of three ships to bear that name). She operated for 20 years with the two companies. She was followed in 1930 by the *Prince William*, which lasted only one year on the Queen Charlotte run.

The latter years of the 1920s were the period of greatest expansion for the Union Steamship Company. The *Cardena* was joined in 1925 by the *Catala*, another vessel which would serve the northern canneries for many years and like the *Cardena*, become an indispensable lifeline of those shore operations.

She was named for Catala Island in Esperanza Inlet, which had been named for Father Magin Catala who had been a missionary at Nootka during the Spanish occupation there in the 1790s.

In 1926, Gosse Millerd Co. bought the *Chilliwack* and converted her to a floating cannery.

Canadian National Steamships introduced three new ships in 1930 and 1931—the *Princes Henry*, *David* and *Robert*. They were the most luxurious yet to enter coastal service in B.C.—primarily on the Triangle (Victoria, Seattle, Vancouver) and Alaska runs. But their participation was short-lived. The *Prince Henry* and *Prince David* were transferred to the Atlantic coast in 1932 and the *Prince Robert* was laid up until she entered war service for the Royal Canadian Navy.

In 1931, the *Cardena*'s route was via Bella Coola and Ocean Falls to Prince Rupert and in the winter she also served Rivers Inlet on the reduced winter schedule.

In 1933, another floating cannery came into being when CP Steamships sold the *Princess Ena* to Francis Millerd. By the time she was converted, however, floating canneries had been made illegal by the provincial government and she eventually reverted to the CPR who then had her broken up for scrap.

CN Steamships sold the Queen Charlotte Islands vessels to Union Steamship Co. in 1940 and thus withdrew from the fishing industry service except for the Prince Rupert and Prince George on their direct Vancouver-Prince Rupert runs. The *Prince Charles* and the *Prince John* became the *Camosun II* and the *Cassiar II*, respectively. The *Cassiar II* was fitted with refrigerator space for frozen fish transport.

In 1936, Barkley Sound Transportation started service in Alberni Inlet and Barkley Sound with the *Uchuck I* and later the *Uchuck II*. This continued until 1960, when Alberni Transportation Co. took over with the *Lady Rose*.

In 1940, Union Steamships purchased the Frank Waterhouse Co. which was a competitor in the cannery freight business. The Waterhouse vessels continued to operate as a separate company picking up the parent company's heavy cargo business and opportunity business. Also in 1940, Union Steamships became the only line to continue serving Stewart.

The war years were busy ones for the upcoast services of both Union Steamships and CN Steamships and the west coast of Vancouver Island service of CP Steamships. There were huge new demands emanating from the takeover of the port of Prince Rupert by the United States military and from the new Canadian airbases at Shearwater, near Bella Bella, at Coal Harbour on northern Vancouver Island and Alliford Bay and Masset in the Queen Charlottes.

The CN's *Prince George* was a total loss from fire at Ketchikan in 1945. She was replaced by a new *Prince George* in 1947, especially with the Alaska tourist trade in mind, but still serving Prince Rupert from Vancouver with one or two major stops in between. This little liner quickly became a favourite for Prince Rupert passengers.

In 1945, Union Steamships retired the *Camosun II* (the former *Prince Charles*), from its Queen Charlotte run and sold her, leaving the *Cassiar II* as the sole vessel on that service. The *Venture* was retired and sold in 1946 and the only other vessels now left for the northern routes were the *Cardena*, *Catala* and *Chelohsin*. But the big event in 1945 was the purchase of three Royal Canadian Navy corvettes. These were converted as passenger/cargo vessels for the northern routes. The first was named the *Coquitlam II* and entered service to Prince Rupert and Stewart in November 1946. The *Camosun III* joined her the following month on a route from Vancouver to Ocean Falls, Prince Rupert and Ketchikan. The *Chilcotin* followed in May 1947, on the tourist runs to Alaska.

Radar was introduced in coastal vessels in 1946. The first to be equipped was the *Prince Rupert*, followed in quick order by the entire fleet.

The *Princess Adelaide*, which had run to Prince Rupert weekly for many years, was withdrawn in 1948 and the CP Steamships were finished with the B.C. north coast routes. And in 1954, the beloved *Princess Maquinna* succumbed to the declining west coast traffic and was withdrawn for good from her run which she had serviced for 40 years. Parts of her route were taken over by the *Princess of Alberni* until 1958 when she was sold to Northland Navigation. Northland ran her as the *Nootka Prince* until she was damaged in an accident in 1959.

By 1950, only the *Cardena* was servicing the calls north of Toba Inlet to Smiths and Rivers Inlets, and the *Catala* was running to Ocean Falls and Bella Coola via Johnstone Strait. Union Steamships brought a number of freight vessels into service under the Union/Waterhouse flag. And these served Butedale and other key fish packing plants. This fleet consisted of the *Cassiar*, *Chilkoot*, *Chilliwack*, *Island King*, *Capilano*, *Eastholme*, *Argus* and *Gulf Mariner*.

The building of the Aluminum Company of Canada smelter and town at Kitimat and the power facility at Kemano was a boon to Union Steamships' northern vessels, the *Camosun* and *Coquitlam*. The Indian village of Kitimaat had been served by the company's vessels monthly for decades and their Masters were familiar with the waters of Douglas Channel.

In the meantime, British Columbia Steamships had entered the freight business on the coast and in 1952, changed their name to Northland Navigation.

In 1955, the *Prince Rupert* made her final trip at age 45 and was subsequently sold to Japanese interests for scrap. Canadian Pacific and Canadian National created a joint service to replace her with the *Princess Norah*, whose name was changed to *Queen of the North*. In 1957, she was sold to Northland Navigation and renamed the *Canadian Prince*. This left only the *Prince George* operating by CN and she served the Alaska tourist run until 1975 when she was heavily damaged by a dockside fire in Vancouver.

In 1956, Union Steamships took over Tidewater Shipping Co., which was successful in the coastal freight business. But in 1958, Union Steamships, bleeding financially and unable to negotiate an increased subsidy for the camps and small communities of the north coast, withdrew its passenger services on the subsidized routes. The *Catala* was put back in service later that year to Johnstone Strait, Port Hardy and Bella Coola. The Union/Tidewater freight routes continued and the *Cassiar* and *Chilliwack* provided limited passenger space to Prince Rupert, the Queen Charlottes and some of the northern ports. But this was the death throes of Union Steamships. In January 1959, the Union's fleet was sold to Northland Navigation, which had been successful in acquiring the federal government's subsidies for the northern communities. The *Cassiar III* became the *Skeena Prince*, the *Capilano III* the Haida Prince, and the *Chilliwack III* the *Tahsis Prince*.

Northland had taken over the CPR's west coast service in 1958. In 1963, they launched a new passenger-freighter for the subsidy runs on the north coast, the *Northland Prince*. But in 1976, she lost the government subsidy and Northland withdrew all its passenger services.

In 1966, B.C. Ferries' *Queen of Prince Rupert* began passenger service to Prince Rupert from Kelsey Bay on Vancouver Island. She was replaced by the *Queen of the North* in 1980, with the *Queen of Prince Rupert* taking over the Queen Charlotte Island service. B.C. Ferries also operates a passenger service from Port Hardy to Namu, Bella Bella, Klemtu, Ocean Falls and Bella Coola.

Virtually all of the upcoast canneries have now been closed in favour of modern centralized plants in Prince Rupert and Vancouver, and the modest passenger services which have inherited the coast are primarily carriers of tourists, as more and more discover the beauties and wonders of the north coast which for so many years was the life and breath of thousands of cannery workers.

The closure of the canneries, and the development of modern air travel, obviated the necessity of the unique passenger vessels that provided the lifeline to these remote points on the map that are no more.

The cannery companies themselves provided some of their own services. As the big packers came into service over the years, they were used to carry freight when they weren't loaded with fish. There were countless voyages up and down the coast each year by these vessels and a considerable amount of freight was carried in this way.

B.C. Packers had their own shipping company. The Packers Steamship Company was incorporated in 1902 to hold ownership of all the vessels which belonged to the new company, The British Columbia Packers Association of New Jersey. In 1928, Wallace Fisheries Ltd. was merged with British Columbia Fishing and Packing Co. Ltd. to form British Columbia Packers Ltd., and Wallace Diesel Ships Ltd. was folded into Packers Steamships Co., Ltd. The ownership of the vessels was transferred to B.C. Packers in 1934, and later Packers Steamships became an operating subsidiary for operation of the coastal freighters *M.V. Cloverleaf*, *M.V. Teco* and *M.V. P.W.* These vessels served the far flung plants of B.C. Packers for many years and accepted freight from other shippers as well. This fleet was sold to Northland Navigation in 1960.

Capt. John Horne spent most of his career in Union Steamships and Packers Steamships. He was Chief Skipper for Packers Steamships when it was sold to Northland Navigation, and he went with Monty Auldous, manager of Packers Steamships, to B.C. Ferries. He started as a young officer on the *Venture* and recalls the days on the cannery runs: "Bones Bay was the last canning cannery on the run of the Union boats on their way south. So Bones Bay was always the top-up cannery for the ships. We would start out with the *Venture* at Namu and we would load maybe three thousand cases and then go down into Rivers Inlet and load another three thousand. Margaret Bay was still canning in the early '40s so we would go into Margaret Bay and get two thousand cases and then we would go on up Knights Inlet to Glendale Cove and get two thousand cases and then come down to Bones Bay and top the trip up. Bones Bay was only around the corner from Chatham Channel and you couldn't go through there on the wrong tide. Of course, being young kids and eager to get home, we used to break records loading so we could make the tide. I remember one night we loaded 1,140 cases of salmon in one hour—all hand stowed.

"The *Venture* was taken off the run at the time that the Union Steamships built the three Corvettes. They restructured the whole northern operation and the *Cardena* and *Catala* came down into the bottom end. The *Catala* was not a good enough handling vessel to use in the "jungle." She could not do places like Chatham Channel and those areas—she just wasn't capable of it. But the *Cardena* was really a modern model of the *Venture* and she was a perfect ship. She could go anywhere.

"In Rivers Inlet, up at the head, you had Kildala and RIC and over on the other side were the remains of McTavish and down towards Wadhams and

Good Hope were two canneries that had disappeared long since. Inrig's cannery was in Moses Inlet. Then you had Beaver and at the mouth was Goose Bay. Beaver was always Dogpatch. It was painted mustard yellow with red trim."

John describes the rigging of the winches on the Union boats: "One of the main reasons for rigging 'Siwash' was because of pipe and logs and all those horrible things we used to have to load into those tiny hatches. 'Siwash' was when you lift the handles (on the steam winch), the hook goes down. If it's rigged so when you lift the handles the hook goes up, it's called 'up for up'. 'Siwash' rigging was a safety thing for the winchman.

"It's fascinating how the loading changed. In the early days, when the *Chelohsin* came in, her hatches wouldn't take a full sized board of canned salmon. So they used what we called racks. It was two metal rails with a long metal handle on each end and you hand-trucked the salmon, five cases at a time into the hold. And they greased it with bacon rind. Then the *Venture* came and we had what we called a board and it took three cases this way and whatever number it took to go to the end. And it was the hardest thing to teach new sailors how to pile the cases. The sailors took this board which had four hooks on the corners, into the cannery and loaded from the piles with our dollies, pulled it outside and hooked it on and took them into the hold and then discharged them again on dollies and stowed them 10 or 12 cases high.

"Then came a thing called the Towmotor—this incredible machine—and we didn't have to go into the cannery anymore. All he did was run out to the ship, drop the load, pick up an empty pallet and run back into the cannery. We would be working both hatches at once. We would load, on average, 600 cases an hour. When it got down in the hold it landed on our dollies and the dollies were rolled aft and the salmon was hand stowed.

"The *Venture* left Wednesday afternoon at two, except during the war, when she left at night. The *Cardena* did the Skeena—she went on Tuesday night at nine. The *Catala* did the Stewart run and she left on Friday night at nine. When the corvettes came in, the *Cardena* used to go Tuesday as far north as Bella Coola.

"The *Cardena* took over from the *Venture* and still left on Wednesdays until about 1947. The *Coquitlam* took over the Prince Rupert-Queen Charlotte Islands run that the *Cassiar* and *Camosun* used to do during the Second World War. They had been the CN ships, *Prince Charles* and *Prince John* and they both ran every ten days to the Charlottes because the amount of military in the Islands was quite significant. When the war ended the *Coquitlam* took the Queen Charlotte Islands run and the *Camosun* took the Stewart run so they were still a Tuesday and a Friday sailing.

"We used to relieve occasionally. I was on the *Cardena* in 1947 when we went aground in Masset Inlet. Until 1949 we had the *Chelohsin* as well. She used to do a lot of the jungle up as far as Sullivan Bay. We went to Simoom Sound, Echo Bay and right around to Allison Harbour.

"After the war, *Coquitlam* did Vancouver to Prince Rupert, Queen Charlotte Islands and back to Vancouver. The *Camosun* did Friday out of Vancouver as far north as Stewart, stopping at Kitimat and Rupert. She had replaced the *Catala* on that run. The *Cardena* did from Vancouver up to Bella Coola, Ocean Falls, Bella Bella, Rivers Inlet, Smiths Inlet and Port Hardy. We used to get into Port Hardy Tuesday morning, left at noon and got into Vancouver in the wee hours of Wednesday. After '49 when the *Chelohsin* was lost, the *Cardena* went on the jungle run and the *Catala* did the *Cardena*'s run."

Capt. John Horne had a special family association with the *Cardena*. He married Patricia Dorman of Bones Bay whom he met while serving on the Union boats. His in-laws had spent their honeymoon on the *Cardena* enroute to Wales Island cannery where Jack Dorman was a bookkeeper. He presented Patricia with her engagement ring on the *Cardena*, and Patricia's sister, Shirley, met her husband on the same ship. Brother-in-law David Dorman named his pleasure boat *Cardena* in honour of the old vessel which was so much a part of their early lives.

Jessie Graham, who with her husband Jim established Duncanby Landing in Rivers Inlet in 1936, recalls the steamboats: "The *Catala* and the *Cardena* were the two main Union Steamships that came to Duncanby. When we first started, we were the 45th call out of Vancouver. They would stop anywhere—you may see a little dinghy come out and they would stop and that would be a call. They would open up those big doors on the lower deck and put off the mail and groceries. We were the 45th call but when we left in 1972, we were the 3rd call. The coast just died—it's a shame.

"In the early days, the *Beatrice* used to come in to Rivers but I don't think it ever came in to Duncanby Landing. We depended on the Union Steamships. They came in every week. They never missed. Boat day was a big day.

"Captain Bowden was on the *Cardena* a long time. They had so few navigational aids. I remember so well, when we were at Goose Bay especially, when it was foggy. They would whistle to tell us they were coming. So we would run in and get a tin basin or something and a wooden spoon and stand on the corner of the wharf and bang that thing. Then they would toot and we'd bang it some more. And they would come in just slow and easy and they'd land just perfectly.

"In the winter time, they wouldn't stop at Rivers on the way down. So if we wanted to go to town, we would go all the way around. In those days, it was about 19 dollars to Vancouver—the *Cardena* mostly, but we had the *Catala* with us for awhile—and we'd go all the way around the Inlet and up to Namu and to Prince Rupert before we headed south to Vancouver. We had a lovely trip and they'd feed you and all for that price."

Princess Maquinna at Port Alberni

Southholme at Sunnyside

Cardena

Officers of the Venture

The Lifelines 157

CN steamship

Grand Trunk Pacific's Prince George

Catala at Carlisle

Northland Prince at Butedale

Chapter 11

DECISIVE DECADES

The 1930s and 1940s initiated profound changes to the fishing industry as they did to every other part of Canadian society. With the creation of British Columbia Packers Ltd. by the merger of B.C. Fishing and Packing Company with Wallace Fisheries in 1928, the salmon sector could look forward to correcting some of its wasteful practices and improving earnings all down the line from the primary producers to the processors. The Fraser River was still awaiting the rescue of an international treaty, but on the rest of the coast, wherever interception by American fishermen was not a factor, the runs were producing well.

Then came the big pink run of 1931, which pushed many producers to the wall and injured those that survived. The generosity of Mother Nature that year coincided with the manifestation of the Great Depression's first effects on European and North American markets. But even more profound events in the offing would leave unexpected marks on the industry.

In the early 1930s, Canada had flirted with a policy of neutrality in the event of war between Japan and the United States. Japan was declaring its imperialistic ambitions in the Pacific and the U.S. was considering the strong possibility of war in order to thwart those ambitions. The U.S. also feared the possibility of Japan invading the west coast of Canada as a base for operations against the United States itself. And the Americans were concerned about Canada's lack of preparedness for the defence of her Pacific coast.

Japanese-Canadians and Japanese nationals had become major players in the fishing industry, particularly in the gillnet and West Coast troll fleets. Ever since they first appeared in numbers in B.C. in the 1890s, their presence had been resented by the white fishermen and to some extent by the Native Indians. There was a very strong anti-Asian bias in the established society at the time. The Japanese soon proved themselves to be excellent fishermen who were efficient producers of good quality product. By the 1920s, Japanese in B.C. had established markets in Japan and China for dry-salt herring and for canned chum salmon. All this fed the racial bias so well established in the rest of the fleet. The canners, for their part, were keen to have these good producers to man their boats on the Fraser and in the northern areas.

In 1923, the federal government responded to the anti-Asian lobby in the province with the Chinese Exclusion Act. They stopped short of legislation in respect to the Japanese and instead, negotiated an agreement with the Japanese government, by which the number of Japanese immigrants to Canada was limited to 400 per year.

Meanwhile, in Japan, the military establishment had taken effective control of the government and in 1931, the Japanese occupied Manchuria, in pursuit of its natural resources. In 1937, Japan invaded China and the possibility of war in the Pacific took on a new and very real aspect. At this time, the U.S. Army even offered to take responsibility for the defence of the B.C. coast, such was their fear of the lack of preparedness. But Canada decided to do it herself and to rely on the new Canadian Airforce as the front line of defence on the coast.

During the First World War, in 1915, the Aero Club of B.C. was formed to train pilots for Britain's Royal Flying Corps and Royal Naval Airforce. This event had a connection to the fishing industry. None other than H.O. Bell-Irving was a founding director, and his son Richard was one of those who took his early training here and became an officer in the Royal Flying Corps in Britain. The Aero Club had one Curtiss biplane and began operations at Minoru racetrack in Richmond. It was soon moved to Terra Nova field in Steveston. The club ran out of funds and came to an early demise, but it can be said to have been the genesis of the RCAF in B.C. In 1917, the Royal Flying Corps established its own training school in Canada but fell short of setting up in B.C.

In 1919, Canada created the Air Board to regulate aviation across the country and in 1920, formed the Canadian Air Force as a non-permanent force. Given the lack of airports in the country, flying boats were the preferred equipment and they came to the Air Force as war-surplus planes from Britain and the U.S. That same year, the B.C. government granted a large parcel of land at Jericho Beach on English Bay, and the site was prepared for the first and the principal Flying Boat Station.

The forest industry and the B.C. Forest Service were the first to use the services of the Canadian Air Force flying boats. But in 1921, the federal Fisheries Department tried this new technology for transporting fish fry to stocking locations and for fishery patrols.

In 1924, the CAF became the Royal Canadian Air Force. Strange, but true, the aircraft (HS2Ls) actually used homing pigeons to relay messages back to base at Jericho Beach. But this practice died after reliable radio communications were integrated into the system.

In 1936, as concern grew about a possible war between Japan and the U.S., and with the rising war probability in Europe, the government ordered a survey of the coast for potential Flying Boat stations and land airports for coastal defence.

In 1937, a seaplane tender scow was established at Bella Bella, which acted as a refuelling base and meteorological and wireless radio facility.

Barkley Sound and Port Alberni were considered vulnerable to attack by Japan as a strategic jump-off base to Vancouver harbour and from there to the United States. In 1938, a Flying Boat weather station was established at Ucluelet, although the planes were still flying out of Jericho Beach. At the same time, construction began on Flying Boat stations at Ucluelet, Coal Harbour, Bella Bella, Prince Rupert (Seal Cove) and Alliford Bay. And aerodromes were proposed at Patricia Bay, Port Hardy, Sandspit and Tofino. These were all ready for duty in 1940, complete with army units for their defence. All of these stations, with the exception of Pat Bay, were in fishing industry territory and would have their effects on the industry.

Canada's entry into the European War in September 1939 brought major changes to the fishing industry. The preoccupation with coastal defence, of course, was accelerated and initiatives like the fishermen's navy had a direct impact. Supplies and materials for the plants and fleets became strategic goods for the war effort, and scarce for civilian uses at home. At the same time, the production of the industry became strategic itself, and the canned salmon pack and the canned herring pack were commandeered by the British Ministry of Food. The production of canned herring was put into high gear as a convenient way to provide nutrition to Allied troops in the field. The advantages of canned fish were never more apparent than during the war—highly nutritious, non-perishable, transportable and, at least in the case of canned salmon, very palatable.

The British Food Ministry had three labels for canned salmon: Group 1 was red and was for sockeye only, but for all grades. Group 2 was blue and was for coho only. Group 3 was green, was called "household," and was for all other salmon species. Canned herring was for the troops and for the Russian people who were beset by the German invasion. Immediately after the war, most of the herring went to UNRRA for feeding refugees or displaced persons.

With their markets assured, the canners problems focussed on production. Everything was in short supply—supplies for the canneries, fuel for the boats, and most of all, labour. The availability of boats themselves was sometimes a problem, as the armed forces requisitioned vessels for their own use. Just some of the well-known boats taken over by the R.C.A.F. were the *Combat*, *Kimsquit*, *Snow Prince*, *Cape Canso*, *Midnight Sun*, *B.C. Star*, and the *Skeena Maid*.

The first Stranraer flying boats arrived in 1939. Like the HS2Ls, they were considered obsolete but they were a great improvement both in range and in carrying capacity. Several of these ugly ducklings survived the war and were part of Queen Charlotte Airlines' first fleet.

By 1940, the Seal Cove Flying Boat base was operational and Prince Rupert was fortified with army and navy units, anti-aircraft batteries, heavy artillery and a submarine net at the harbour entrance. The city, with its major deep sea harbour facilities and its trans-Canada railway, was considered an obvious target in the event of a Japanese invasion.

That same year, the Canadian Aircraft Detection Corps was organized with volunteers in isolated parts of the coast (many of them, fishing industry ports), trained to recognize aircraft and to report their movements. Another important event in 1940 was the introduction of radar, which, once it was available for general use, would change navigation safety on the coast as nothing had before.

At the end of 1941, with the Japanese sneak attack on Pearl Harbour, the United States was suddenly in the war and Canada was at war with Japan. The war in Europe had seemed distant to British Columbians except for the armed forces personnel that were being trained and shipped overseas and except for the production of war materials and equipment that by then was in high gear. But Pearl Harbour and the subsequent lightning strikes by the Japanese forces from Hong Kong to Singapore, the Philippines and Burma, brought the war close to home. The whole coast was put on high alert, with blackouts, training of civilian Air Raid Precaution (ARP) units and training of militia for guerilla fighting in the mountains.

Early in 1942, both the American and Canadian governments decided to evacuate people of Japanese origin from their west coasts. The removal of the Japanese fishermen caused a major problem for canners who found their fishing fleets decimated. The boats were still available because the assets of these evacuees had been seized and were later sold by auction. But the men to man the boats were not available as both the armed forces and the war production effort were demanding all the manpower (and womanpower) possible. Part of the solution was the import of net fishermen from Great Slave Lake, which established a multigenerational tradition in the B.C. fishery.

In June 1942, a large Japanese force occupied two of the most western Aleutian Islands, Kiska and Attu. Prince Rupert became the main staging area for American forces in the defence of Alaska and in the expulsion of the Japanese invasion force. The U.S. Army virtually took command of Prince

Rupert and its port facilities, and built an army base at Port Edward.

The effect on the fishing industry was immediate. Nelson Brothers had opened a new cannery on the Ocean Dock in Prince Rupert in 1940. The dock was commandeered by the U.S. Army and the cannery was forced to move. The Nelsons built a new cannery at Port Edward, next to B.C. Packers' reduction plant. Building materials were almost impossible to buy, and Nelson Brothers moved a defunct mill from Esperanza Inlet to the site, and this became one of the largest plants on the coast and remained so for many years. The presence of so many American servicemen and some of their families was a boon to Prince Rupert, and it encouraged the expansion of fisheries cold storages in the city. But the biggest positive effect on the industry was the facilities and buildings left behind when the Americans eventually left.

In the meantime, the threat of invasion grew all through 1942 and into 1943, when Japanese reverses in the war in other parts of the Pacific drew their attention away from North America. The presence of Japanese submarines on the coast was the most obvious manifestation of the danger of invasion. The shelling by a Japanese submarine of the Estevan Lighthouse in June 1942 brought the hot war home to Canadian soil. Several ships were sunk in the entrance to Juan de Fuca Strait—the *Fort Camosun*, a British freighter; the *Ocean Vengeance*, an American freighter; the *U.S.S. Grunion*, a U.S. submarine; and the American freighter, *Coast Trader*, which was sunk by the same submarine that shelled Estevan Light. There were many submarine sightings, for example, in Esperanza Inlet, at Tofino, at Bella Coola, near Port Simpson and Victoria.

The I-class Japanese subs carried small air craft, the Yokusuka E-14Y1. The wings of these planes folded for storage in small hangars on the deck of the submarine. They were launched by catapult from the deck and on return to the sub, landed on the water and were hoisted aboard by crane. They were used for reconnaissance missions. In February, 1942, one was sighted over Prince Rupert and later, several sightings were reported over the Coal Harbour R.C.A.F. station. Post war information indicated that there were many undetected E-14Y1 flights over U.S. and Canadian territory.

In 1943, the first Canso Flying Boats arrived on the B.C. coast. These were far superior to the Stranraers and would play a part in postwar coastal air travel for many years. That same year saw the opening of the new land airports at Comox, Tofino, Port Hardy and Sandspit, the latter three of which would revolutionize postwar travel on the coast. A perforated steel runway was built on the beach at Masset. With these airports and the Flying Boat stations, many isolated fishing and logging communities were suddenly in the air age and within easy reach of B.C.'s major centres. The site for the city of Prince Rupert, obviously, was not chosen with air travel in mind. There was no suitable site for runways in easy access to the city and it wasn't until the 1960s that the airport on Digby Island was opened by Transport Canada. Even then, the airport was, and still is, a ferry ride away from the city. In the meantime, after the war, regular air service to Prince Rupert was established in a round about way. Canadian Pacific Airlines flew DC-6s from Vancouver via the airport at Port Hardy to Sandspit airport. Passengers were then conveyed by Canso flying boat across Hecate Strait to the seaplane base at Seal Cove. The death of the coastal passenger steamer service was thus foretold, but it was slow in coming because of the inconvenience of the indirect flights.

The evacuation of Japanese people from the coast in 1942 continues to be a controversial action, especially in respect to those who were Japanese Canadians. Public opinion is pretty well unanimous in condemning the seizure of assets and their subsequent disposal at fractions of their value. But the justification or otherwise of the evacuation of all people of Japanese origin still evokes doubt and debate. It occurred after many years of anti-Asian and anti-Japanese feeling among the white and Indian population. And there had been concern in the military establishment about the security of the new airbases that were being built in the 1930s in remote parts of the coast, which were also the locations of villages established by Japanese fishermen who had been shunned in the larger centres.

There were many legacies of the war to the people of the coast. The new airports brought regular air transportation to Port Hardy and the Queen Charlotte Islands and Prince Rupert. And they made possible the operation of small company-owned or chartered float planes which could fly company officials from plant to plant in quick order to supervise their widespread coastal operations. They could also deliver spare parts to the fleet when needed and could even deliver them to the side of the vessel at sea. The need to depend on the weekly steamer from Vancouver or Prince Rupert was becoming a thing of the past. The isolation of the canneries and their villages was disappearing.

The buildings and equipment abandoned by the U.S. forces at Prince Rupert were snapped up by the canneries at bargain prices, making it possible to improve the living conditions in the cannery villages. Both Butedale and Namu became the proud owners of R.C.A.F. crash boats which were used for dispatch boats for their fishing fleets. These boats were 70 feet long and were powered by two 1350 HP Packard engines. They could go "like stink", but in doing so, would burn fuel at a prodigious rate.

The Coal Harbour Flying Boat station was closed after the war and eventually became the whaling station for Western Canada Whaling Co., a consortium of B.C. Packers Ltd. and Taiyo Gyogyo Fishing Co. of Japan. Alliford Bay Flying Boat station was closed and most of its assets transferred to the airport at nearby Sandspit. The station had been built on the site of the Maritime Fisheries cannery, built in 1912. The plant and equipment had been bought by B.C. Packers in 1938 and transferred to Pacofi, which they were rebuilding.

Industrial relations took a decisive turn in 1945 with the formation of the United Fishermen and Allied Workers Union. There had been sporadic attempts at organizing the fishermen since 1893 when the Fraser River Fishermen's Protective and Benevolent Association came into being. The early canners took it upon themselves to agree what the prices for raw fish should be. They formed "combines" for this purpose and even for determining selling prices for the finished product. These agreements were not hugely successful because then, as now, there were always some operators who felt their interests were better served outside the fold. So the agreements were always short-lived and had changeable memberships. Nevertheless, the economic power remained with the canners for many years and the fishermen were takers of prices rather than price setters. There were many attempts to counter this with various organizations and with strikes and strife.

But it wasn't until the UFAWU was formed that the fishermen, shoreworkers and tendermen came together as a more or less cohesive unit. As so often happens in labour relations, the owners' practices made it possible for the organizers to bring the labour sector together. As also so often happens, they deserved what they got but they didn't deserve as much as they got! From this time forward, the unilateral power of the canners ceased and their ability to manage their business was severely challenged.

The war brought big changes in communication technology. The radio-telephone ended the isolation that the upcoast canneries had lived with for so many years. It was now possible to communicate ship to ship and ship to shore. And in no time, every cannery and every fishing vessel was equipped. The chatter on the Fishermen's Band was a constant while the boats were fishing and as they kept in touch with one another. Cannery managers could keep in contact with their boats to make sure their catch was picked up and to let them know where the best fishing was taking place.

Radar was introduced to the fleet after the war and sonar technology soon produced the depth sounder which proved so valuable in herring fishing. These advantages were adopted by the steamships as well and improved the safety of navigation on the coast enormously.

Ranking with all the other events of the 30s and 40s was the agreement finally reached between the U.S. and Canada for joint management and rehabilitation of the Fraser River sockeye resources. The International Pacific Salmon Fisheries Treaty was signed in 1937 and the Salmon Commission was created that same year. The first fishways at Hell's Gate were completed in 1945 and the restoration of those great runs which had been desecrated by the 1913 and 1914 slides had begun. Other fishways were added at Hell's Gate in 1946, 1947, 1952 and 1966.

Chapter 12

NOT THE SALMON FISHERY

When Atlantic Canadians say fish, they mean cod. When Pacific coast Canadians say fish, they mean salmon. And the salmon resource was the solid foundation on which the fishing industry in British Columbia was built.

The other fisheries became important as well, and although they were ancillary to the utilization of salmon, they made possible the multi-purpose plants and the efficiencies of year round operations.

The **halibut** fishery was its own world as the nineteenth century became the twentieth. Pioneering companies, in particular, New England Fish Company out of Boston, had developed markets in eastern Canada and the United States, and as market demand grew, and the high production of the virgin stocks on the Atlantic coast declined, they went further afield to develop new grounds. The halibut resource of the American slope of the North Pacific promised to be at least as prolific as that of the Atlantic coast. The opening of the Northern Pacific Railroad and the Canadian Pacific Railway made it possible to deliver fresh Pacific halibut by express train to the eastern markets.

The halibut fishery would be the beginning of The Canadian Fishing Co., Ltd. which was purchased in 1909 by Nefco and became, along with Anglo-B.C. Packing Co., B.C. Packers Ltd. and Nelson Brothers Fisheries Ltd., "the big four" that dominated the B.C. fishing industry for decades.

U.S. and Canadian halibut fishermen prosecuted the fishery together, from small boats and then—east coast style—from dories carried by steam driven motherships with long distance travelling capacity and mega-ton carrying capacity. This joint development began on the banks off Oregon, Washington and British Columbia, largely in what were then international waters (territorial seas extended only three miles from the coast). But the fishery was poorly controlled in the early years and overfishing severely damaged the resource in these easily accessible grounds. In 1915, the Department of Naval

Services (which then included fisheries) was concerned about depletion of the resource. The producers were urging a closed season in the winter, but nothing came of it. The fishery moved progressively north onto virgin stocks, and the overfishing with it until finally, the governments of the two countries formed the International Pacific Halibut Commission—in time to preserve the stocks in the north, but too late to conserve those in more southerly waters. (The international treaty that created the Commission was signed in 1923 and was the first treaty that Canada ever signed in her own right—foreign relations having been handled on her behalf by Britain until that time.)

One of the major failures of Canadian fisheries diplomacy (and there have been many), in the post Law of the Sea period, was its inability to retain a right to harvest the jointly managed stocks in what had become Alaskan waters. The Americans had done their share—perhaps more—to deplete the halibut stocks off B.C. The Canadians had done their share to preserve those off Alaska. Logic would permit Canadians to continue to benefit from the results of the joint I.P.H.F.C. work. But logic is never a factor in fisheries negotiations with the U.S., unless it speaks to their own interests. That isn't rhetoric—it has been demonstrated year after year and issue after issue since 1783.

Herring is primarily an inshore fishery and Canadians have managed to deplete that resource by themselves—not totally through greed and irresponsibility, but also through a misunderstanding, even by the scientists, of what fishing pressure the stocks could sustain.

The early herring fisheries were for salting and curing in the early 1900s. Nanaimo was one centre with oar-powered boats fishing double seines for the salteries there. The Japanese were heavily involved in this industry and supplied markets in the Orient. Many tons of dry salt herring in 300-pound boxes were processed and shipped to Japan and China. In the retail market, the fish were sold individually and the wood and nails from the boxes were saved and used as well. This market died in the 1930s, probably as a result of the Sino-Japanese war.

The west coast of Vancouver Island also was an early centre with dry salt and Scotch cure herring being produced in plants in Barkley Sound and at Nootka.

There was a huge flurry of herring canning during World War II, with Britain buying everything produced for the armed forces and for the civilian population and for food aid to Russia. Herring in tomato sauce in one-pound flats was the norm and while it was nutritious, it was not delicious and with the end of the war, the market collapsed.

The main utilization of herring for many years was for processing in

Herring double seines at Nanaimo

reduction plants into high-protein fish meal and oil. Reduction plants were built originally for pilchard processing and herring, being primarily a winter fishery, complemented the other, at least on the west coast of the Island. But reduction plants were built specifically for herring in the 1930s in other areas, e.g., Port Edward, Butedale, Namu and Steveston. When the pilchard runs ceased in 1945, the west coast plants also depended on herring until one by one they were closed in favour of the mainland plants.

Technology doomed the herring reduction fishery. Seine fishermen are always innovative and when they introduced echo sounders and powerful pitlamps to the fishery, they were able to attract the fish away from the reefs and shoals that provided a natural protection. The scientific wisdom of the day held that herring could not be overfished because the fishery would become uneconomic before the stock would be in biological danger. But they hadn't counted on the deadly efficiency of the pitlamps. Depletion became all too apparent and the herring reduction fishery had to be closed.

This coincided with the opening of a hugely lucrative market for herring roe in Japan. Japanese companies had been buying whole frozen herring, but it was not generally known that it was being processed there for the roe. About 1970 or 1971 the Hokkaido Fishermen's Co-op approached Ross Nicholson of B.C. Packers and Joe Antonelli of the Prince Rupert Fishermen's Co-op, to buy some roe herring from the boat, to be frozen and shipped to Seattle for processing there. This was arranged and the first catch came from Khuzeymateen Inlet, near Port Simpson, where the roe content was the required 12 to 14 percent. The next year, Marubeni Co. and others arranged for the herring to be processed in B.C. plants and sent their skilled technicians from Japan to ensure that it was done properly. These first small shipments were extremely profitable and the herring roe fishery was born. Of course, everyone wanted to participate in it and the Department of Fisheries was hard pressed to control the fishing effort in order to conserve the stocks that once had been so plentiful. The fishery officials' role is now very specialized and the fishery itself is likened to a gold rush with openings measured literally in hours or even minutes. The lowly herring has become one of the most lucrative of the resources.

In the long-term picture of the industry, the **pilchard** fishery was transient. The stocks were pelagic and at the northern end of their range in B.C. waters. In fact, they were probably north of their normal range and were in these latitudes only because of the intrusion of warm waters created by the *el Nino*s of the day. But in the first half of the twentieth century, *el Nino* was not known or, if suspected, not well understood.

There was a well established pilchard fishery in California, but the presence of these sardine-like, oily fish in Vancouver Island waters was not apparent until after the First World War. And besides canning them, the industry took them for production of fishmeal and oil. Reduction plants sprang up on the west coast of the Island in short order and a thriving industry was

Pilchards for canning, Koprino, 1928

established at such locations as Nootka, Ceepeecee, Ecoole and Kildonan. By 1927, there were some 26 pilchard reduction plants operating between Barkley Sound and Kyuquot, some very large and some quite small. In 1940, fishing had moved outside the inlets and the very small plants with small vessels had closed, leaving the fishery to the ever larger seine boats. The pilchards disappeared from B.C. waters altogether after 1945 and the stock failed in California as well. For awhile, the reduction plants continued to process herring but the west coast catches came to be transported to the mainland plants and only Port Albion near Ucluelet, continued into the late 1950s.

Apparently, the pilchards are not extinct as many had feared, and they are once again appearing off the west coast of the Island.

Albacore **tuna** off B.C. are also an anomaly associated with warm water intrusions. At various times and for a brief period in the 1960s, these southern fish were abundant enough to support a canning operation at Kildonan plant. But this fishery lasted only a few years

Making money from **groundfish** in B.C. has always been a challenge. Local markets in Vancouver, Victoria and New Westminster were early established for fresh fish. The same occurred in Prince Rupert as that city grew from its railway construction days. The Campbell Avenue fish dock on Vancouver's waterfront was the focus of the local market and over the years, numerous small enterprises branched into processing in addition to supplying the local and interior markets.

But the Pacific slope of Canada does not have the massively extensive continental shelf that the Maritime provinces and Newfoundland abut. So the Pacific groundfish resources are much smaller than those on the Atlantic. Only J.S. McMillan Fisheries and for awhile, the Prince Rupert Fishermen's Co-op can be said to have made an enduring success of the groundfish business. Jack McMillan and his sons are associated with groundfish processing more than anyone in the province. B.C. Packers invested heavily in this area in the 1960s, building a state of the art plant at Steveston to process "prepared products" from salmon, halibut and groundfish, but this initiative did not succeed and the plant is gone. The Co-op has also failed and J.S. McMillan is left as the only major player, with plants both in Vancouver and Prince Rupert.

A fishery has been established off the coast for so-called underutilized species, particularly hake and pollack, which don't have a ready market in Canada. Canadian trawlers catch the fish and deliver them to Polish and Russian motherships, which process them at sea and transport them to their home markets. The Hake Consortium has been a boon to the B.C. dragger fleet.

Shellfish are abundant in B.C. waters and have sustained a processing and marketing industry for many years. The dungeness crab that inhabits this coast, particularly in the vicinity of the Queen Charlotte Islands, is unrivaled for flavour. Similarly, the tiny Pacific pink shrimp have an unlimited demand. There are many varieties of clams—razor clams, butter clams, little necks, geoducks—and the unique abalone supports a small fishery by divers. Crab, shrimp, clams and abalone are regularly processed at Campbell Avenue and North Vancouver fish docks and both the Prince Rupert Co-op and Nelson Brothers Port Edward plant have been processors of the northern dungeness crab. But the crab and clam story is really the story of the Simpsons and Queen Charlotte Canners Ltd. which is contained in Chapter 19.

Dogfish is the most abundant shark species in B.C. waters. It is a predator of salmon and other commercially important species and a fouler of nets and gear. Properly processed, its flesh is palatable and versatile. But without timely and correct processing, the flesh becomes tainted with ammonia and is inedible. Because of the problems the dogfish create for other fisheries, there have been many attempts to find a viable use for them. They were eagerly sought after in the 1920s, 1930s and 1940s for their livers, which are extremely rich in vitamin oil, and liver plants were built all over the coast. This reached a climax during World War II when Vitamin A was a strategic material for the health of the armed forces. But its very value led to the invention of synthetic Vitamin A and the liver oil industry came to a screeching halt.

After the War, the federal government offered subsidies for a dogfish fishery and for the development of a useable product. A modest dogfish industry continues and this once-despised fish has taken its place as a desirable product.

The first commercial **whaling** operation in B.C. was out of Cortes Island in the Gulf of Georgia in the 1860s. It lasted about 10 years before the whale population became too scarce to hunt further.

With the completion of the Union Pacific Railroad, San Francisco became the centre of Pacific coast whaling.

Steamers came from there and around Cape Horn from the east coast, many of them operating out of the Hawaiian Islands. They prowled the North Pacific and harpooned from small whaleboats. They flensed the blubber alongside, took the whalebone or baleen and spermaceti, and discarded the carcasses. The blubber was rendered on board to produce the oil.

Pelagic sealing for fur seals had been prosecuted for many years in the 19th century, but this came to an end with the International Fur Seal Treaty at the turn of the century.

In 1905, some of the sealing captains who had been sailing out of Victoria formed the Pacific Whaling Co. In the next three years, they built three shore stations—Page's Lagoon (near Nanaimo), Sechart, and Kyuquot on the west coast of Vancouver Island. John Macmillan, father of Ewen Macmillan, was one of the principal investors.

The whaling ships came from Norway with Norwegian crews. They were named the *Blue*, the *Black*, the *White*, the *Brown*, the *Green* and the *Rose*. The *Grey* was added as a company freighter/tender.

In 1910, the company opened Rose Harbour Station on Kunglit Island, and Naden Harbour Station, both in the Queen Charlottes. Page's Lagoon was closed by then because of a lack of whales in the Gulf. In World War II, the Japanese market was lost and the fleet was tied up.

In 1947, B.C. Packers, Nelson Brothers and W.F. Gibson and Sons formed Western Whaling Corporation. They purchased the Rose Harbour property from the company, which had now become Consolidated Whaling Corporation. The next year, they purchased the Coal Harbour Flying Boat Station from the Canadian government's War Assets Disposal Corporation, and this became their principal processing plant. In 1950, the company was sold to B.C. Packers Ltd.

In 1961, B.C. Packers teamed up with Taiyo Gyogyo, one of Japan's major fishing companies, to form Western Canada Whaling Corporation, which became the owner and operator of the Coal Harbour Station and the company's three boats.

They operated until 1967.

The B.C. whaling plants produced whale oil, whale bone, bone meal, and whale meat. After the war, the whale meat was frozen for the Japanese market.

EARLY HALIBUT VESSELS

Dory schooner

Prospector

Not the Salmon Fishery 175

Manhatten

Kingfisher

Flamingo

Roman

Celestial Empire

New England

Halibut crew, circa 1910

The catch unloaded

Chapter 13

THE BELL-IRVINGS AND ANGLO-B.C. PACKING COMPANY

Henry Ogle Bell-Irving was born in Lockerbie, Scotland in 1856. He was well educated, qualifying as a civil engineer and practising for four years in Europe before coming to Canada in 1882. The Canadian Pacific Railway was then building west from Winnipeg and Bell-Irving took a job as a survey engineer on the project. This took him across the Prairies and through the Kicking Horse Pass, the Eagle Pass and on into Shuswap country. He was also a bit of an artist and left some interesting watercolours of Shuswap Lake and the Adams River country that would be an important part of his life in future years. At some point he left the westward construction and walked, with his backpack, 50 miles on the Cariboo Trail to meet the Onderdonk construction crews working eastward from the coast. On the way, he was robbed by bandits of everything except his survey instruments.

H.O. Bell-Irving reached Vancouver in the fall of 1885, with the completion of the CPR and set himself up as an architect for a short time. A man of tremendous energy and many talents, he soon went into partnership with R.P. Paterson in the general merchandise import-export business. Paterson was in the whiskey business, and the partners became agents for some pretty important whiskey and spirits brands, some of which are still familiar today.

He was an alderman for the fledgling City of Vancouver in 1887/88, the year after its incorporation, and was the Chairman of the Civic Board of Works.

In 1889, Bell-Irving and Paterson became agents and financial managers for Hobson & Company, who were building a cannery on 57 acres of land at Steveston. It was to be known as the Frasermouth cannery, but this was soon changed to Garry Point cannery. The partners also appear to have had shares in Hobson & Company. The company had other canneries and the agency arrangement applied to them as well, for a period of three years. Bell-Irving & Paterson were to receive 5 percent commission on buying and 5 percent on selling. This was H.O.'s introduction to the salmon canning business. It is interesting that in London, he was warned "to be careful of Hobson & Co., as they are reported tricky." This is also an indication of how well the financial community in England was plugged into the business community in British Columbia. Of course, at that time, the U.K., rather than the United States was the prime source of capital for Canadian business.

Bell-Irving & Paterson were the first to ship canned salmon direct from B.C. ports to England, rather than by the regular route of shipment via agents in San Francisco. In 1890, on one of his many trips to London and Scotland, Bell-Irving chartered the 879-ton Hudson's Bay Company sailing ship, *Titania* in London (one of the fastest of the tea clippers), loaded it with general cargo, including tinplate for the canneries, and sent it around Cape Horn to New Westminster. There, Bell-Irving & Paterson had amassed canned salmon from various canneries and loaded it for the return trip to England. The risks associated with shipping around the Horn were great. For example, in the 1905 sailing season, of the 130 square riggers that sailed from Europe for the U.S. west coast by way of the Horn, only 52 reached port intact.

Up until this time, canned salmon was often sold three or four times between B.C. and London, most of it through Victoria and/or San Francisco. The *Titania* shipment was the beginning of a regular trade that lasted into the new century, and tall ships loading salmon became a familiar sight in New Westminster and Steveston. In 1902, Bell-Irving stopped chartering sailing vessels and shipped via steamer from then on. Shipments were made to Australia and Valparaiso, Chile and later to Shanghai, Hong Kong, Rangoon and Japan. In fact, the Orient was the first market for canned pink salmon and salted "dog" salmon or chums were shipped there in the 1890s. They also shipped canned salmon to eastern Canada via the CPR and established markets there.

At the same time, Bell-Irving had become the municipal engineer for New Westminster and was in charge of laying some of the early water mains and sanitary sewers in the Royal City. His cargoes from England included pipe for these projects.

In 1890, new canneries were springing up on the Fraser and upcoast at a steady rate. H.O.'s early involvement in the salmon industry on the Fraser convinced him that the business was fragmented and poorly organized. He records a meeting of the Fraser River canners in New Westminster on June 21, 1890 in which he was representing the Hobson cannery. "Mr. Wadhams (E.A.), Secretary, T. Ladner in the Chair. On discussion that the price of fish be fixed at 8 cents, it was general opinion that ought to be the price. It was about to be moved that the price be 8 cents, only to be increased after calling another meeting with three days notice to the Secretary, when I suggested it would be well to hear whether the meeting was prepared to consider fair distribution of boats. Todd proposed that each cannery should have 20 government boats, but Ewen and Young would not agree and the meeting broke up without anything being decided."

He conceived the first amalgamation of canneries and the vertical integration of fishing, canning and shipping. He approached a good many of the canners with this in mind and on December 22, 1890, the Anglo-British Columbia Packing Company was formed with its head office in London. Bell-Irving had arranged financing in England from some of his wealthy cousins and in particular, James Jardine Bell-Irving. H.O. was not immediately a shareholder himself, although H. Bell-Irving and Company later became shareholders in Anglo-B.C., and eventually one of the major shareholders.

Bell-Irving was tireless and meticulous in his efforts for the new company. But his real genius was in having Bell-Irving & Paterson appointed Anglo-B.C.'s "managing agent." A few years later, in 1893, the partnership was dissolved and H. Bell-Irving and Company was formed to take over this role. (It was re-organized as H. Bell-Irving & Co., Ltd in 1901.) They were paid a nominal fee for management and a commission on all sales of product. H. Bell-Irving & Co. also represented Fidalgo Island Fishing & Packing Co., which H.O. had established as a subsidiary of Anglo-B.C. Fidalgo operated canneries in Puget Sound and Alaska. H. Bell-Irving & Co. never had a loss in its 75-year history and paid a dividend every year. Thus the Bell-Irving family fortune was established and sustained.

The formation of Anglo-B.C. Packing Co. Ltd. involved the purchase of nine canneries—seven on the Fraser: Garry Point, Britannia, British-American (Fraser), Canoe Pass, Wadhams, English (Phoenix) and British Columbia Packing Co.—and two on the Skeena: North Pacific and British American (Skeena) at Port Essington. The cannery costs in 1890 were $2.55 per case, made up of materials (tin, solder, lacquer, acid, boxes and labels): $1.00 per c/s; fish: 0.85 per c/s; Chinese labour contract: 0.50 per c/s; white labour 0.20 per c/s. White labour included a watchman for twelve months, foreman for six, engineer for two, bathroom man (steambox) for two, retort man for two, cook for six, bookkeeper for eight and assistant bookkeeper for six months. The Chinese labour contract covered all the other cannery employees. One sheet of tin, imported from England, made 24 tops or bottoms or 6 bodies. It took 10 lbs. of solder to each box of tins. The tins were hand-cut and -soldered by skilled Chinese labourers.

The boxes—shooks and ends—were shipped from Royal City Mills and Brunette Mills in New Westminster.

H.O. Bell-Irving's contemporaries in the industry were such well-known cannery men as Alexander Ewen, Thomas Ladner, E.A. Wadhams, Marshall English and Jacob Todd. He became a power in the business and social life of B.C. and Vancouver.

In 1894, he was president of the St. Andrews and Caledonian Society when Earl Aberdeen and Sanford Fleming were their guests at a Halloween supper.

In July 1891, he was in Rivers Inlet to investigate the possibility of Anglo-B.C. building a cannery there. He describes the "Wannock" cannery: "McNeil, proprietor; Draney, manufacturer. 6,000 cases packed to date. Fish running well since the 12th. More fish than they can handle, last day or two. Building about 200 feet by 55 feet. One retort. Building fairly good. Fish knife worked by machinery. Counted 28 boats tied up—all gillnet fishing. Water fairly muddy. A number of Indians around."

He went on to RIC, which was also operated by Draney (Robert Draney who later also built Namu and Kimsquit canneries).

This trip was aboard one of the Boscowitz steamers and it went on to Lowe Inlet cannery in Grenville Channel, operated by Robert Cunningham of Port Essington, and then into the Skeena. He stopped at Balmoral cannery, where he noted that a waterwheel was used to hoist salmon, and that there were 300 fishing licences allowed on the Skeena—200 to canneries and 100 to outside men. There was a price "contract" on the Skeena of 9 cents per fish (sockeye) or 6 cents if the cannery supplied the boat and net; 3 cents per tray for fillers and 11 cents per hour for "wipers." (Wipers were employed to clean the cans after filling and before lacquering.)

Early the next year, in spite of the favourable signs, he made a decision not to build in Rivers Inlet.

Bell-Irving was a keen outdoorsman and an avid hunter of birds and trophy animals like grizzlies and mountain goats. His trips upcoast sometimes gave an opportunity to head off into the bush to hunt. In this way, he also discovered the fascination of the salmon migrations to the spawning grounds and he became a student of the natural—and unnatural—forces that affected the strength of the various runs. At one time, he even argued for a complete closure of Fraser River fishing for two or three years for conservation. This showed his commitment to the long-term health of the resource at the expense of short-term exigencies—something for which neither fishermen nor canners are famous.

In June 1894, he was again in Rivers Inlet where he noted, "Indians do a lot of loafing, bringing in only what they think is right." Later, he noted that there had been "a surplus of Indians that year. Many went away."

He visited the Victoria cannery, "11 miles from Wannock," where a machine filler was being used. He noted that Namu "is a very small place. No good. Drainey (sic) packed last year 3200 cases." Rivers Inlet fishermen were paid $40-45 per month. He examined "a site at 3 Islands for cannery building behind shelter of 1st island."

In December he was in London for the meeting of Anglo-B.C. Packing Co., where it was decided to build the cannery on Rivers Inlet. This would be the Good Hope cannery built in 1895.

In May 1895, Bell-Irving left for Rivers Inlet on Canadian Pacific Navigation Company's *Danube*. The new plant, which he no doubt had had a hand in designing, was under construction. He went on with the *Danube* to the Wannock and British Columbia (RIC) canneries where he met " Kirkland and McTavish." He made an arrangement with Kirkland for his steam tug to make "two trips per day, morning and evening, empty scows out, full scows back – 40 miles per day." Back at Good Hope, he noted he could "use 15 to 20 Japs to shingle, cut cordwood and fish after."

Then came the hunting trip while the cannery construction proceeded. Apparently, Kirkland was to pick him up and take him to the Wannock River on the steam tug. His journal notes on May 7, "as Kirkland's steamer not come in, left with Ben and an Indian in rowboat. Arrived at Owikeno—Kirkland's—at 7:30 p.m. McTavish out for Siwashes. Kirkland arrived shortly after with steamer, having called at Good Hope and found we had gone." The next day, "Got Tinshop George and Lazy Louis with canoe at 10:15 a.m. and started for Lake (Owikeno). Arrived lake at 11:30 a.m." And later, "came to big ram. Siwashes made a mess of it and spoilt my chance which was a sure one." He evidently was successful because he skinned and salted some goat heads. He was back in Vancouver on May 12.

On these hunting trips, he also noted the many spawning rivers in Owikeno Lake and the many natural hazards that he believed limited their production. On one such trip in 1896, he was delayed in the lake and missed the *Danube* and had to wait five days at Good Hope for the *Coquitlam* southbound. One can imagine him pacing the dock in frustration in those days before radio-telephones.

On May 17, 1897, he left Vancouver for Rivers Inlet again aboard the *Danube*. He arrived at Wadhams at 9:30 a.m. on the 17th and at Good Hope at 11:30.

He describes operations in his new cannery: "Cleaning and washing all done in gutshed before fish sliced by circular knives. Slicing done in cannery and pieces taken direct to filling tables. 24 Chinamen and 24 cluches (sic) in gutshed, 48 in all. 50 fillers, 20 toppers, 8 test kettle and 12 in bathroom. When making cans, 13 seamers and 8 toppers. One man cutting tops, cuts 5 boxes tin per day."

On his hunting trip to Owikeno Lake that year "for bears and goats," he noted that the Owikeno Indians could man only 25 boats for fishing. He was told that "long ago, Siwashes were very plentiful. Always fighting with Bella Coolas."

Bell-Irving was well aware of the Puget Sound salmon fishery and that it depended largely on Fraser River stocks. He lobbied for use of traps in B.C. similar to those at Point Roberts. In November 1895, he formed Fidalgo Island Packing Company as a subsidiary of Anglo-B.C. and built the cannery there (near Anacortes) the next year. They had traps at Point Roberts and Anacortes. Anglo-B.C. had two experimental traps for a short time at Boundary Bay until they were banned in B.C. in 1900 (except for Sooke and, for a short time, the northern traps).

Fidalgo extended its operations into Southeast Alaska with the Ketchikan cannery built in 1901, and to Cook Inlet, and continued in operation until it was sold in 1963.

In 1896, Henry Bell-Irving was in San Francisco negotiating for a can factory to be built in Vancouver, for which H. Bell-Irving & Co. would be agents. This came to fruition the next year when the "Automatic" can making plant was opened in New Westminster. Anglo-B.C. was a major shareholder with 200 shares, but Pacific Sheet Metal Works was the majority shareholder with 465 shares. Various Bell-Irvings also held shares. This was the first departure from cans hand-made at the canneries, but the latter continued as the preferred method for many years. The Automatic Can Factory could make 60,000 talls and 20,000 to 25,000 halves and ovals per day.

There were often attempts by the canners to work together to reduce competition or to improve the efficiency of their operations. For instance, in 1892, after the big pack of 1891, Bell-Irving records an "agreement to reduce pack at each cannery by 50 percent of capacity on the Fraser River and 25 percent on the Skeena." But in January of 1893, "Rithet called with Ladner—says combination on Fraser impossible as to reduction of pack. Wants us to agree with Ewen to keep price of fish to 6 cents. Said would be agreeable to do it."

On a trip to the Fraser River in February of 1893, on the *City of Nanaimo* (a paddlewheeler operated by the Mainland and Nanaimo Steam Navigation Company between, Nanaimo, Vancouver and New Westminster), he met with Tom Ladner who reiterated that they agree on six to seven cents per fish, the fishermen to furnish the nets. In June, they met again and agreed on a maximum price of seven cents per fish.

In July, he went from home in Vancouver to Phoenix cannery by buggy and noted that "English only got 12 Siwashes—has about 200 Japs. Has 21 white and Siwash outside boats and says Japs have about 46 licences and 18 nets. Indians paid $2 and $2.25 to fish company boats." Then in a prophetic note, he adds, "Fishermen's Union 'playing devil'. Want $2.75 and $3."

In September 1894, "Winch (R.V.) came and talked about a combination of Fraser River canners. Suggested that all new canneries combine."

There were strikes of fishermen in 1896 on the Skeena, at Rivers Inlet and on the Fraser. Bell-Irving notes in July 1897, "Steveston meeting of fishermen last night. Want 15 cents. Reported white men threatened to shoot Japs if fish for less. Saw Jap at Phoenix who said Olie at Federation had been shot at in the Gulf yesterday."

The canners eventually got together in 1900. A "pool" was arranged to which 42 of the 46 canneries on the Fraser subscribed. The pool members agreed on the allocation of the number of boats that each cannery could fish. They also set the price of fish and appointed four officials to travel the river and carry out the instructions of "the committee." The members were required to take fish only from their own boats and, to discourage fishing outside the river in the Gulf of Georgia, ruled that no cash advances were to be made in the Gulf.

In 1901, the pool became the Fraser River Canners' Association, comprising all the canners on the Fraser River. An executive committee of seven was elected and a "working committee" of three appointed. The main business of the committee at first was the rating of the canneries for the number of boats to be fished. Subsequently, they were to agree on the price to be paid for fish.

The new united strength of the canners had its antithesis in a growth in militance by the fishermen, which resulted in the famous strike of 1901 on the Fraser. Violence erupted after two fishermen left the Phoenix dock to fish and were beaten by the strikers. This resulted in the militia regiment, Duke of Connaught's Own Rifles being brought in to keep order. The Bell-Irving records state, "After a serious strike resulting in lawlessness, violence, intimidation, marooning of Japs and net-cutting, a settlement was made on a basis of 10½ cents for sockeye."

Henry Bell-Irving was often pre-occupied with the decline in the Fraser River stocks, beginning around the turn of the 20th century. He advocated a three-year closure of the sockeye fishery to permit the stocks to recover. This idea was not well received by his colleagues or by the government and nothing came of it. In 1919, the company did not operate any of its Fraser canneries. Britannia was converted to a shipyard, Phoenix was maintained for warehousing and the others were dismantled.

The 1920 Fraser run was "the worst failure on record in B.C." In 1921, the H. Bell-Irving and Co. records stated, "Results this year certainly indicate that the salmon canning is no longer going to be as important a factor on the coast as it has been in the past." (They were looking at herring as an alternative and Anglo-B.C. had gone into jam-making on Vancouver Island with the purchase of King Beach Manufacturing Co.)

In 1923, Anglo-B.C. operated only Glendale, Good Hope, North Pacific and Arrandale. Their B.A. cannery at Port Essington burned that year. In 1928, they entered the pilchard reduction industry when they opened their Caledonia plant at Kyuquot.

Anglo-B.C. introduced the company flag in 1899. Attempts had been made to identify a company's boats by painting on the hulls. But the distinctive flag was a superior method and was soon adopted by all the canners. In time, the company flag became a source of pride on the fishing grounds and instilled a sense of community in the various company fleets.

H.O. Bell-Irving died in 1931. Sadly, he did not live long enough to see his efforts and those of other canners finally result in a viable treaty with the United States for the management and rehabilitation of the Fraser River sockeye.

He was succeeded by his son Richard, who had been a Lt. Colonel in the Royal Flying Corps in the First World War. Richard Bell-Irving, like his father, was well connected in Great Britain and was instrumental in the creation of the British Preferential tariff which was instituted in 1932, and which gave Canadian canned salmon a tariff preference in British Empire countries. He passed away in 1962, and was succeeded in turn by his son, Ian. During Richard Bell-Irving's tenure as president of H. Bell-Irving and Co. Ltd., he was supported by Peter Traill, who had become secretary of the company in 1916. For years, until his retirement in 1968, he was the benevolent "eminence grise" of the company, and largely responsible for its ultra conservative approach to the business during those years.

Ian Bell-Irving spent many of his school summers working in Anglo-B.C. plants and, at one point, was manager at Arrandale cannery on the Nass River. Like his father before him, he was in charge of sales for the company. Under his presidency, the company sold the Fidalgo operation and in 1966, tried diversification into the herring reduction business in New Brunswick. With bank financing becoming tight, Anglo-B.C. sold its northern B.C. operations to Canadian Fishing Co. In 1968, the Phoenix plant on the Fraser River was sold to Canfisco and the Anglo-B.C. seine fleet was sold to Nelson Brothers Fisheries. In 1973, the company was wound up and a major factor in the history of the B.C. fishing industry ceased to exist.

Through all its years, Anglo-B.C. Packing Co. had been served by a team of loyal and capable employees, many of whom spent their entire careers with the company. There were many, but a few outstanding names should be acknowledged: Frank Lord, Malcolm Robertson, Bill Matthews, Bus MacKenzie, Ole Phillipson, Norm Corker.

Chapter 14

THE DORMANS OF BONES BAY

Bones Bay was a typical example of a cannery community and how it molded the lives of those who lived there. It was typical of what we might call the second generation plants, built in the 1920s and 1930s as regional plants or bases for the major companies. Bones Bay was Canadian Fishing Company's Johnstone Strait plant and headquarters for both its gillnet and seine fleets in that important salmon fishing area. It also had buying camps in the area for troll salmon.

The history of Bones Bay is closely tied up with the story of the Dorman family. The plant is unique, in that it had only one manager for the whole of its operating life. Jack Dorman supervised its construction and its ultimate closing down. He carried on after processing ceased, and while the plant continued as an important fishing station for the company. He and his wife brought up their four children at Bones Bay and Vancouver, and their lives were largely shaped by their experiences on the coast.

Jack Dorman was a character in his own right. He was short in stature and had the bantam rooster personality that so often goes with that. In fact, "the little rooster" was one of his nicknames, along with "cock of the walk" and "Johnny Bones."

He was born in Port Gravelle, Nova Scotia in 1889 on a scratch farm. He moved to B.C. in 1903, following his Klondike-tested father, who had tried his luck earlier in the goldrush. By that time, the father and an uncle were in the logging and lumber business in the Kootenays and Jack joined them there. Unfortunately, the mill burned and Jack returned to Vancouver to make his living delivering milk by horse and cart. In the meantime, his eldest sister had come west as a school teacher and in time, the family followed.

His first job in the fishing industry was as bookkeeper for Wallace Fisheries at Kildonan in Barkley Sound, where we know he was in 1914. Later, during the First World War, he was at Claxton cannery on the Skeena River with the Wallaces. One of his stories of Claxton was about Jimmy McKillop, a jolly Irishman who later became a well beloved chief officer and briefly captain on the Union Steamships vessels. Jimmy was on the dock, using one of those long crosscut saws to saw through a creosoted timber. He had the timber projecting out over the bullrail for the cut but Jimmy was standing on the river side of the cut!! He realized his mistake just in time.

Somehow, Jack moved to The Canadian Fishing Company and in the spring of 1926, we find him travelling with his bride on the *S.S. Cardena*, bound for Wales Island cannery in Portland Canal on the Alaska border, where Canfisco had its Nass River cannery. This plant was purchased that year after the company had leased it for the previous two seasons from M. Desbrisay & Co., from whom they also bought the Gulf of Georgia plant in Steveston. Salmon traps were permitted at Wales Island at that time because the Americans were fishing traps on their side of the border and of course, intercepting Nass River sockeye as they do today, further out to sea. Canfisco's parent company, New England Fish Company, had the cannery at Hidden Inlet in Alaska, across Portland Canal from Wales Island and the Wales Island staff were responsible for that operation as well. Borders and customs were less formal in those days. At Wales Island, Jack was bookkeeper under another well-known character, Ted Quisenberry, who later became manager at Tallheo cannery and at Home Plant. It would have been a Mutt & Jeff team because Quisenberry was as tall and lean as Dorman was short and stocky.

In 1927, Jack was moved to the old cannery in Shushartie Bay at the north end of Vancouver Island as manager. Shushartie had been purchased by Canfisco in 1923, along with Butedale, on Princess Royal Island, Margaret Bay in Smiths Inlet and Lagoon Bay on the Queen Charlottes. Jack's next task was to build the new Canfisco cannery at Bones Bay on Cracroft Island, dismantle the cannery at Shushartie, and transfer the equipment to the new plant.

So Bones Bay was one of the company's first new plants. It was as modern as it could be at that time and was strategically located near Alert Bay and the great seine and gillnet fisheries of Johnstone Strait and the inlets of Vancouver Island and the mainland.

The routine, as for virtually all the seasonal plants, was that the manager and the core crew went from Vancouver to the plant in the spring, usually April, to prepare the nets and other fishing gear and to ready the plant for canning. In the fall after the salmon runs had ceased, they would return to Vancouver. The manager and bookkeepers would finalize their books and records at head office and even "settle" some of the fishermen who would

The Dorman family with Charlie Birch

have extended their season in the south. The key employees would be employed at operations in the southern areas—Vancouver or Steveston—or in the herring reduction plants. Both trips would be made on the steamships, particularly the Union Steamships which served the people of the coast for many years. This was the Dorman family's life for more than 30 years. They had four children, two of whom were born in the hospital at Alert Bay—the spring or summer babies—and the other two in Vancouver—the winter babies. David Doman, a spring baby, likes to say he made his first trip to Bones Bay in his mother's womb. That was in 1938.

As kids growing up, with about half their year in the wild country of the coast and the other half in the city, they had the unique advantage of the best of both worlds. They were privileged, of course, being the manager's children, but they learned the sea and boats at an early age and knew the pleasures and wonders of unspoiled forests. From the time they were old enough to work, they were always assured of a summer job and spending money for the winter.

Their playmates were the children of skilled workers who also had the same schizophrenic lifestyle, and the Native Indian children who came to the cannery from the Johnstone Strait villages. Later on, some of their luckier high school chums would also be hired for the summer canning season. There is even the story of the interior of the cannery being painted in Prince of Wales High School colours by the "happy gang."

There was also a downside to these annual migrations, in that the cannery kids missed the summer time activities in the city. But if this was a handicap, it was lost on the Dormans.

One of the most interesting places for a young boy was the netloft. It had a special atmosphere with its big spaces, its hardwood floors polished to a sheen by the dragging of countless nets, and its smells of linen and cotton web, cutch and tar. David learned to make up corklines and leadlines and to hang them to the gillnets. Before the introduction of nylon nets after World War II, the nets were linen and the lines were cotton. The corks were cedar, milled into elliptical shapes and waterproofed with hot tar. Every cannery had its cork tarring operation, where the big lumps of tar would be melted in vats and the corks dipped in bunches. They would then be strung out to dry on the railings of the ubiquitous boardwalks. The odour of hot tar was an unforgettable smell of spring at the canneries.

The corks were strung on cotton lines and tied at regular intervals as the corkline was hung to the gillnet selvedge. The simple little hanging bench was universal in the industry—definitely low tech, but efficient for all that. Similarly, with the leadlines. The lead weights were formed right onto the line by means of moulds through which the line was strung. That done, the leadline was hung to the bottom of the net and it was ready to fish. The quality of the hanging could mean the difference in how a net would fish and many of the best hangers were followed by their reputations and sought after.

The Dorman boys learned these skills at an early age, just "hanging around" the netloft. They also learned how to nail boxes where speed was of the essence because the work was done by piecework. During the war, labour was scarce and the boys were put to work. Even the RCMP constable would make boxes during his off hours and competition was stiff to see who could make the most in the shortest time. Until after the war, canned salmon was packed in wooden boxes, 48 pounds to the case and the manufacture of box shooks and ends was a thriving industry for mills both in the Lower Mainland and up the coast. Like everything else, the knocked-down boxes would be shipped to the cannery by steamship or packer and made up at the cannery. After World War II, fibre or cardboard boxes, durable but much lighter in weight and easier to form, replaced the wooden boxes.

The boys, of course, learned to operate boats which were a natural part of their lives at Bones Bay—first as deckhands and as they grew older and more competent, as skippers, with responsibilities for servicing camps and packing fish to the cannery or large packers. They were responsible for the quality of the fish they carried. David tells of one instance where cleanliness aboard the boat backfired on fish quality. As a teenager, he was running a small packer from Bones Bay to camps at Echo Bay and Simoom Sound to Alert Bay. "We were having problems with bad fish and the company thought it was all stuff that had been taken out of creeks. So I had to segregate all of the fish. But what had happened—I had come out of there and gone to one of the big packers and they had lost 10,000 fish because they had thrown mine on top of the load and it all went bad. So I had to segregate all this fish and I came out and we unloaded onto the deck and they looked at it. They said 'This fish, where did it come from?' 'From Echo Bay.' 'Tell me everything you know about Echo Bay.' I said, 'For one thing, it's the only camp with no fish odour in it whatsoever.' 'How do they clean it?' 'The guy uses Rinso.' And that was what was causing the fish to rot. There's something in the chemicals and the fish touches it and it's gone, right now!"

There was time for exploring in the wilds as well. Garth tells of encounters with grizzly bears on the flats at the rivermouths in Kingcome and Knight's Inlets, where he was imagining himself on a deserted island. In fact, he was, and the danger of being alone in such places was part of the adventure that these young boys enjoyed.

While the boys operated boats, the girls worked in the cannery and the office. The pulse of life during the hectic canning season became second nature to them.

The 24th of May was always **the** holiday at the upcoast canneries. Dominion Day and Labour Day were statutory holidays, but the season was well in progress for both of those and getting away was usually impossible. But the Queen's birthday was the time for a break before the canning season began in earnest. Usually it was a picnic on a beach within an easy run of the cannery. Whoever was at the cannery by that time piled on the cannery workboat and headed out to one of these idyllic spots that were known only to the coastal people. From Bones Bay, it would be the old Wilson place at the back of Minstrel Island, or to Potts Lagoon. From Namu, it would be Koeye River or Hakai Pass; from Rivers Inlet it would be in Owikeno Lake near the Wannock River, and so on. But recreation was a must, time permitting, during the canning season too, and the weekend dance was an institution.

In the early days, the fishermen fished from Sunday evening at 6 p.m.— the boats would be on the grounds ready to fish when the fishery officer fired a gun or a cannon or sounded a siren, letting them know they could set their nets, which everybody did in a rush, in order to be the first at the best sets—until Friday at 6 p.m. Later, as the fishing effort and efficiency increased, the five-day week would be shortened to four or even less. The fishermen used the weekend to attend to their nets—bluestoning and mending on the netrack floats provided by the company. And they were always in camp or at the cannery on Saturday night and most places had a dance in the netloft. This was a pretty risky business, considering that nearly everyone smoked and that the liquor flowed pretty heavily but the fire potential was watched very carefully and there was surprisingly little problem of that type. There was always someone in the camp that could play musical instruments and they were in great demand. The weekly dance was an important outlet for both plant workers and fishermen after long hard hours during the week and the lack of diversion that is typical of isolated places. And cannery management knew it and went out of their way to provide the opportunity for "wholesome" fun.

The weekends could be a problem, especially if the fishing week was less than five days. The standard recreation for the fishermen, once their boat and net problems had been taken care of, was drinking. Liquor had to be brought in from Vancouver, Prince Rupert, Ocean Falls or Minstrel Island, but it was always available and always in use on the weekends. Most of the partying was in good fun, but inevitably there would be drunkenness and fights and sometimes, worse. Very often the Indians made their own home brew and the village would rock until it was all gone.

Minstrel Island had a hotel and beer parlour. It was said to be the 12th largest bottle selling beer parlour in all of Canada!

Some of those dances were pretty formal. Tricia Dorman recalls, "The ladies wore long dresses and we spread that liquid wax stuff on the floor of the netloft. And we threw linen gillnet covers over the seine nets so that these dresses wouldn't get dirty.

"Woodward's would send up a huge carton full of evening dresses. The girls would all come down and try them on in our living room and choose the ones that they would like to take, pile the other ones back in the box, mark it to Woodward's and it went down on the boat the next week with the money for the dresses they'd bought. There was no band, but there was always somebody who could play—there would be a piano accordion, banjoes, rhythm bones, spoons, guitars, washboards."

Shirley Dorman adds, "I can remember going to the dances as a little girl and falling asleep on the nets. And people would come and ask us to dance even though we were small as a grasshopper. And we did."

Peter Seifert, who was assistant bookkeeper in 1947, tells another version of the weekend dances. "Bones Bay was the hub for all these other people coming around because we had lots of cannery girls. And as it happened, we had an ex-Mounted Police, his name was Lefty, and he was our guard because on the weekends, we would have groups of boats coming from the different logging camps with all the men trying to get to the cannery girls up on the hill. There was Mr. Dorman and Lefty standing there fighting off the men and the girls were fighting to get down. They (Mr. Dorman and Lefty) were nice about it though, and he was a very convincing young man and he was able to control the loggers."

And Garth Dorman relates "the story about the three loggers that terrorized the cannery one Sunday afternoon. When my father tried to get control of it, one of them picked up a two-inch pipe and stabbed Dad in the face, broke his glasses, cut his nose and his upper lip right through, broke his plates. He was a small man and he was down on the ground. And mother apparently came around the corner at that time with a 30/30 carbine in her arm and told the logger who was about to hit my father again, 'Sir, if you hit him again, I will shoot you.' He looked up at her blearily and said, 'Lady, I think you might,' and there was a click, click as mother put a shell into the chamber and said, 'You have that right.' He looked at her for a minute and said, 'Lady, if you'll kiss all three of us, we'll leave,' and she said, 'Done.' And she kissed all three of them and they left."

The cannery was expanded and modernized in 1943. A new concrete dam was built to provide a more reliable water supply, and a new office, dance floor and recreation room were built. There was an old saying in the cannery business that if a company spent a lot of money on a plant, you could bet that they would decide to close it soon after. It was coincidence of course, but this is what happened at Bones Bay. It canned for the last time in the 1948 season. But this was not the end of Bones Bay plant. It carried on as a fishing station into the 1970s, when it was finally abandoned.

The Bones Bay operation was intimately tied up with the Native Indians of Alert Bay. Most of the seine boats were fished by Native crews. This was not unique to Canadian Fishing Company, but was true as well of the Anglo-B.C. Packing Company and B.C. Packers operations in the area. Jack Dorman had a close relationship with the Native peoples and could speak Chinook passably well. He was instrumental in helping them become owners of the boats they fished.

The members of the Cook family at Alert Bay were a dominant force in the Canfisco operation. The founders of the clan were Stephen and Jane Cook. Stephen was a Kanaka who came to Seattle on the lumber ships that ran between Seattle and the Hawaiian Islands. Jane was said to be a granddaughter of the famous Indian chief Seattle. Their sons Chris and Reg were seine boat captains, and Herb was fleet dispatcher for the plant. The family was large and one of the leading families at Alert Bay.

David Dorman recalls, "Dad sent me to Alert Bay to get some money. I was running the *Sunbury II*, collecting up in Kingcome Inlet. I was really quite chuffed with myself because I was considered trustworthy enough to go and do this. It wasn't until several years later that I realized the elaborate precautions he had put in place.

"Of course, I was on the boat alone. Enroute there, I met nobody and when I got to Alert Bay, I tied up at the BA Oil float, where we always went. I walked off the float and one of Dad's skippers, Harry Brown, who also had a taxi in the Bay, met me and said, 'Where you goin'?' I said, 'I have to go up to the bank.' He said, 'Well, I'll take you up there.' So he took me up there. He said, 'Are you going anywhere else?' I said, 'No, I'm just going to the bank and then back to the boat.' So he said, 'Well, I'll wait for you.' When I walked out of the bank, Harry was there and Herb Cook was there having a chat and the RCMP officer was there. I took my bag of money and climbed into the cab and went back to the boat. The RCMP wasn't far behind me. I fuelled the boat up at the BA float and away I went.

"Between Alert Bay and Bones Bay, I met nine boats—all of the Cook family were enroute and saw me and actually talked to me. I had $50,000 cash. So it was a young boy's great adventure with high responsibility, but there was a great deal of support put in place, and it was several years later that I realized fully how it was done."

David Dorman went on to be an airline pilot with Canadian Pacific Airlines. His first job as a commercial pilot was flying Bob Payne, who was then president of J.H. Todd and Sons, around the coast. Ironically, David's father, Jack Dorman, had given Bob Payne his first job in the fishing industry as skipper of one of the Bones Bay collector boats. Another circle closed.

How did Bones Bay get its name? The story is that after Captain Vancouver's expedition left the area in 1792/93, smallpox wiped out a great many of the Indians and Bones Bay was a place they came to die. Some of the bones are still there, but the Indians never seem to have claimed it as a sacred area, probably because it was a horrible death area.

Chapter 15

THE EWEN AND MACMILLAN FAMILIES

Alexander Ewen is considered the father of the salmon canning industry in B.C. There were other earlier examples of salmon canning prior to his first cannery at Annieville on the Fraser River, notably Captain Stamp's abortive attempt at Sapperton and James Symes' few cases in 1863 at New Westminster. Ewen is also noteworthy in that his family were pioneers of canning on the Skeena River at the venerable Cassiar Cannery, the last one to operate on the Skeena River proper.

Alexander Ewen was born in Aberdeen, Scotland in 1832 and emigrated to Canada in 1864. It was an advertisement placed in the Scottish papers by a Mr. Annandale of Victoria that brought him around the Horn by sailing ship to the colony of British Columbia. Annandale was planning to operate fishtraps, and Alexander Ewen was thoroughly conversant with this method of fishing, having spent years fishing north of Aberdeen, where the traps were placed outside the bounds of the spawning rivers. However, he was not happy after a year or two working with Annandale, and the story was that the greatest reason for his unhappiness was that Annandale was not honest, which was a word that he took very, very seriously.

He started up a fish and game store on Columbia Street in New Westminster. He provided the fish himself, by gillnetting in the river, and he bought the game—deer and ducks and geese—from the Native Indians in the area.

His daughter, Mrs. John Macmillan, recalled her vivid memory of this store. The building was built up on pilings and was fairly long and narrow. The lower end of the building was occupied by Indian women, who in season, were picking the game or cleaning the fish that Ewen had brought in. There was no shortage of either fish or game. She told of the Indians coming down from Pitt River with buckboard wagons, loaded to capacity with ducks that had been shot in the Pitt Meadows area. According to Ewen Macmillan, "The favourite method of shooting in those days was not exactly sporting. It consisted of the Indian owning several lengths of pipe, and the method of operation was that a charge of powder was put in one end of the pipe and the pipe was stuffed full of stones and nails and anything else that was suitable. The Indians would set these guns out where the ducks came in to feed and in the evening, they would light the fuses and retire and pretty soon there would be several loud bangs. In the morning, the squaws would be sent out to pick up the ducks."

Alexander Ewen teamed up with James Wise, who was a commercial fisherman, in an enterprise to salt salmon. Wise was also associated with the fish and game business. Then, in 1870, the two of them joined with Alexander Loggie and David Hennesy to start a salmon cannery at Annieville. Both Loggie and Hennesy had had experience in the lobster canneries of New Brunswick. They called their company Alexander Loggie and Company, and theirs is considered the first commercial salmon cannery in British Columbia. The partners started off by engaging a competent tinsmith, James Knowles, who was the canmaker for the new enterprise. The can parts—bodies, tops and bottoms, were cut out of sheet metal by hand and soldered together. The cannery was really an adjunct to the salting of salmon, at which Alexander Ewen was an expert, and both operations concentrated on spring salmon. The first packs were sold to the U.K., through an agent in London.

But the cannery at Annieville was not appreciated by the neighbours, and so the operation was moved briefly to New Westminster. In 1876, Alexander Ewen formed Ewen & Company. He bought Lion Island, just downstream from New Westminster and built his new cannery there. He also had the foresight to buy a section of land—640 acres—on Lulu Island, opposite Lion Island.

His grandson, Ewen Macmillan, was named Alexander Ewen Macmillan for his grandfather. Ewen recalls, "My grandfather operated the cannery from New Westminster. He would drive back and forth by horse and carriage every day. He arranged for a cousin by the name of Livingston to come out from Scotland to run the farm.

"So he was sitting with a cannery on an island and 640 acres of what is now very valuable land behind the cannery. So he was becoming quite a dominant force in the political situation in New Westminster and he arranged to build a bridge—the first bridge from New Westminster to Lulu Island. My grandfather, with a few other men, put up the money to build the bridge across the North Arm. So this gave him good access to the cannery and he was able to make much better time on his trips to and from.

"One story that my grandmother told me was of my grandfather being all dressed up to go to church, but insisting on taking time to go out to the cannery on Sunday morning to make sure that everything was running alright. When he went out there, he became pretty impatient with one of the Chinese workers who was pughing fish on the floor. My grandfather got pretty irate—he seemed to be a little bit of a short-tempered man anyway—and he insisted on giving this Chinaman a lesson in pughing fish. So he clambered over the boards in the gutshed and started to show the Chinaman how to pugh fish and make sure he pughed them in the head and so on. And just about this time a large shot of fish was coming into the gutshed by an elevator. I guess he had forgotten all about this because suddenly while he was in the midst of giving his demonstration, a load of fish came down the elevator and he ended up in a most undignified position on the floor in his best go-to-church clothes. The story that I heard from my grandmother was that by the time he got home, he was still mad at the Chinaman, he was a little bit mad at himself, but not too much because I suspect that he thought he wouldn't have to go to church—but my grandmother insisted that he had to change his clothes and they both went off to church.

"There's another story—a story of a strike at the cannery. The Chinese crew had gone on strike and my grandfather didn't really put up with strikes—they interfered with things! So my grandfather, as the story goes—and I'm quite sure it's well documented—proceeded in a very ostentatious way, to fill a large metal can with gasoline. Then he headed straight for the China House and started splashing the gasoline around in very copious quantities around the very foundations of the China House. Having accomplished this circle, he then ostentatiously pulled out a box of matches and said, 'There now, if you sons of bitches don't get going and get down there and go to work, I'll burn you out!' That ended the strike."

At some point, he and Daniel Munn acquired the Bon Accord cannery, which was opposite and upstream from New Westminster. Later they built the Sea Island cannery. He was also interested in railways, as were so many others in that railway building era. He and others built the B.C. Southern Railway from the Great Northern at Blaine to South Westminster. He was also involved in the Kaslo-Slocan Railway.

While other canneries were built on the Fraser in rapid succession, the Ewen cannery at Lion Island remained one of the largest operations in both canning and salting salmon. By the turn of the century, Alexander Ewen was not well and the question of succession became a preoccupation. He had three daughters but no sons, and in those days women were not usually considered when it came to managing business. So in 1902, he accepted the opportunity to amalgamate his firm with other canneries under the British Columbia Packers' Association of New Jersey. The initiative for this venture was provided by Aemilius Jarvis, a financier from Toronto, and Henry Doyle, who was general manager of the Doyle Fishing Supply Company, founded by his father, and son-in-law of another cannery pioneer, Marshall English. Ewen's company was the core of the Association and he was its first president. He was never happy with the arrangement, however, and according to his grandson, being responsible to a board of directors was not his style. "He had never been used to anybody telling him what to do. It was just too much for him. And my mother said she could remember him sitting in an armchair in the kitchen, wrapped up in blankets to keep himself warm and cursing and complaining about the day that he ever amalgamated his company with anybody." In fact, both he and Doyle resigned their positions in 1904 because of interference from the bankers on the board, but Ewen was persuaded by the new general manager to stay on. This icon of the salmon canning industry died in 1907.

His daughter, Isabella, married John Macmillan and they continued the family interest in the salmon business. John Macmillan's story is linked to the Skeena River, but like his father-in-law, he too started out in Scotland. He was born on the Isle of Arran near the mouth of the Clyde, where his family was trying to eke out a living farming on lands belonging to the Duke of Hamilton. One branch of the family gave up and moved to the mainland where the two eldest boys were apprenticed to a bookbinder, and from there rose to eminence and ended up founding the famous Macmillan book publishing company. That branch also produced a prime minister of Great Britain, Sir Harold Macmillan.

Ewen Macmillan describes what happened to his father's branch of the family: "My father's side stayed on the Island and the Duke gave them a hotel in Loch Ramsay to run. My father and his brothers and his father had all been good horsemen, specializing in that day in large, heavy horses—Clydesdales and Percherons. A lot of these horses were shipped overseas—a large number went to New Zealand and Australia—and it was common for them to send somebody the horses were accustomed to on the boats. My father's older brother made several trips to Australia and New Zealand with these horses. They were acting as sort of brokers, buying the horses from the local farmers and then arranging for sale.

"My father, the younger one of the family, was kind of pushed to one side a bit. But he was indentured to a farmer on the Isle of Arran who was very successful, and it was decided there was nobody better for him to learn about the farming business from. So that was a great idea. The only problem was that the farmer had three young daughters. So my father, being a true

Macmillan, was quite impressed with these three daughters and, from what I've heard, I suspect that one of the daughters became suspiciously pregnant and my father was in very bad odour, to such an extent that he left the island in quite a hurry.

"He got himself out to the Scottish west coast and knowing about his brother's going to Australia and New Zealand with horses, he managed to get himself a job on a sailing ship. In other words, he got out of Scotland before he was shot. This developed into my father becoming a pretty good seaman, which would be natural because it was in the blood of those people over there. And he ended up on these wool clippers that were sailing to Australia and making all these wonderful voyages."

On one of these trips, in 1894, John Macmillan ended up in Portland, Oregon. There he met Peter and John Wallace, who also had emigrated from the Isle of Arran, and who were now well-established in the fishing business on the Columbia River. Peter Wallace was engaged in freezing spring salmon and steelheads, using salt and ice. The fish were transported by refrigerator car on the Northern Pacific Railroad, to Chicago and New York for the U.S. market, and to Portland, Maine for export to the British and French markets, by refrigerated ship.

John Macmillan was engaged by the Wallace brothers as outside man between the Columbia River and Puget Sound, "where the fish were in great quantity," and where fishing by double seines (two flat-bottomed boats, propelled by oars, to each net) was just beginning. He also erected traps for them at the mouth of the Cowlitz River. The company started mild-curing spring salmon on the Columbia in 1895.

At the same time, he made his first trip to the Fraser River, where Duncan McKenzie was freezing sturgeon for the Wallaces at Bon Accord cannery. John worked there in the winter and one summer season at the Ewen/Munn cannery on Sea Island. He established fishing stations for sturgeon on the Fraser and Pitt Rivers, but it was slow going. Ewen recalls, "My Dad was enamoured with all these salmon. He had never seen so much fish and he thought that the sturgeon business was really for the birds and that there was much more money to be made in salmon. But the salmon business on the Fraser was well-established by that time. Between my grandfather and others, there wasn't much chance for an outsider to get into the situation.

"So, he reported accordingly to the Wallaces and, just about this time, another Scotchman appeared on the scene (they seemed to have built up a network). He was a shipwright who had been building tugboats on the Fraser River and he was a friend of the Wallaces. The new triple expansion steam engines were giving much more vibration than the old steam engines, and the tugboats had to be built stronger to withstand it. So this fellow had gone north to the Skeena River and found a supply of yellow cedar crooks and he used these for natural ribs in the boats. He was building a tugboat, the *Alexander*, at Port Essington, and in the process, he had seen large quantities of beautiful spring salmon in addition to all the other fish. This had caught the imagination of the Wallaces, whose whole background was as fresh fish men."

So they decided to investigate and in the spring of 1898, John Macmillan and John and Peter Wallace arrived at Port Essington, on the *S.S. Tees*, skippered by Captain Joe Gosse. They took over the cold storage shed at the Cunningham plant and began buying salmon and making mild cure. The fish were bought for 25 cents each, and the smallest sides were 10 pounds each. They were put up in 800-pound tierces. Ewen Macmillan tells an amusing story, "The Wallaces had provided him with sufficient money to buy the fish, and in their wisdom it was all in gold coins. He started to try to buy the fish but the Indian fishermen would have nothing to do with gold. The only money they would take were 'Cunningham dollars' which, of course, were stamped out of brass or bronze. So he had the problem of exchanging his gold coins for Cunningham brass dollars which must have caused him some anxiety!"

The following year, they moved their operation to Balmoral cannery, which at that time, along with Inverness, was owned by Turner, Beeton & Company of Victoria. The Wallaces were now interested in the canning business and the two brothers and John Macmillan, took a Sunday trip in a sailboat downriver to look at Carlisle and Claxton canneries. Claxton had a small cannery opened in 1892, and a sawmill that was still operating. They liked the look of Claxton because of its water power and they bought the operation that winter. In 1900, they rebuilt the cannery and added the cold storage for freezing and mild curing.

That same year, after touring Alaska, "prospecting for fish locations," John Macmillan sailed from Port Townsend, Washington, for Sydney, Australia as a sailor. There he got mixed up with the 5th Contingent New South Wales Bushmen and went with them to the South African War.

Ewen picks up the story: "This was the Boer War. And for the rest of his life, there was nothing that my Dad loved better than a war. He loved wars. He thoroughly enjoyed them. The New South Wales Bushmen was a mounted group and he did very well because he was really the only man who knew much about horses. He was a splendid rider and on top of that, he knew how to look after horses. So Dad had a wonderful time in the Boer War, survived it and came back to civilian life in 1902 and was discharged in Australia."

He wasted no time in returning to B.C., and his first year back he worked for North Pacific cannery, putting up smoked salmon in one-pound flat cans.

In 1904, he married Isabella Ewen and went to work again for Peter Wallace at Claxton.

(John Wallace had parted company from his brother. In 1911, he built the Butedale cannery and sold Arrandale on the Nass River, to Anglo-B.C. Packing Co.)

John Macmillan had had some experience in Astoria with timber cruising and registration of timber claims. He was the kind of person who made friends easily, and at Claxton he had become friendly with the fishermen who came over each season from the Queen Charlotte Islands to fish the Skeena. And from them he learned about the great stands of Sitka spruce on the Islands. So he visited the Islands to have a look for himself. His transportation was the big dugout canoes that the Haidas used for fishing. And he started cruising timber in the off seasons and registering timber claims. These claims eventually came to the attention of Brooks and Scanlon out of Minneapolis, who founded the Powell River Company. And they bought Macmillan's holdings for "a considerable sum of money".

Armed with this financial gain, supplemented by his wife's inheritance from her father, Alexander Ewen, they bought the Cassiar cannery on the Skeena Slough.

Ewen Macmillan explains, "My father was not made to concentrate on any one thing for very long and the idea of ever managing the Cassiar Packing Company never entered his head, which was probably a very good thing because he engaged Jim Lamb who had been working for another canning company up in Port Essington. Jim Lamb had come out from the east and was a trained millwright and had adapted himself very well to cannery operations. He was the ideal man to put in charge of the cannery because there were a lot of hard times to come and Jim Lamb could stretch a dollar further than any man I ever knew."

John Macmillan made an attempt to negotiate the purchase of the Strathcona cannery in Rivers Inlet and forming a Cassiar and Strathcona Canning Co. But his partners at Cassiar were not interested and he arranged the purchase of Strathcona by Wallace Fisheries instead.

Ewen Macmillan continues, "The First World War broke out and that put an end to my father's activities in the salmon business, because he liked the war far better. So my sister was two days old when my Dad left for war. And the Cassiar Packing Company was left to fend for itself as far as my Dad was concerned.

"At that time, he had a bookkeeper by the name of O'Hara, who departed with a great deal of my father's money before the war was over so that, financially, the First World War was not very good to my father. But the conditions and the fun of the war were just great. He ended up being quartermaster general for the Canadian Expeditionary Force and made lots of trips to London and got to ride to hounds in all the famous hunts and just really had a very good time."

On his return, John Macmillan went into the whaling business for several years by investing in the Victoria Whaling Co., which was later changed to Canadian North Pacific Fisheries. He was involved with a German scientist, Ludwig Rissmuller when they purchased five or six whalers and brought them out from Scotland. "Dad was very emphatic that these whalers should all be given good Scottish names but the German Rissmuller was equally determined that they should be given German names. The net result, to satisfy everybody: the whalers were named the *Red*, the *Blue*, the *Gray*, the *Green* and the *White*."

The ownership of The Cassiar Packing Company remained in the Macmillan family for most of its operating years, except that the Wallace family (friend of the family, Andy Wallace of Burrard Drydock, not related to the fishery Wallace brothers) had become shareholders when they had injected some much needed cash during one of the difficult periods the company experienced over the years. Eventually, the salmon roe business attracted the attention of Marubeni Company of Japan (as it did many other important Japanese firms) and the opportunity arose for the other shareholders to be bought out, leaving only Ewen Macmillan in sole ownership with Marubeni.

Alexander Ewen Macmillan was born in Vancouver in 1910, the third generation of his family in the fish business. He had not intended to spend his life in this way. He tried university without much success because, according to him, he discovered girls there and there wasn't enough time for studies and girls both. The time was the late 1920s "and at that time, the stock brokerage business was going very strong, and a lot of my friends who had not gone into the banks had gone into these brokerage houses. And those were the days when you could buy penny stocks and sell them in a couple of weeks' time and double your money. And I thought that sounded pretty interesting. The exciting point was that these schoolmates of mine who had gone into the brokerage business were accumulating enough money to buy automobiles. And if you could buy an automobile, you did much better with the girls than without an automobile. So it was just through a process of logical deduction that I came to the conclusion that the thing that I needed was an automobile and that in turn meant getting into a brokerage house."

And this he did, with a small firm, Hugh M. Fraser and Company on Hastings Street. Fraser was in the process of winding up the affairs of the

Municipality of Burnaby, which had gone bankrupt. He remained there earning some very good training, but little else—and not enough to buy a car—until the Depression began. "Hugh M. Fraser and Company decided they had to cut their staff. I was kept on, but a couple of senior men to me were let go, and I woke up to the fact that I was still working, but at no increase in salary, and I was doing my regular work plus the work of the two men who had been retired. For the first time in my life, I questioned the fairness of this thing and I approached Mr. Fraser about the problem. I plucked up my courage to suggest that under these conditions and at the salary rate they were talking, they really couldn't afford me as well. They agreed with me on that, so we parted company. So my career as a stockbroker and an accountant and everything else came to an abrupt halt. I made the rounds of the other brokerage houses and found they were in similar situations and everybody was being laid off and I was one of thousands."

So, in 1931, Ewen Macmillan went to work for Jim Lamb at Cassiar Packing Company. "My first thought of going north was that this was just a temporary situation because this Depression was not going to last very long. But I ended up by spending the rest of my active working life on the Skeena River. Looking back on it, I'm very, very glad that it happened. It made a very interesting life, I met a lot of people of all races, Indian, Chinese, Japanese and everybody else you could think of and I was very fortunate, because all those people were good people, hardworking people, and from every one of them I learned something."

Ewen Macmillan learned the cannery business from the ground up, literally. "Jim Lamb worked on the theory that in the fishing business you only worried about the year ahead. You forgot about the year behind you and you didn't look more than a year ahead, because by that time you may be out of business anyway. So the obvious thing was to just keep things propped up and held together. So we didn't drive many piles—that was expensive—mostly, we used mudsills and set-ups.

"My first job was with Nathan Lawson, a Native from Port Simpson. We'd tow a pile under the cannery at high tide, sometimes it was in the middle of the night. And at low tide, we'd dig a trench in which you put another old pile and you made a mudsill. And you cut a pole the appropriate length to let you jack up the beam you were trying to support. And judging on the state of the mud under the cannery, you took a wild guess and jacked the beam an inch above level, sometimes, three inches. Then you placed the pile and the mudsill sank a little bit and if your judgment was right, when you were finished, it was level."

Most of the Cassiar crew came from the Native Tsimsian villages up the

Skeena River. Arrangements had to be made for their transportation and to see that the Indian village at the cannery was ready for their arrival. Ewen was always involved in that and in the early days, he learned the timekeeping and piecework control once the cannery started operating.

After the canning season, he, like everybody else, returned to Vancouver. There he took welding and machine shop courses at Vancouver Technical School. (It is an interesting fact that many of the men who became senior managers in the industry took their schooling at Vancouver Tech during the period that the father of Jimmy Sinclair, later to become federal Minister of Fisheries, was principal there.) Ewen became a proficient machinist and filling machine man and then lineman. This was in the era of the Johnson 4-spindle machines, and steambox.

After 10 years of this apprenticeship under Jim Lamb, Ewen found himself running Cassiar cannery when Jim Lamb became ill. His right hand man was Roy Gurd, the seasoned bookkeeper. But within two weeks of Jim Lamb leaving for good, Roy Gurd also became ill and died soon after arriving at the hospital in Prince Rupert. So Ewen was suddenly on his own with a canning season facing him. And he made it work, with some help from his bankers and the company's accounting firm. Each day, Ewen spoke by telephone to his bankers in Prince Rupert. The problem was, the phone was a party line, and everyone on the line apparently listened in every day and knew the state of Cassiar's line of credit and salmon pack.

"Once I had become acclimatized and resigned to my fate that I was on the Skeena River and it looked like I was going to be there permanently, I became partly fascinated by the life and I became completely happy in it and evolved a lifestyle around it that worked very well. For instance, I was always able to get away shooting in the fall and important things like that.

"One of the things that sticks in my mind was the cannery crew arriving from upriver. Until the railway came in, in 1910, most of the cannery help on the Skeena River was supplied by Natives from the Queen Charlotte Islands. The railway changed all that very quickly. The CNR would put on special trains for them and the ladies would come down in the spring before the start of the fishing season to get themselves settled down. And everything came with them. All their possessions. Everyone had two or three big galvanized washtubs filled full of clothing, with an oilcloth tablecloth stretched over top, tied down tightly so that nothing would come loose.

"Every family had three or four large dogs. These were kept in the baggage car along with the other luggage and one of the exciting parts of the whole thing was watching the dogfights as the dogs got unloaded and found all their enemies. The Natives never used actual sleigh-dogs. They were packing dogs and they were amazingly strong and could carry large packs. In later years when I went up into that country, I could see them working and it was amazing how much the dogs could carry. But the dogs were pretty precious possessions and they were pretty carefully guarded and their owners never allowed the fights to continue very long in case a dog got hurt. Eventually the dogs would be corralled by their owners and led off down into the village and we never saw them again during the summer.

"Another highlight was when the Union Steamship came in to the cannery with the Chinese crew. The Chinese crew at Cassiar in those early days probably comprised of 40 or 50 Chinese. They, again, would bring all their possessions. They had all travelled steerage class on the Union boats, either the *Cardena* or the *Catala*. All the belongings would be dumped out on the dock and all the groceries for the China House, like all the sacks of rice—basically a season's supply. There would always be a crateful of piglets. The theory was that they fed the pigs on the slops from the messhouse and as the pigs grew, they were eventually butchered. When they arrived at the dock, there was always some joker in the crew that would manage to pry a bar or two loose on the crate and let the pigs out onto the dock. It would then be like a Chinese fire drill, everybody trying to get the pigs back into their crate. So that spiced things up a little bit.

"We regularly worked a six-day week and nobody thought anything about that. There was only so much time to get the plant and the boats ready for the season, and there was a lot of work to be done. The only holiday we really had was the 24th of May. That was the big holiday of the season. Every cannery closed down and took the holiday. That comprised of doing several things and you tried to vary them. Prince Rupert was the closest place to go and at that time, the big halibut fleet was operating out of Prince Rupert. These were good, big boats with crews to match. They were a bunch of good, hardworking men. And the inevitable place for them was the red light district which was flourishing in those days and was a model of how a red light district can be run in a city without any problems whatsoever. Unfortunately, our excursions into the red light district were curtailed somewhat by our lack of money. We could at least get into the drawing room, where you were served drinks, but any further, more exciting expeditions were forbade because there was not enough money in one's pocket.

"The other thing to do was—we'd take a cannery boat to Prince Rupert, but often we'd keep on going to Port Simpson, where the Natives always had a celebration, a ballgame, sports and so on. We knew everybody in the villages and these were thoroughly enjoyable visits. We would spend the whole day at Port Simpson and there would be little feasts and suppers for us and then we would sail back to the cannery in the evening and that really made a very nice day.

"This was the days of the Chinese contractors. They supplied all the Chinese labour and also looked after the payroll for the whole cannery crew except the machinemen and the netmen who were on a company payroll. It was quite a large payroll and the Chinese contractor took full responsibility for it.

"A lot of the pay was done on piecework, especially on the hand-filling of the cans. This was done by so much a tray. The women were standing at a table where the cut fish, which had gone through the gangknife, were distributed to them. The tray was at about eye-level and as the woman filled each can, she would place it in the tray. And as she filled a tray, a Chinese employee would punch her ticket and remove the tray and replace it with an empty one. They developed a rhythm with tremendous dexterity and could fill the cans at an amazing rate. So there was a continuous process and it worked surprisingly well. At the end of the day, each woman would carefully pin the punched ticket to her uniform and keep it until it was fully punched when it would be exchanged for a fresh one.

"The actual payday didn't come until the end of the season. All the women would gather at the door of the China House and go in one by one to the Chinese bookkeeper and his assistant and get paid their season's wages. There were no modern calculating machines—all the calculating was done with an abacus which was both fast and accurate.

"There was a surprising amount of harmony throughout this whole operation. The contractor knew all the women by name and I rarely heard of any dissension. At the end of the season, when the last cases were filled and the plant was put away for the year, the Chinese contractor would sit down with us and we would agree on the exact number of cases that the cannery had produced. And he would be paid so much a case for the cannery labour according to the rate which had been agreed upon before the season."

The standard case at all canneries was 96 half-pound cans in a wooden box. After World War II, the canneries switched to fibre boxes of 48 half-pounds or the equivalent in quarter-pound or one-pound cans. But the standard case, for statistical purposes remained at 96 half-pound cans.

Most of the sockeye pack was in quarters and halves. One-pound talls were used for sockeye, but usually only for special orders. The talls were used primarily for pink and chum salmon. Some of the Skeena canneries produced a one-pound oval pack, but although this was an especially prime product, it took considerable labour and skill to make a presentable pack.

At times, the canneries couldn't handle all the fish that were caught. In spite of all the best efforts to get them canned before they spoiled, sometimes they had to be dumped.

"In 1930, the year before I got up there, there were stories of them dumping whole scowloads of pinks at the different canneries. And there was simply nothing else you could do about it.

"In any of these big runs, you were working with a limited quantity of cans and there would be some wild trading around between canneries to get ourselves out of jackpots. But the cooperation among the canneries on the Skeena and the different managers was a heartwarming thing. You never turned anybody down unless you were absolutely desperate. Later on we had a reform line, but not in the early days.

"North Pacific had a can-making plant, the only one on the Skeena in my time. We had a long-standing arrangement with them to take a supply of cans every spring. We would take a small scow and a gasboat down to North Pacific. The cans were stored in their wooden boxes and we'd slide them down planks to the scow and tow it back to Cassiar. In addition, we would get supplies up from Vancouver on one of the freight boats, but North Pacific, for years and years, supplied us with made-in-North Pacific cans and they were good cans.

"The entire cannery was designed around the dock. All the freight needed was loaded from a steamship onto the dock, then into the cannery. And when the pack was completed and you were shipping out, you moved it out of the cannery, across the dock and onto the steamship. (It wasn't until we got into the war years that we started shipping by rail.) So, of course it was inevitable that during the season we had small freighters of several different shapes and sizes that came up from Vancouver and made the rounds of the canneries. The Union Steamships were the main ones, because they had a regular call into the cannery on a mail contract, and a passenger contract where they had to service the canneries.

"In the early years, there were older boats like the *Tees* and older Union boats like the *Venture*, but the ones I was involved with were the *Cardena* and the *Catala*. It was usually the *Cardena* and she continued the service all through the winter. The navigation by those skippers was something to marvel at. In the fog and the rain and the snow, of which there was plenty on the Skeena River, all the navigation was done by using whistles, counting the time between blowing the whistle and getting the echo back, so it was a pretty hairy process. They did put them up on the rocks every now and then, but the boats were designed with flat, double bottoms, so they went up on the rocks quite nicely and usually got off with only a minor embarrassment.

"The skippers were wonderful men. They would bring children up from the south after their holidays and deposit them at the different plants. All those children were well cared for on the boat.

"One of the things that I've marvelled at in later years was their seemingly inexhaustible supply of food. We would board the *Cardena* in Vancouver on a Tuesday evening, and if we hit a mail run, which we usually tried to do, we did all Rivers Inlet, and every possible cannery there and then Butedale and Kitimat and points in between and by the time we would arrive in the Skeena Slough at Cassiar, it would sometimes be noon on Sunday. So that was a long time to be on a ship. They could not have been overly endowed with refrigeration, but they invariably turned out the regular three meals a day, plus an afternoon tea at three o'clock, plus a mug-up in the evening before you went to bed. And somehow or other there was always food on the table and lots of it.

"The trips up north in the spring and down south in the fall were full of pleasure, in that you stopped at every one of these small canneries and you knew all the crews. And with freight loading and unloading, there was always time to spend in the cannery. And whatever area of the cannery you were interested in, whether it was the Iron Chink or cutting machinery or closing machinery, the appropriate man would be very pleased to show you the improvements he had made during the year, with the idea, and genuinely so, that you could take his idea and use it the next year. There was a great spirit and everybody was friends and everybody was glad to see one another.

"There was one other delightful thing that comes to mind with the Union Steamships. We were subject to what was considered a very rigorous sanitary inspection from Victoria, once a year. This consisted of several things, the main thing being that a tour had to be made of the cannery and the village. It was mostly concentrated on the cannery, but certainly, the village got its share of regulations. One of the outstanding regulations was that all the privies in the whole establishment had to be situated over water. That was a very serious matter. So the experts from Victoria would get themselves over to Vancouver and on to the *Cardena*. And they would have a very pleasant trip up the coast, stopping at all the canneries on the way up and eventually get to the Skeena. The beautiful part of doing the inspection on the Skeena River was the 24 foot tides and that there was no way that the Union boats would tie up at any of those canneries and take a chance of going dry. So it was essential that they didn't get in any later than a half high tide and that they were out of there before the tide was more than half down. So that worked just lovely. The delegation would get off at the cannery and solemnly tour the plant and solemnly inspect every privy and see that the base was well covered with water. Due notes were made in their notebooks that everything was in order and they would get back on the *Cardena*, back into the comfort of their staterooms, the *Cardena* would blow its whistle, untie its lines and away it would disappear and that took care of that inspection business. By the time the *Cardena* was three or four hours out of sight of the cannery, every privy in the place would be high and dry underneath. But nobody ever suffered as a result.

"There was another serious incident having to do with sanitation and the disposal of the offal from the cannery operation. All the time that I was at Cassiar, conscientious efforts were made to gather the offal. There were special bins underneath the cannery that would be filled during the day. And the reduction plant at Port Edward had a self-propelled scow that would come around every twenty-four hours and empty the offal bins. The system worked very well until we got into heavy canning and then the offal tanks were never quite big enough and would sort of spill over.

"So we were somewhat alarmed when this edict came out of Victoria that something had to be done about the offal. Just by luck, at the same time that this news came out about the big cleanup on the Skeena River, we got help from a completely unexpected source. The naturalists who had considerable power in Victoria were becoming very much aware of a shortage of bald eagles in British Columbia and were very concerned about this shortage, and the publicity they managed to drum up was really quite intense and the situation became well-known. Between Cassiar and Sunnyside, there was a long spit that came out that probably had been left from a slide on the mountain behind us. And this had formed a small reef that at low tide would be exposed.

"So when the offal inspectors arrived from Victoria, I made sure they stayed for low tide. We inspected the surroundings under the cannery fairly completely and the situation was not very good. However, in the most dramatic manner that I could manage to summon up, I insisted that this whole group—there were about twelve of them—take time off and follow me down the railway track for a fifteen- or twenty-minute walk. And there on the reef, there must have been three hundred eagles feeding on the offal. Somehow or other I never heard anything more about the offal problem—it seemed to solve itself.

"In addition to the Union Steamships, there were other small, independent lines operating out of Vancouver. My fondest memory is of the old *Salvor*, owned by Gulf Steamship Company. She was a peculiar looking ship—her stern was built very high to provide crew accommodation and the skipper's quarters and the galleys. Her foredeck was quite large and she had good rigging for handling freight on and off. She was pretty slow—her engines were tired out—but she faithfully made the trip up and down. Jim Lamb was always able to negotiate a special rate, which was better than the Union

Steamships, so we used her a good deal for bringing up cans and taking the canned salmon south. She was built exactly like a scow, completely flat bottomed, so nobody worried about her going dry. Everything was loaded and unloaded by hand-truck.

"Captain Jorgensen, who was a Native from Alert Bay, was skipper of the boat and he had a mate by the name of Tommy. So over those years, we had become good friends. And here was the *Salvor* sitting safely on the mud in front of Cassiar cannery and no supervision was needed, as the crew had been on her for years and knew exactly what they were doing for loading the boat. So there was not much doubt in Jorgensen's mind and in Tommy's mind that they deserved to be entertained. And the idea of entertaining them was to take them up to the guest suite, which served us well over the years, and open a bottle of Scotch and proceed to enjoy the day. Socially, I would have to partake of a reasonable amount of the Scotch but I would have to excuse myself to see that everything was running properly in the cannery. But Tommy and the Skipper had no concern about anything at all. And when it was finally time to get them back on the boat, I would try to get them to eat something from the messhouse. Tommy had a surprising capacity and always remained in quite reasonable shape. But Captain Jorgensen would have given in to his enthusiasm and would get wheeled down to the dock either in a hand-truck, or on Tommy's shoulder. By the time the ship was fully loaded and eventually sailed out of the river, they always made the trip quite safely. Jorgensen was a first class skipper and ended up by being a coast pilot and did a wonderful job there."

Cassiar was one of the meeting places for the early contract negotiations. These were very informal in those days and in sharp contrast to the marathon, brinkmanship, power play negotiations that developed between the Fisheries Association of B.C. and the United Fishermen and Allied Workers Union in the 1950s and 1960s. Typically, senior executives of the large companies, like Bob Payne Sr. of Canadian Fishing Co. and Sam Murray of B.C. Packers, would travel north from Vancouver on the *Canfisco*, Canadian Fishing Co.'s equivalent to today's corporate jet. They would stop in Rivers Inlet and other large points like Namu and probably Klemtu, and gather all the local managers together for the conference. The local Union representatives at the various canneries would have meetings ahead of time, to determine what they wanted for salmon prices and the Native representatives would do the same. All the important men from the various bands would attend the meetings at Cassiar, even from as far away as the Nass River.

The conference would go on all day or even two, during which the parties would hammer out an agreement on prices. There would be plenty of

The Canfisco, early 1930s

beverages to lubricate the talks and for a few years, that was how the negotiations were carried out.

Preparing for the new season was always a busy and exciting time. Ewen describes it, "At Cassiar cannery in particular, the main object of the game was that after the winter, which could have been pretty rough—lots of snow, lots of wind, not to mention rain—there were an awful lot of things to be propped up so that it would last for another season. This was everything from sidewalks to roofs on houses. So that required a little bit of work and time. And we always had a force of good Indian carpenters.

"And then there was always something new that had to be built—either a new Indian house or, certainly, a new lean-to. Lean-tos were our favourite piece of architecture. We built some magnificent lean-tos and some magnificent sidewalks.

"In the spring, I would go down to False Creek with Jim Lamb and our favourite place was the Alberni Lumber Company, which was located on False Creek just off 1st Avenue. They had a huge parking lot along First, in which their lumber was stored. The owner's name was McCrae and his son and I went to school together in the West End so I knew the family slightly. McCrae and Jim Lamb were good friends. Jim's trick, which he taught me, was to look over the piles of lumber and if a pile was covered heavily with soot and cinders, that was the pile to try to buy because it had been there for a long time and was well-seasoned. So rather than dickering around with so many thousand feet of wood, he would buy it by the pile.

"And these piles consisted of 2 by 12s for sidewalks, 2 by 4s for building your lean-tos and a great quantity of 6 to 8 inch shiplap. With shiplap, you could build just about anything. You put up a few studs and you nailed the shiplap to them and you had a wall. If you wanted a table, you sawed some shiplap into different lengths and with four 2 by 4 legs, the rest of the table was shiplap. And beds—we made hundreds of beds out of shiplap. So the lumber was duly shipped up to the cannery so that it would be there when the crew arrived.

"The next item was to make sure that all your gillnets had been delivered. They were ordered in the fall and they all came from England, so you had to be sure they had arrived in proper order and been shipped up to the Skeena. That was very important. There were a lot of fine men in the business at that time—Dick Leckie and his family and Colonel Tait and his family. The Reddens came along later, but the oldtimers like the Gundry people were out here. Ted Gundry came out from England and spent some time sizing up the situation and stayed in Vancouver for a few years. We became good friends.

"The next order that you had to be sure of was a supply of double-boiled linseed oil because the linen net was unfishable unless it was soaked in linseed oil to stiffen it up. And then you had to have paint—if you decided you had enough money that you could afford to paint something. You had salt for just about everything and it was very efficient at keeping the smell down. And there were literally a hundred and one things that had to be ordered and shipped up to the cannery.

"So with all this ordered and shipped, you had to get yourself down to the *Cardena* and sail north for another season. This would be in April. Then the cannery had to be put into operating shape. The American Can Company owned the filling machines and vacuum sealers. They had a service boat that travelled up and down the coast with troubleshooters and a generous supply of spare parts. Every few years, these machines would be overhauled at their plant in Vancouver during the winter and all would have to be in place and in working order before the fishing season opened.

"Preparing the nets was probably the most important thing. After all, if you were going to make any money at all, your nets had to be in good shape. At that time, the nets were owned and supplied by the cannery. We had a netboss by the name of Renny Noble, a great big man and when I first knew him, I was scared to death of him. He had a voice like a bullhorn. First the nets were selvedged—the borders of twine, top and bottom, to which the lines were hung. This was done by Japanese men. (Later, the selvedge would be done at the net factory.) These men would sit on the floor of the netloft, in pairs, facing each other, the depth of the net apart, and knit the selvedge twine to the first row of meshes. They were amazingly skillful and two men could do two or three nets a day.

"Then they had to be oiled and this was always a dicey time. We had made an oiling machine which consisted of a trough six feet long, two feet wide and two feet deep and there were two washing machine rollers on each end of it. This was powered by a small engine and you fed the net through the first set of rollers, down into the trough where it was held near the bottom by other rollers and it was immersed in this double-boiled linseed oil. Then it went through the second set of rollers, which squeezed out most of the oil.

"Then the critical part was getting them properly dried. They would be hung from the rafters in the netloft, properly spaced and you made sure there was always a wind going through the building, which incidentally was never much of a problem. If they were not properly dried, the knots would slip and there were many agonizing times over that. There were two or three things that could go wrong. Sometimes we got bad batches of oil, where the oil wouldn't dry for days and days. Other times, it was the weather—too much wet weather and they wouldn't dry. A lot depended on that and there was a lot of money involved in all those nets.

"As the cannery grew, and we accumulated more fishermen, we probably hung in the neighbourhood of a hundred sockeye gillnets every year. These would catch sockeye and pinks and in those early years, it was almost 95 percent sockeye fishing. But coho and chum fishing in the fall called for a different size mesh and so, a separate net.

"So finally having declared the nets dry, the next performance was to hang them on the lines. So the lines had to be prepared. They were all cotton lines in those days and the corks were made of cedar and had to be tarred so they would keep their bouyancy. Noble would set up a big tar pot down on the river bank, boil the tar and dump the corks in the tar, maybe a dozen to a string. Then they would fish them out again and hang them on the edges of the sidewalks. We had lots of sidewalks which would all be strung with lines of corks and we almost achieved a festive appearance around the place! The leadlines were made by passing the line through moulds in which you poured molten lead at regular intervals. The lines had to be stretched. The idea was to avoid any rollups when the net was fishing and this was an art that you depended on your netboss to carry out.

"The hanging was done mostly by Native women. Noble had about a dozen ladies who came with their husbands to the cannery early in the spring. About half came from the Nass and half from the Interior around Hazelton—Kitwanga and Kitwancool. They would hang the nets under Noble's supervision.

"Just a word about the boats. I came up to the Skeena in 1931 and the industry was just starting to change over from sailboats to gas boats. The sailboat was a conventional 26 or 28 foot Columbia River gillnet boat with a centreboard and one mast with mainsail and a jib that came down to the forepeak of the boat. You could sail them fairly close to the wind and you could tack quite well in them. My first memory of those boats was when we would go north with my Dad just for two or three days or a week. In those days we towed all the sailboats out to the fishing grounds by large gasboats or more likely, by steam tugs.

"Fishing always started at 6 o'clock on Sunday night and continued until 6 o'clock on Friday night. Cassiar Packing Company had a deal with a steamboat by the name of the *McCullough*, a big steam tug. She would tow the boats out to Tugwell or Kitson Island, depending on the tides or where the fishermen wanted to fish. They would drop off the towline one at a time and everybody would start fishing and the *McCullough* would stay there as a sort of mothership. It was one of my early delights. The *McCullough* was resplendent in that it had a Chinese cook in a full apron and a big white hat that I found very impressive. We would go out in Jim Lamb's runabout to check the fishing and then head for the *McCullough*. For my sister and me, the main joy in the whole trip was that as soon as we scrambled aboard the *McCullough*, we headed for the galley. Chinese cooks all seem to be good at making apple pies and my sister and I would sit and eat great slices of apple pie while my Dad and Jim Lamb would confer with the skipper and size up how the fishing was going.

"The average Columbia River sailboat was supplied with a small tent and at night they would put down the boom so that it made a ridge along the length of the boat, and put the tent over the boom at the fore end of the boat. They had the old square five-gallon cans (I'm sure these were the same sort of cans the Nass River Natives used for packing the eulachon grease over the grease trails in the spring). On the boats, they would fill the bottom of the can with sand, puncture holes in the can above the sand. They would gather twigs over the weekend and these would be stowed on the boat and used for fuel. And that's where they did their cooking.

"When they got back to the cannery after having been out for the week (they either rowed and sailed back or were towed back by the tug), there were two things they had to do before they went home. The first thing was to get the net into the bluestone tank, which contained a solution of copper sulphate. It was used to kill the algae on the nets. As it was, it was hard enough to make them last through the season and if the sun ever got to them with this growth on them, it would rot the linen nets overnight. The skipper and his boat puller, who did the rowing and the hard work, would pull the net up onto the dock, load it on a hand truck and get it into a bluestone tank, put a weight on top and make sure it was completely covered.

"The second job, which was basically the boat puller's responsibility, was to get the blankets that they had been using all week up to the boiler room and get them over the boiler so they could dry out. And they would have to walk the length of the cannery to get to the boilerhouse. And as long as I live, I will not forget that sight: the men going along the dock with their blankets over their shoulders and the water coming out in steady streams all the way to the boilerhouse. We had racks built over the boiler for them to hang the blankets so they would be dry enough by Sunday night. That's one sign of how hard the fishing was.

"The conversion of the boats to power was, as far as I was concerned, a very funny humourous side of the whole thing, yet it was deadly serious. Power boats were still not allowed in Rivers Inlet, but on the Skeena, around 1930, probably because of the tides, we were allowed to put engines in the boats. And here we were with about 50 boats, some of which had been built for us by Andy Wallace. There was no way we were going to be able to buy 50 engines in one year and put them in the boats. Not only was there not enough money, but there wasn't enough time. Jim Lamb had begun accumulating engines and when I arrived the next year, there were probably six or eight installed. Jim, as usual, never bought anything new—that was a foolish extravagance—so every one of those engines had been purchased second-hand. We had Yale engines, we had Frisby engines, we had Palmer engines, we had Standard engines. On most of these, the engine and the clutch were two separate units, so you had a few lining up problems. And most of them were the old make and break spark plug systems running from a coil. Jim Lamb didn't have a clue about engines and neither did I. But old Herman Boeing took hold of the situation and the other cannery machinemen, especially our foreman, Harry Taylor, had worked on farms all their lives and were reasonably conversant with engines.

"The main trick was to find carpenters that could convert the boat. We had one Japanese carpenter, Mr. Aramoto, who kind of specialized in knocking out the stern of the boat with very little disturbance. Then a stern post would be installed and the stern reshaped, so it left being a sailboat stern and became a conventional power boat stern. An engine bed was built and then it was a matter of fixing a stern bearing to the stern post and running the shaft through the bearing and into the hold of the boat and through a couple of bulkheads and finally reaching the engine, which was then ready to install. Then there would have to be a steering system and a netguard and a shoe. So it was quite a performance just preparing the boat for the engine.

"Most of these engines were single cylinder. The Palmers were two-cylinder and had more power, but the Yales and Frisbys were larger. Now we were suddenly away from the necessity of towing the boats from one point to the other, but once started there was no end to it. You bought more engines and converted more boats and then bigger and better engines and bigger and better boats. Then someone came up with the idea of the powered drum which meant the fishermen could stop hauling the net by hand.

"At first these were built on old Model T transmissions. But soon Easthope was building boat engines and also manufactured a drive especially for gillnet drums. The drums we built ourselves at the cannery out of wood, but the transmissions came from Easthope.

"As we replaced the older engines, our fleet gradually became pretty well completely powered by Easthope engines. The single cylinder engine became a two-cylinder engine by the simple expedient of just adding one more cylinder on it. And then there were three cylinder engines and then it became four and they developed a fairly powerful engine. By the time Vivian got into the two-cylinder engine, they were beginning to realize the importance of the diesel engine and they were switching to bigger, heavier engines that were not suitable for gillnet boats and basically they gave up the small engine business and Easthope dominated the picture."

Supply of water was always a problem for the canneries on Inverness Slough. The mountains behind are very high and the streams drop straight to the river.

On the south side of the river the mountains had readily accessible lakes that could be fairly easily tapped so canneries like Carlisle and Claxton had reliable supplies of good water. Similarly, at Port Essington. Anglo-B.C. Packing and B.C. Packers formed a joint company in 1912 to claim the water rights on Cunningham Lake behind the town. But the canneries on the Slough had a more difficult time. As the smaller canneries began to close, Cassiar would gain some fishermen. Ewen explains: "We had Cassiar up to a state where it was canning well over 100,000 cases a year, whereas when I first went there in 1931, probably 20,000 cases was it. And we just had to do something about the water. Our water supply for years had been supplied by a creek that came down from the top of the mountain and in dry spells (there were some), would dry up alarmingly. We had a storage tank that we used to make sure was filled with water every night before we went to bed. That would last us at least a few hours into the day. We dreamed up all sorts of schemes which were either impractical or impossible or too expensive.

"Richie Nelson had built a cannery in Prince Rupert on the old Ocean dock. When the war came along, Richie got pushed out of there by the U.S. Army. He started to build in Port Edward but in the meantime, he tried to get all the help he could from the other canneries, some of which were not very cooperative. But Richie and I were old friends and I assured him that we would can any fish that we possibly could. I had figured I could make some money canning his fish, but most of his fish was going to B.C. Packers, which I got a little upset about. So I got after Richie and told him he had to give me more fish. He reciprocated by snowing me under with fish to the point that the cannery was almost a day and night operation. Harry Robins, who was manager at Port Edward, came down to check on the situation, probably being concerned about our water supply situation. I told him there was nothing to worry about. Our water tank was getting a little low, but there were heavy fogs at night at that time of year and the fogs would condense enough water on the top of the mountain and there would be sufficient water to fill the tanks and everything would be alright. Somehow or other we got through it, but it was pretty iffy times.

"We eventually solved the problem. We toured the top of the mountain very carefully by helicopter and found two good lakes up there. We built a dam at the top, taking care not to tell anyone what we were doing. By this time, plastic pipe was available, whereas our previous efforts had been with wood stave pipes which were horrible things. So we were able to put in a full eight inch line from the mountain top down to the level of the Skeena River, run it along the track for about two miles, to the cannery at comparatively small expense. We were twenty or thirty years late, but now we had a reliable supply of water.

"The Second World War caused an awful lot of changes in the operation of the fish business. One of the largest ones—we woke up one morning and found that the whole industry had been commandeered by the British Ministry of Food. They expected to get our entire production and all of it had to be shipped from the west coast to the east coast by rail. So here we were with a set of cannery buildings that were designed for delivering over the front dock to the boats. All of a sudden we had to get this same salmon all the way up the long dock, up a ramp and to the siding so we could load it on the railway cars. We didn't have much of a siding, because you had to pay the railway rent for it. Harry Robins was firmly ensconsed at Port Edward and was sitting pretty. Port Edward had been originally planned as a townsite, so they had lots of sidings. So Harry would always order some extra cars for me that he would park on his siding and as we used up our reserve and needed another car, I could always phone Harry and after a certain amount of grumbling and complaining, he would send me out an empty railway car.

"The crew held pretty well together. We were told right at the beginning that with the cannery having been taken over by the British Ministry of Food, all the operating personnel would also be taken over as an essential service. This opened up what I must admit was an avenue of thought that on the whole looked pretty good. There was undoubtedly the possibility that if you went to war, you were going to get shot, which I didn't like, but there was also the possibility that if I didn't, I could continue my hunting in the off-season. My only problem was to get gasoline. I had introduced Norman Nelson to hunting on the Prairies and Norman was an expert at getting gasoline. We got gasoline at every airport in the Interior on our way down to the Prairies. It was all high octane and the cars that we were using to drive down never ran so well as they did during the war. So we didn't lose our hunting trips.

"In addition, our bills were always paid on time. We had to worry a little bit about short supplies, but the fish were still coming up the river the same as they did before the war. But it always bothered me that we were so well off while so many tragedies were taking place overseas."

Ewen Macmillan was third generation in the Pacific coast salmon industry. But his connection is even deeper than that. He married Kathryn McMillan (note the spelling), who had also been brought up in the fish business. Kay was born in 1914 at Port Essington in the small hospital run by the Methodist Church. Her father, Pat McMillan was lineman at the Cunningham cannery, which was part of the B.C. Fishing & Packing Company's operation. A few years later, he became foreman at Balmoral, which was a much larger cannery, located at the junction of the Skeena and Ecstall Rivers. Later he became foreman at Sunnyside under Tom Wallace—then to Lowe Inlet cannery for a year, then Oceanic for one year, and finally Claxton where he was manager.

At Port Essington, there were three canneries at that time: Cunningham, Skeena Commercial and Anglo-B.C.'s British American.

Kay recalls, "It was a very peculiar life. We lived in a very small house with a chicken yard in front. It was on the sidewalk that led to the cannery. We were right on the main street, which was a wooden street. Every Sunday the Salvation Army Band would come down the street blaring its instruments and that was a big event in my young life.

"The people were very nice. I remember a few of them—Mrs. Moray lived across the street from us and there were the Harris'—Mr. Harris was in the Cunningham store. The ladies were very genteel, of course—they had a great many tea parties. And mother sang. She had a beautiful voice, so she was quite in demand for singing in the choir and the various concerts that they had.

"We would come down to Vancouver after the season and lived with my grandmother—Dad's mother. She had a big house on Bayswater Street which she had bought after grandfather died. Before that, they farmed McMillan Island in the mouth of the Fraser, which is now Iona Island.

"Then we'd pack up again in the spring and go back up north. Eventually, mother did get her own house, but until that she was a very peripatetic lady, because she would have to pack up when we left the cannery because we would never know at which B.C. Packers cannery Dad would be working next season.

"Or some winters we lived in Prince Rupert, where my mother had two sisters. So I went to school in Prince Rupert and Vancouver and when I reached high school, we stayed in Vancouver every winter and I went to Magee High School. By then, all I wanted to be was a nurse. So in 1933, I went into training at Vancouver General and graduated in 1936. During my two weeks holiday, I would visit my parents, who at that time were at Claxton.

"Dad started out in the cannery business when he was a very young man. He had apprenticed at Easthope as a mechanic and machinist. He started out at Dominion cannery on the Fraser after he and mother were married. From there he went up to Cunningham cannery and from there to Balmoral. To get anywhere from Balmoral, we had to take a boat to Port Essington, and then by ferry to Haysport and by train from there to Prince Rupert.

"We had three boats at the cannery—the *Klatawa*, the *Wawanesa* and the *Michael*. On Sunday afternoon it was great to go out on the towboats. Unfortunately, it was usual that we were bucking the tide and usually it was quite rough and often I got seasick. And for some reason or other they always served us sardine sandwiches.

"Our house was part way up the hill. We were surrounded by bushes so we did a lot of berry picking. We had a garden in tubs and mother grew nice roses there. But it seemed to me that I lived a very unsupervised life—we were allowed to sort of run free. The houses were well away from the river, but we spent a lot of time running around the dock. Further along the Ecstall, there had been a homestead of people by the name of Hewitt and we used to walk down there. Eileen Binns and I—her father was bookkeeper—would wander all over the place.

"Further down on the Ecstall side of the River, there was an older cannery called Alexandria and there was a boardwalk to it down through the woods. We would go down there and play on the piledriver and I don't think anyone knew where we were half the time. We didn't know it at the time, but I think everybody watched us. I fell off the dock one time but nobody knew that because I hung onto the top of the piles for dear life until my friend pulled me out.

"My cousins would come out from Prince Rupert and stay with us. One time we were playing on a boat. I fell overboard and I was going past the stern when my cousin Bill grabbed me by the hair and pulled me in the boat. Those were sort of growing up days.

"Then, when we got to Claxton of course, I was going to high school and I was much more sophisticated. We played a lot of cards and the boys from the office would come up to the house and I had a lot of good friends out from Prince Rupert. I would go up and down to Vancouver on the *Cardena* or *Catala* and everybody would look out for me.

"Then I went into training for three years and after a short stint in the hospital, I went up to Prince Rupert where I had two aunts. I went to work for Dr. Geddes Large. I lived with my aunt and her family. She had two boys in the navy and she would take navy boys in as part of her bit for the war. One of these was a Lieutenant by the name of Eddie Lee who had gone to school with Ewen Macmillan. And he brought Ewen to dinner at the house and that's how we met. At that time, I was very busy with other people, but eventually we got together. I think Ewen wanted to marry me because I was an R.N. and he needed a First Aid Attendant at the cannery. I had had my teeth fixed and I had a fur coat and I had a 50 dollar Victory bond, so I was rich. We were married in the spring of 1942. We had a few days honeymoon and then the big collapse came when they rounded up all the Japanese and Ewen had to come back and look after his boats and his Japanese fishermen. It was a very harrowing experience.

"One of the reasons we got along so well was that I knew cannery life and what a cannery wife should be, and I think that's what made it work out so well.

"We had three children. I had decided they would be two years apart, so they were born in '44, '46 and '48. They had to be born in the first of the year because I didn't want to have them during the season and Ewen had to go shooting in the fall and then it was Christmas. And I had to have them in fairly good time before we went north in March or April. So Kim was born on January 20th, Leslie on the 31st and Don on February 2nd. So we were going up and down the coast with three children, two years apart. And we would trail up and down the wharf with a baby in the buggy and the others on harness.

"We nearly lost Leslie once. I tried to keep a red coat on them so I could see them if they were playing outside the house. One day we were down on a scow, fishing. The kids loved fishing, catching bullheads, and so on. I missed Leslie, she was two at the time, and I thought she had fallen in the river. I ran around looking and yelling and then I noticed the square opening in the deck of the scow, and I saw a little red coat away at the end of the scow—she was down in the hold. It was low tide so the water had all run down to one end of the hold. Luckily, there were some men working on the dock, so Bob Smith crawled in and pulled her out. It was lucky that she had the red coat on. It was the only time we had a close call with them.

"We had our four-room house with the lean-to for the bathtub (I had said I wouldn't get married without a bathtub), and when Leslie was born, we had to put another lean-to on. The house was on mudsills and the railway was right behind and every time a train passed, the house would shake. Any visitors we had thought they were in an earthquake.

"I can still remember that at low tide, there was just mud in front of our house. The kids loved it. They'd put on their gumboots and go out and play in it. More than once, Ray, the cook, would come out in front of the messhouse and there would be a kid stuck in the mud—slop, slop, slop, he'd go out and grab the kid.

"Our front door was never locked. You just stepped in the front door and the bedroom door was on the right. Several times, we would wake up and there would be somebody standing at the foot of the bed. I remember one night, early, early in the morning, I woke up and there was Mrs. Tom Smith standing at the end of the bed peering at us, her eyes blackened and everything. But they knew the door was open and they'd just wander in.

"Peter Williams was the medicineman. He knew a lot about Native medicines. Anyway, he did an abortion on his daughter and he came to get me because it had gone wrong and she was bleeding too much. We had to get her on a boat and rush her into Rupert. There was a Mr. Snidel, whose appendix burst. We had to take him into town on the boat. He didn't come back.

"The train to Rupert went by about 11 o'clock at night. If the kids got sick and we felt they had to see the doctor, we'd get someone up-river to tell us when the train was coming and we'd hang a lantern out to get it to stop. Ewen would phone Ross Brothers taxi and they would meet us at the train and we'd go off to the aunt's.

"We always had dogs and when we went north in the spring on the *Cardena*, it was like a safari. We'd have two dogs and three kids and trunks full of stuff to last us till fall. If I had a baby in diapers, Roy, the steward, would take them down to the boiler room, wash them and hang them up to dry. One year, Ewen bred our two dogs and we had eight puppies to take down with us on the boat. We had them in two crates. Every morning, Ewen would go below and he'd haul the pups out of one crate into the other one while he cleaned out the crates and hosed it all overboard.

"Later, when the kids were older, we would go up just for part of the season, sometimes on the old Canso flying boat. Before the airport was built on Digby Island you flew to Sandspit on the Islands by land plane and then took the Canso to Seal Cove in Rupert harbour. Or sometimes the Canso would fly all the way to Vancouver. When it landed in the water the kids were terrified. They thought it was going to sink, and so did I.

"They were good years and when we stopped going up for the season, I missed it."

Cassiar remained family owned and independent of the big four companies until the end. In the end, it was the last cannery to operate on the Skeena River itself.

Chapter 16

THE FRANCIS MILLERDS

Francis Millerd was born in Cork, Ireland in 1884. He arrived in B.C. rather by accident and was destined to be one of the leading pioneers in the salmon canning business. He was to have a remarkable career with many ups and downs that reflects the dynamics of salmon canning in the early years.

He had three sons, Francis W. (Frank Jr.), James (Don) and William (Bill). Bill was in the R.C.A.F. during World War II, and was killed in action overseas. Frank and Don became well known figures in the industry. Don's son, Don Jr., carried on the family tradition and is today operating salmon processing enterprises.

Frank Jr. recounts his father's story briefly. "In 1907, he was discharged from the Irish Cavalry regiment, fighting in the Boer War with the British. He decided to emigrate to Australia which seemed to be where everybody was going. The ship he was on had some sort of trouble and it came up this way instead of going across to Australia. And while they were here, he was walking around the town, of course. He was walking along Water Street and he saw this sign in one of those little store fronts that said "CLERK WANTED." Well, he'd been a clerk on his school holidays in Cork, just to fill in at the store. So he thought maybe he'd qualify as a clerk so he went into this little place. He told them who he was, that he'd been around, that he was from Ireland, and he'd been in the Boer War and so on, and he said he thought he could handle that job as a clerk.

"So the fellow said, 'Maybe we'd better give you a try.' And the fellow that he talked to was Bell-Irving, the old man Bell-Irving. H.O., the original. He said, 'Well, if you'd like to give it a try, we'll send you out to one of the canneries.' So they sent him to the Fraser River and then up to Knight Inlet. He was there for two years and he found that he liked the fishing industry.

"So then he had met Captain Gosse, who had built Glendale and they started up together and ran a pretty successful operation for quite a long time. Finally they broke up as most partnerships eventually do, and he built a cannery out at Steveston. He had trouble financing it but he eventually got going.

"One of the things he had thought about was a floating cannery. So in 1924, he made a deal with T.W.B. London, who owned the property where Great Northern Cannery is, to outfit a sailing ship there and make it into a floating cannery. Everybody was sort of scoffing at this. But Dad went ahead— he always liked to bulldoze ahead on any idea that he thought was good. He got this five-mast boat that had been abandoned down in Hawaii somewhere— they had run into trouble with the steering and they had to leave it there. So there was some fellow arranged to tow it up with the old tug Lorne and they towed it up to Vancouver. Dad looked at it with two or three other guys and they cut down four of the masts and just left one of the masts up and made a floating cannery of it. It had a one- pound tall line.

"They took it up to Masset and they canned 41,000 cases in about four weeks, which was kind of a record at that time. Of course, they were working night and day. They were right near the B.C. Packers Shannon Bay cannery and they didn't like it very much. Some of the canneries, I guess, tried to talk the Fisheries Minister into not allowing these floating canneries, because they could see in the long run he would probably be moving the cannery from one place to another (which he intended to do), and to can on the different runs of fish as they became available, which would then make a shortage of fish going to all these different shore canneries. So they went after him on the fact that he didn't have a licence that would permit him to do this.

"They closed him down but he said they were wrong and he went to court. Up to this point, the Dominion government had always issued fish canning licences, but Dad and his lawyers said that according to the original B.N.A. Act, the provincial governments had the right to issue licences for canneries. The federal government said they had the authority and they were going to close him down, which they did. And they went all the way up to the Privy Council fighting it. It took about three years. He won the case, he proved that he was right, that the provincial government is the one to issue licences for fish canneries. And that is the way it is today.

"Well, in the process of all this, he went broke because he spent all his money on courts and lawyers. So that would bring him up to 1928 or '29. He didn't have any canneries for awhile; he just operated a couple of fish stores and he went to work for one or two of the canneries as a bookkeeper and just kept going. And he didn't really get involved in the cannery until 1935, when the Great Northern cannery was available. Bob Gosse, the son of the old captain, had been running it, but he didn't think that he wanted to keep going any further, so Dad took it over and in 1936 he started canning a lot of chums.

Great Northern

The Depression was on and a lot of the other canneries were closed and weren't canning anything so he got the chums at a pretty good price and he was able to can them and send them to Australia and make a few dollars. In fact, he did quite well on it and that was the start of the Great Northern cannery.

"Then, in about 1938, he started to can herring, which was luckily a good move because as soon as the war broke out, the British Ministry of Food wanted all the canned herring they could get. He was the only one at that point that had the know-how to can herring which he had remembered from the old Gosse-Millerd days. He encouraged the other canners to do the same because they needed this canned herring for the war effort. So they had tremendous big packs, not only the salmon but about two or three hundred thousand cases of herring was canned in the industry at that time.

"So that's the way it went and he kept running different things. He canned some sardines for awhile but he always kept the salmon going. We had camps up the coast in Rivers and Smiths Inlets and different places and he had quite a few fellows who fished for him and some fellows who he financed their boats and he had a pretty good operation going.

"We had a plant up in Prince Rupert (Seal Cove) for a couple of years but it was in a bad place and we just ran it mostly for canned clams. We did put in a little plant at Redonda Bay and we used to get fish from Bute and Toba Inlets. Well, there's no fish in Bute and Toba now; it was fished out because of the fishing in Johnstone Straits. When they opened Johnstone Straits to the seine boats, they let them fish a certain number of days on the fish that were there but they didn't have the right track on where those fish were going and they were all mixed. So eventually they fished them all out—Loughborough, Bute, Toba—all good runs and they're gone.

"We packed fish to Great Northern from as far as Rivers Inlet, first in ice and then in chilled seawater. We had camps in Jones Cove in Smiths Inlet and Finn Bay in Rivers. We had collectors and camp scows there.

"Then the government brought in a lot of new regulations for the canneries—cement floors and closed ceilings, for example, and a whole bunch of other things. We were in a non-conforming zoning in West Vancouver and we couldn't make any changes to the cannery, not even to improve it. We wanted to put in a cold storage, but they wouldn't let us do that, so it got to the point that we decided if we couldn't improve it, we couldn't use it, we'd better sell it, so in 1967, we did.

"We arranged with Queen Charlotte Fisheries to custom can for us and we carried on. But Dad died in 1976 and Don died in 1977, so we thought the best thing was to close up and we sold the company."

Francis Millerd's first canning company was Gosse-Millerd Packing Company, which he formed in 1909 with Captain Richard E. Gosse. Capt. Gosse had been a cannery builder, but not a cannery owner until he built the plant at Sargeaunt's Pass at the mouth of Knight Inlet in 1907. In 1910, the Sargeaunt Pass plant was moved to Glendale Cove in Knight Inlet. In 1911, it was sold to Anglo-B.C. Packing Co. Gosse-Millerd Packing Co. became one of the largest canning companies on the coast. In 1914, they bought the Fraser River canneries of Canadian Canning Co. and in 1915, they bought the Bella Bella cannery from East Bella Bella Canning Co., who had opened it in 1912. In 1916, they built the Sunnyside cannery on the Skeena. In 1918, they built the herring cannery and curing plant at San Mateo in Barkley Sound and in 1920, they bought the McTavish cannery in Rivers Inlet. In 1921, the company name was changed to Gosse-Millerd Co., Ltd. and in 1922, the partners separated and Francis Millerd left the company.

In 1924, Francis Millerd formed the Somerville Cannery Co. Ltd. He thus acquired the Somerville cannery on the Nass River and built a new cannery at Sointula and one in Ferguson Bay in Masset Inlet. He also operated in Ferguson Bay, with the *Laurel Whelan*, the floating cannery which he moved from place to place, including Quatsino Sound and Rivers Inlet. In 1926, he built a plant at Jedway on the east coast of Moresby Island.

In 1927, Francis Millerd changed his corporate name once again and incorporated Millerd Packing Co. Ltd., which acquired the properties of Somerville Canning Co. The new company added to these with a saltery at Port Alberni in 1927, a cannery at Barnard Cove on the Nass in 1928, and another saltery at Finn Bay in Rivers Inlet in 1928.

That same year, B.C. Packers Ltd., which had been formed by the merger of B.C. Fishing & Packing Co. Ltd. and Gosse Packing Co., Ltd., acquired the assets of Millerd Packing Co. Ltd.

Francis Millerd had put himself in financial difficulty while making legal history. He challenged in court the jurisdiction of the Dominion government to license processing plants, and argued that this was a field belonging to the provincial governments. He won at each stage, including the Privy Council in England. But in so doing, he bankrupted himself and so he sold out to the new B.C. Packers Ltd.

That same year, 1928, his plans to build a cannery at the foot of Bidwell Street, in Vancouver's Coal Harbour, which had been opposed by the Parks Board, came to fruition. In 1929, he built a one-line cannery at Port Alberni. In 1930, the British Columbia Fishermen's Cooperative Association (formerly Sointula Fishermen's Co-op) acquired both the Bidwell and Port Alberni canneries. Francis Millerd was hired as manager of their operations.

In 1935, he took over the Great Northern cannery and formed Francis Millerd & Co., Ltd. In 1943, he re-opened the cannery at Seal Cove, primarily for clam canning, and established the plant at Redonda Bay in Bute Inlet, which operated intermittently. Shortly after, Great Northern became the company's sole processing plant. In 1969 it was sold to the federal government and became the site of the Pacific Environment Centre and later the Biological Sciences Branch of the Department of Fisheries and Oceans.

Francis Millerd was active in the fisheries at the national level. He served as president of the Fisheries Council of Canada from 1951 to 1954, the only president to serve more than one term.

Francis Millerd passed away on November 30, 1976. The company that bore his named passed out of existence in 1978.

He left a legacy, however, that at this point encompasses three generations. His sons Frank and Don worked with him in the company, and in time, took over the management. Don died shortly after his father and the family decided to sell the plant, and was able to do so to the federal government. Don's son, Don Jr., bought some of the assets and thereby established himself in the salmon processing industry. He has been true to his heritage and today is president of Batchelor Bay Management Ltd., which processes salmon.

Chapter 17

THE NILSSENS

When Richie Nilssen and his family arrived in Canada in 1905, the Immigration Officer said, "We call that Nelson around here." They were so grateful to be allowed into the country that they didn't object. Probably, it should have been Canada that was grateful, because the Nelson brothers came to be one of the leading families in British Columbia's fishing industry and Richard (Richie) Nelson was its leading man.

Richie was born in a small farming community near Tromso, Norway, north of the Arctic Circle in 1896. His family were farmers and fishermen, a combination that was often repeated in the early days in B.C. There was a failure in the Norwegian cod fishery and the farm could not sustain the family, so they decided to emigrate to North America. The two older brothers came out first and managed to make enough money logging to finance the rest of the family's trip to British Columbia. They came by ship to Quebec City and then by train to the coast.

They arrived in New Westminster and settled on the south side of the Fraser River at Sunbury not far from where the first commercial salmon cannery had been built in 1870. Sunbury was a significant Norwegian community and the new immigrants duplicated what they knew at home in terms of their living quarters, their attraction to farming and fishing and of course, the Lutheran Church.

The Nelson brothers started fishing in skiffs on the river. Richie made himself useful in the small netsheds that the fishermen used and by the time he was 13 or 14, he was putting scraps of web together to make himself a net which he would fish himself from his rowboat to provide food for the family.

Norman, 10 years older than Richie and the only source of income for the new immigrants, went fishing halibut in the Bering Sea on the dory schooners. He did fairly well and after a few years, he and Richie went fishing together, first gillnetting for salmon on the Fraser and then halibut fishing on their own halibut boat, which they called the *Bayview*. They prospered well enough to send Richie to Pacific Lutheran College in Washington State.

The first commercial venture of the family began in the 1920s when Richie and Norman started buying troll salmon at Kyuquot and transporting them to Seattle. They would take turns—one would stay at the camp, buying and dressing the fish, while the other ran the boat to Seattle, often by himself—a 50-hour run through treacherous waters. Eventually they hired a helper at the camp. He wasn't very good at arithmetic, so the Nelsons arbitrarily set the price of fish at ten cents, and all he had to do was move the decimal point. This seemed to work and that man became one of the many long time Nelson loyalists.

They were quite successful in this operation, so that in October 1929 they incorporated Nelson Brothers Fisheries in New Westminster and grew from there, with Norman Nelson as president and Richie as secretary-treasurer and managing director. In 1932, they had the opportunity to lease St. Mungo cannery on the Fraser, within shouting distance of home in Sunbury. St. Mungo had been built in 1931 by Sunbury Packers Ltd., owned by Marshall English Jr., Capt. J.D. Williams and one of the Draney family. That year they packed mostly half-pound oval cans of sockeye. In 1933, Nelson Brothers bought the cannery.

In 1934, they bought Ceepeecee, a pilchard reduction plant in Nootka Sound on the west coast of Vancouver Island. It had been built by the California Packing Company of San Francisco in 1926, who had made the classic fishing industry mistake of building a plant without providing a supply of fish. Richie had done some work for the company and they offered the plant on very favourable terms. Nelson also acquired in that deal the services of Del Lutes, a consummate reduction plant man and one of the fabled characters of the industry. They shortly acquired two more west coast plants at Ecoole and Toquart.

Ecoole has been gone long since, but it is still strong in the memories of some of the old-timers. It was built by Butterfield (later to become successful Vancouver florists), Mackie and Gregory (B. Gregory of Port Alberni). Art Miller went there as a child of three in 1916. His father had gone overseas early in the war, and was skipper of a naval ship on convoy duty in the North Atlantic. The Ecoole people needed employees who knew how to preserve fish and Art's mother, a native of Scotland, knew the Scotch cure for herring. So she was engaged to work at Ecoole and to recruit other Scottish ladies. They moved there from New Westminster, children and all.

In 1938, Nelson Brothers bought Masset Canners Ltd., a salmon cannery at Old Masset which had been built in 1926. In 1940, they opened a cannery on the Ocean dock in Prince Rupert Harbour with Harry Robins, who was destined to become a household name in the northern fisheries and a long-time Nelson loyalist, as manager.

All this growth apparently put the young company in a difficult financial situation and in June 1941, they sold the company to B.C. Packers Ltd. This was undoubtedly the best kept secret in the B.C. fishing industry, and arguably in all of B.C. business circles for the next 28 years. The new owners decided that Nelson Brothers would continue to operate as an entirely separate entity and in competition with its parent. And this they did, under Richie's management, until some time after Weston's had acquired ownership of B.C. Packers Ltd. and was required to reveal details of its subsidiaries. In the meantime, Nelson Brothers Fisheries Ltd. appeared on B.C. Packers public records only as X Company—a remarkable thing considering that B.C. Packers was a public company. Only the most senior of the B.C. Packers executives were aware of the true relationship between these two of the industry's leading companies.

At the time of the sale, Norman Nelson resigned from the Nelson Brothers board and Richie became president with a new board of directors. Each of these had "alternate Directors," who were the three chief executives of B.C. Packers.

Richie Nelson seemingly carried on as if nothing had changed. In 1951, a "competitor" had shown an interest in buying the company and as a result, it appears there was a sale of a one third interest back to the Nelson family.

In 1942, when Prince Rupert became the staging port for the U.S. Army in the effort to defend Alaska against Japanese invasion, they needed the Ocean Dock and so Nelson's cannery was evicted. B.C. Packers were operating their reduction plant at Port Edward, at the mouth of the Skeena Slough and this became the site of Nelson Brothers new cannery. With building materials being critically short, Richie and Harry Robins found an old abandoned sawmill at McBride Bay on the west coast, which they bought and dismantled and then hauled to Port Edward. Because the building had been a mill, the layout was unusual for a cannery. The Iron Chinks were on the ground floor but the canning lines were on the second floor. The setup worked well in spite of the fact that the raw fish had to be elevated to the cannery and that leakage of water from the canning lines to the ground floor was an on-going challenge.

Port Edward had always been intended as an industrial area from the time Prince Rupert was first established, and it was well suited for such a purpose. Nelson Brothers had to share it for a few years with the U.S. Army, but it became the premier fisheries operation in the north for many years.

In addition to the salmon cannery, Port Edward had a reduction plant with a capacity of 1,000 tons per day and it had a crab cannery that ran all through the spring and summer at least two or three days per week. There was a shipyard and machine shop and netlofts and floats and company-provided accommodation for close to a thousand people.

Nelson Brothers now had major canneries on the Fraser and the Skeena. They never did have a cannery in the central area, although they had camps to service the fishermen at strategic places including Rivers Inlet and Johnstone Strait. The *Samson IV* and the *Samson V* were former paddlewheel snag boats from the Fraser River and the *K5* was a smaller vessel, formerly a ferry. These camps were fitted out with machineshops, netloft and store and were tied up to shore where fresh water was available. Nelsons relied on big, fast packers and meticulous icing of the fish to transport their catch either north or south. This procedure and the closure of small canneries had already begun when Nelson Brothers first became a factor in salmon processing. And of course it continued unabated to the present.

But St. Mungo had a problem with this system. The big packers entering the Fraser often encountered thick fog, which meant delays in reaching the plant which was well up-river. This could affect the quality of the fish and often meant extra labour costs as the crew waited around for a boat to arrive at the cannery. A new cannery, closer to Steveston was indicated and this became a reality in 1958 with the opening of Paramount cannery on the old Colonial cannery site. Here they built a modern cannery and a reduction plant, and later a big boat basin inside the dyke.

Richie Nelson had many strong points, but probably the most valuable and remarkable was his ability to earn and keep the loyalty and respect of his fishermen and his employees. His experience as a fisherman and seaman and his personality, his boundless energy and interest in detail all combined to make him the fishing industry icon he became.

Sometimes people took advantage of the trust that Richie placed in them. Such was the case in what might be called the Bobolink Affair. In 1955, it came to light that two of Nelson Brothers' senior employees had allegedly been defrauding the company by running a logging camp on the Nass River, using Nelson Brothers equipment. It came to light when the *Bobolink*, one of Nelson's big fish camps, similar to the *Samson*, sank on the Nass in November. This was the first Richie knew of the operation and he wanted to know what the *Bobolink* was doing there at that time of year. Allegedly, all their cables and gear and supplies were charged to the company.

Richie was an innovator. He saw the value of diversification in species utilization and in new product development that would make better use of the capital invested in plant and extend the season for employees. One of his ventures was salmon and rice croquettes, a take-off on traditional Norwegian fishballs. This operation began in 1950 at St. Mungo and was operated by a young Jack Elsey, who would later become the owner of Millbanke Fisheries in Bella Bella. This was probably the first introduction of stainless steel equipment and super attention to sanitation in a fish cannery. It was a good product, but it was never a great success because the investment in marketing was not forthcoming.

Nelsons had greater success in their attention to fast delivery of raw fish and in their superior services to fishermen on the grounds. In the latter case, the company Cessna, with pilot Ralph Hansen, had it all over the competitors for years, in servicing fishermen upcoast and in transporting company executives to the fishing operations.

Nelson Brothers Fisheries grew and became one of the "big four" in its own right. They were in the forefront of the development of refrigerated seawater on fish packers that revolutionized the industry and doomed the outlying plants and the cannery village culture. This system was actually developed or invented by the Fisheries Research Station of the Department of Fisheries—Stuart Roach and John Harrison, working at Francis Millerd & Co.'s Great Northern Cannery. But the application of it was undertaken by a number of the larger companies, experimenting with their own installations and with the vacuum unloading systems that went with it. There were many bizarre incidents, like nearly sinking one of the big packers at Port Edward (courtesy of Sonny Nelson) and blowing out the bottom of Vancouver Harbour at Canfisco's Gore Avenue site (courtesy of Bob Payne and Tommy van Snellenberg).

In the 1950s, Richie began to involve the next generation of Nelsons. His two sons, Dick and Bill and Norman's son, Norman Jr., always known as Sonny, had all worked in the plants during their student days. As youngsters during the war, they would work in the packing room and later operated some of the salmon collectors on the river—the *Avon* and the old war-surplus landing barges, the *Fraser Chiefs*. Dick and Bill graduated from the University of British Columbia, but Sonny had only one intention in life and that was to be a pilot, and so he passed up the university option.

Dick went on to take an MBA at Harvard Business School and was about to join Standard Oil in Calgary. At this point, Richie asked him to come to work for Nelson Brothers and, in 1955, he did just that, working on the refrigerated seawater experiments. That fall the Bobolink affair erupted and Dick became Manager at Port Edward.

Dick recalls those first years at Port Edward. "It was a big operation—something like 150 gillnetters and about 45 seine boats fishing for us. 1955 had been a poor year so things were quite depressed. I remember Guy Williams (later Senator) was one of our fishermen on the *Adelaide J.* and his gross stock was 900 dollars. So it was pretty bad.

"It was when drum seining was first starting and Canadian Fishing Company seemed to have mastered the art of drum seining quite well. I envied Clare Salter (Canfisco's northern Manager), because we had a joint packing operation going and when we reported the fish catches every night, they were averaging about twice as high as Nelson Brothers. But nobody quite knew what was the best way to run the drum seines. The Martinolich's with Canadian Fish had sort of invented the system. The thought was that you had to get the drum as low as possible so at great expense, we were faced with putting wells in all 45 seine boats, later to find out that wasn't the right thing. But we did gradually get it worked out and we came even with the Canadian Fish seine boats. Stu Shelly was the manager of the seine boats at Port Edward at that time.

"Anyway the operation at Port Edward went quite well. It had a very large Indian village—a thousand people at times. It was quite a violent period. There were all kinds of accidents, fires and fights. Stu and Charlie McKinnon, our personnel manager and I had to stay up every Saturday night to 2 or 3 a.m. to see that there wasn't any really bad stuff. The different bands, some of whom had been enemies for centuries, would start fighting with each other. We had a running battle with the bootleggers to try to get them to stop doing business. In those days, the Indians were not allowed to drink. We had to meet the 12 o'clock bus from Rupert and anybody caught with liquor, it had to be taken away from them and that sort of thing.

"Many of the Indians lived there year round. They were from Port Simpson, the Queen Charlottes, the up-river Skeena villages, etc. You had to be very careful how you laid out the housing because some of the tribes fought with each other all the time.

"We also had a Japanese village. Nelson Brothers were one of the first, if not the first to take back Japanese-Canadian fishermen after the war. Others were slower to do this because some of their white fishermen said they would refuse to fish with them."

The Japanese were housed in buildings abandoned by the U.S. Army after the war.

In 1962, Richie got the opportunity to realize on another of his ambitions—to operate a cannery in the fabled Bristol Bay, Alaska. He formed Nelbro Packing Company and bought a floating cannery with a tie-up place in Bristol Bay. Dick Nelson and Walter Sedgewick (Nelson Brothers head cannery man, who had also had responsibility for the construction of Paramount cannery) were in charge of building the new cannery and, in 1963, Dick became manager and continued in this position until 1970, when he became president of B.C. Packers Ltd.

In the meantime, the company also branched out into the herring fishery on the Atlantic coast and built a big reduction plant at Port aux Basques, Newfoundland.

In 1964, the executors of the estates of H.R. McMillan and Gordon Farrell, who had been the main shareholders of B.C. Packers since the 1930s, decided to sell their shares. These were acquired by George Weston Company of Toronto. But this was not known publicly until 1967, when Combines Branch authorities in Ottawa, forced Westons to disclose their holdings, including B.C. Packers. Even then, the fact that B.C. Packers owned Nelson Brothers was not revealed until 1969.

Bill Nelson was less involved in the fishing industry. Like his brother and cousin, he worked during his school holidays in the plants and on the boats and he was the first manager of the Paramount plant. When Dick went to Alaska, he served a brief stint as president of Nelson Brothers Fisheries. But top management wasn't his bag and Bill left the industry for the investment business.

Norman Nelson, Jr. (Sonny) had not intended a fisheries career. He qualified as a pilot just at the end of the Korean War and the airline market was flooded with pilots. So with no flying job offers, he went to Port Edward for the summer and became gillnet manager. And in 1962, he became manager of Port Edward.

This was the time of the joint packing and canning operations of the large companies. They were an attempt at achieving efficiency in the industry and utilizing the various assets to better advantage. They were a huge and complicated process involving both salmon and herring operations.

Sonny, along with the likes of Clare Salter and Billy Malcolm was responsible for the northern joint packing. At the same time, Nelson Brothers bought out McCallum Sales, who owned the Masset crab plant and this came under the Port Edward area of operations.

Sonny remained at Port Edward as manager until 1969, when he was transferred to Vancouver as production manager for Nelson Brothers. But shortly after, Dick Nelson became president of B.C. Packers and he asked Sonny to become manager of Pacific operations for B.C. Packers Ltd.

Chapter 18

THE INRIG AND HOGAN FAMILIES

Both the Inrig and Hogan names were well-known as cannery builders and operators. They were linked through their work but also by marriage, when Mary Inrig married Lew Hogan in 1921.

Frank Inrig came to B.C. about 1890 and his wife came out in 1896 (they knew each other in Scotland), to marry him. They were married at the mission in Kitkatla, near present-day Prince Rupert by the Reverend Gurd, the minister there. Frank Inrig was foreman at Standard cannery. In 1904, he became manager at the Cunningham cannery at Port Essington (then owned by B.C. Packers Association). Briefly, he became manager at Bella Coola and then, manager of B.C. Packers canneries in Rivers Inlet. At first, he was based at Brunswick cannery, and in 1910, moved to Wadhams from where he managed Wadhams, Brunswick and RIC. This was a challenging job, given the distances in the Inlet, but Frank had a "speedboat" that did probably 18 knots, and every day he would run it from Wadhams to Brunswick to RIC and back. There was a foreman in each plant, of course. They raised four children there—Mary, Jessie, Jim and Alex and they all came to be associated in their own ways with Rivers Inlet and the north coast.

In 1925, Mrs. Inrig died at Rivers Inlet and about that time, Frank decided to leave B.C. Packers and build his own cannery. In 1926, he built a cannery well inside Goose Bay, near the mouth of Rivers Inlet. It operated only in the autumn of that year canning fall fish. In the spring it became obvious that it was in the wrong place because the pilings were infested with toredos. So in 1927, he and his partner, Alec Rutherford moved the plant and rebuilt it at the present Goose Bay site. In 1928, he sold the plant to Canadian Fishing Company (who operated it continuously until 1957, the last of the canneries to operate in Rivers Inlet). He continued as manager until 1931.

In that year, he built the Moses Inlet Cannery (Inrig's cannery), about

The Frank Inrig family at Wadhams

three miles inside Moses Inlet. It operated in the 1932, 1933, 1934 and 1935 seasons, but timing was against them and in 1935 they became one of the victims of the Depression and heavy packs. Like so many others, the cannery was closed and never reopened.

Mary Inrig had married Lew Hogan, who had a machine shop, gas station and store in Moses Inlet across from the cannery. In 1935, Jessie Inrig married Jim Graham, who was bookkeeper at Goose Bay the first year it opened and who moved with the Inrigs when they went to Moses Inlet.

We will tell of the Hogans later but for now, let's follow Jim and Jessie Graham. The Inrigs had a home in Vancouver and up to this time, had always spent their winters there. After the 1935 troubles, this was all that Frank Inrig had left.

So Jimmy Graham was out of a job, and he and Jessie decided to set up their own business in Rivers Inlet. Jessie says, "I remember saying to him, 'You know, I've spent every summer of my life in Rivers Inlet, but I've never seen a winter there and I'd love to see a winter there.' So he said, 'Why not, maybe we could start something up there.' So right away he got busy and thought a gas station would be the natural thing to start on because there were just one or two there then. So that's what he did. We took up some property and we went up early in '36. And that's where we stayed forever."

The Grahams chose Duncanby Landing because they were familiar with it and liked the location. When they had lived at Goose Bay, they would go there on occasion to swim at the beach. There was another connection. Frank Inrig had built a shack there in 1926, and at first he had planned to locate his new cannery there after the sale of Goose Bay. But there wasn't a secure enough supply of water to run a cannery and they chose Moses Inlet instead.

When Jim and Jessie landed at Duncanby in the spring, there was nothing there but the shack and this became the basis of the lovely home they eventually built. With Frank and Alec, they built a float and a gas station and a store right away and then made a deal with Standard Oil, who at that time weren't represented in the Inlet—an arrangement that lasted until they left in 1972.

Frank Inrig had named the place Duncan Bay after his friend Tom Duncan who had been his engineer at the cannery at Port Essington. Jim and Jessie wanted a regular mail sack via Union Steamships and duly applied to the

Jessie and Jimmy Graham

Duncanby Landing

post office. There were already one or more Duncan Bays on the B.C. coast, so they had to use another name and Duncanby Landing was the choice.

The Grahams were very popular with the fishermen, as were the Dawsons at Dawson's Landing. In spite of the services provided by the canneries, the fishermen patronized the Grahams and the Dawsons. Over time, the Grahams added to the amenities they offered. They opened a restaurant and installed showers and washing machines and even a sauna for the fishermen, and all for free.

The Union Steamships *Catala* and *Cardena* were the main steamships that serviced Duncanby and Rivers Inlet. In 1936, Duncanby was the 45th call out of Vancouver, including whistle stops and rendezvous with rowboats in the middle of a channel somewhere. The boat came in every week, both north- and southbound in the summer, and northbound in the winter. Union Steamships were the lifeline for all these ports of call. Getting out of the Inlet in the winter meant boarding the boat northbound and sailing all the way to Prince Rupert before heading south for Vancouver. This was no inconvenience, because these vessels were mini-liners and the service was exceptional. After World War II when the company brought their Corvettes into service, the schedules were changed and the *Catala* and *Cardena*, as a rule, ceased to do the runs to Prince Rupert and beyond.

Navigation on the coast with all its channels and islands and underwater hazards in those days was exceptionally skilled. Radar was not known until after the war and navigation in the fog was by whistle and sounding line. Jessie tells of times of heavy fogs when the boat was approaching Goose Bay or Duncanby, those on shore would hear the whistle and then would gather on the dock and set up a clamour with pots and pans so the skipper would know how close he was to the dock. And they would glide in as if the visibility were 100 percent.

Jessie Graham recalls, "It was an interesting life. I loved every minute of it. We were very lucky at Duncanby—there were very few accidents and that sort of thing. But we did have a boat explode there. If I had been one second later, I would have been one of the pieces.

"That was an exciting time. It was Harold Malm, the Canadian Fish manager at Margaret Bay in Smiths Inlet. It was early morning when he pulled in to gas up. He was going to Sointula—he was a Sointula man. Usually Jim was at the gas station night and day, but he wasn't there yet, for some reason, and the gas boy wasn't there either, so I was there. We had a restaurant there too and the two ladies we had as cook and waitress that summer were from Sointula too. They were lovely ladies. So they were up early to get ready to serve breakfast, and I was up.

"And this boat came in, so I went down and he got filled up okay and I said to Harold, 'The two ladies from Sointula are up already and I bet they'd like to say goodbye to you or maybe give you a letter to take since you are going to Sointula. I'll run up quick and tell them you're here. I'll send them right down to say goodbye to you.'

"So I ran up the ramp. I was just getting to the top and Bingo! something went off. I turned to look back and there was a dinghy way up in the sky and a man with it. He was blown straight up and he landed straight down. Of course, everybody heard that and everybody came running. Jim was down there right away and of course, the girls from the restaurant. And on the pilings and on the wharf where I had just arrived were big pieces of glass all around. There were two men on the boat—a young fellow who was the deckhand. And he had been blown into the water, so he wasn't burnt or anything—he just had to swim to get back to the float. But Harold, he had landed back on the boat and he was hurt. He didn't show it at first. He was pretty tough. The boats that were next to him had to cut themselves free from the wreckage and get out of there. The floats were full.

"And the two men were taken up to the house. I remember they took the boy up and laid him down. He wasn't hurt but he seemed to be in shock. Harold seemed to be in pretty good condition but he couldn't walk. They put him in a chair in the living room and gave him a drink right away and he sat there and talked and he seemed pretty good. But his feet were smashed. He must have landed straight down on his feet. They say he wouldn't have lived at all if he hadn't been right over that engine at the time. As soon as I saw the explosion, I ran for the gas tanks and shut them off, and a good thing because the hoses were still running as a result of the explosion."

Jimmy and Jessie sold out in 1972 and retired to Tsawwassen.

Mary Inrig was born in 1897, the first white girl born in Metlakatla. Lewis Hogan was born in Nova Scotia and at 16, his father sent him out to B.C. to help his brother Arthur, who had become a paraplegic. Arthur ran the machine shop at Bella Bella for many years—a very knowledgeable person and well known to everyone in the area. Then he became mechanic at Brunswick cannery. When Lewis arrived at Brunswick with him, Frank Inrig gave him a job as deckhand/engineer on the cannery towboat and later, in the cannery. When Frank moved to Wadhams, Lew Hogan became the foreman at Brunswick.

Mary and Lewis were married in 1921 and had six children. Robert, Mary and Dick were born in Vancouver (winter babies), and Kate, Lewis and Charlotte were born at Rivers Inlet. The Rivers Inlet hospital was located at the original Green's cannery site, very close to Brunswick Cannery.

When Frank Inrig left B.C. Packers in 1926, to build Goose Bay cannery, the company replaced him with three people. He had been manager of all three of the company's plants and now each plant had its own manager. Lew Hogan became manager at RIC, at the head of the Inlet, near the mouth of the Wannock River. He was manager for the seasons of 1927 and 1928. Bob Hogan recalls, "That was a delightful part of our life. Dad had been foreman at Wadhams and there were three of us kids at that point. And we went to RIC and lived in the manager's house. RIC in those days was a beautiful cannery. God, it was lovely up there. There was that nice area up around Owikeno Lake and all the rivers and that. And I can always remember, the manager's house had honeysuckle all over it and it smelled so beautiful in the summertime. It was my Dad's first cannery manager's job and he enjoyed it."

In the fall of 1928, Lew Hogan was approached by an English company to build a cannery at Humpback Bay on Porcher Island in the mouth of the Skeena River. Lew was the kind of man who could turn his hand to anything. According to his children, he had a grade four education but he could do anything. "One minute he'd be doing the bookkeeping, the next, he'd be out in the blacksmith shop, then he'd be in the machine shop, next minute, he'd be down buying fish. It just seemed to be natural for him." And he became a piledriving expert and he would be called on to drive piles at all the canneries in the Rivers Inlet area.

Lew took a bargeload of equipment and people up to Porcher Island in the fall of 1928. He designed and built the cannery and had it operating in time for the 1929 sockeye season.

Porcher Island cannery is unique in design. The standard design for canneries was post and beam, with huge hip roofs sloping down from the two- or even three-storey peak, to the top of the first storey walls. The Porcher buildings had two-storey walls and an interesting roof, gracefully curved toward both sides from the centre. No one knows precisely why this was done, but there is no doubt it was Lew Hogan's own design without the benefit of architects. The design gave considerably more room in the upper parts of the plant. There had been a small farm at the head of Humpback Bay and this land was incorporated into the cannery site. The creek carried pink salmon and the bay was well-known for its dungeness crabs.

Lew Hogan liked to experiment and he built a "good sized smokehouse" and put up experimental packs of smoked salmon. He had a line of tips and tails—an early attempt to improve the utilization of the whole fish that predated the standard industry practice. And he installed a one-pound oval can line that produced a specialty pack of whole sockeye cutlets—probably the genesis of the "middle cut" brand that became so famous in England under the John West Company.

The cannery operated from 1929 to 1932, then succumbed to the Great Depression. The Canadian Fishing Company bought it in 1934, but never operated it as a cannery, using it only as a fishing station and outpost for Carlisle cannery, and later for Oceanside cannery at Prince Rupert. But during

Porcher Island

those years, the Hogans thought they were on the top of the world. They had a nice home in Vancouver where they spent each winter—standard upcoast cannery practice—and the children enjoyed the excitement and discovery of cannery life in the summers, made all the more amenable because of the advantages that went with being the manager's kids. Bob Hogan recalls, "It was a great life. We were favoured and looked after. Dad bought a speedboat from somebody in Prince Rupert. It went about 18 knots and we thought that was terrific and we used to go out to the beaches on the north end of Porcher and we'd go over to Lawyer Island where the lighthouse was and we'd have picnics and so on. It was the greatest place in the world. And we always knew we were going back to the city in the fall."

But that all came to an end in 1932. With the Skeena cannery closed, the Hogans returned to Rivers Inlet. Frank Inrig, Mary Hogan's father had just built Moses Inlet cannery which itself was in trouble and could not provide employment for all the family. Lew Hogan decided to try his luck at gillnetting, but the first big Rivers Inlet strike of 1932 caused the loss of most of his season. Forever innovative, Lew decided to build a machine shop and he chose Saltery Bay on the south side of Rivers Inlet, across from the mouth of Moses Inlet, and this became the home of his family until 1939.

He and his brother-in-law, Jimmy Inrig, salvaged the lumber from a building between McTavish cannery and R.I.C. and towed it down to Saltery Bay. The building was about 100 feet long and 30 feet wide and it housed the store, machine shop and the house. It was a nice place, but not very nice in the winters which were particularly vicious in those years. There were open joints in the flooring and the north winds which blew right at the building out of Moses Inlet, would come through those cracks. Lew Jr. recalls, "They had terrible north winds and it would pick up the waters into spray and spray it on the trees and the trees would all be covered with ice, back maybe 200 feet from the shore, through the whole Inlet. One year while we were at Moses Inlet cannery, the whole Moses Inlet froze over and there was about two feet of ice. We built a sled for our dogs and they towed us kids all over the Inlet."

But in spite of the Depression and the difficulty of collecting accounts from the fishermen, the Hogans made a success of their business. It was a family affair, with everyone working and in some seasons hired help as well. During the winter they would make netguards in the machine shop and build up an inventory for the summer fishing season—and they had an A-frame rigged up that was capable of lifting the stern of a gillnetter to install the netguard or to remove netting caught in the propeller—a common occurrence where fishing boats were concentrated.

Food was no great problem. The steamboat would bring in the staples

Hogan's Machine Shop at Saltery Bay

and hunting and fishing produced the rest. There was deer meat and fish and ducks and geese and a lot of this was canned and preserved for the winter. And there was no shortage of wood for heating and cooking. The stream provided power for lights and tools by means of a waterwheel, so there was non-stop electric light at no cost.

Schooling for the children was a problem. It had to be by correspondence so it depended absolutely on the parents to be the teachers. The Hogan kids were more fortunate than most in that situation, because their mother had a university degree and put great stock in the importance of education. Others in the Inlet were not so lucky. So the Hogan children were well prepared for school when they started to return to Vancouver again for the winters. But they still feel that the isolation and the lack of schoolmates that city children take for granted had lasting effects on the social side of their lives.

Mrs. Hogan tried desperately, and unsuccessfully, to have her children enrolled in the Indian residential school in Alert Bay. She strongly resented that the government would provide the Indian children with a good education, free room and board, new clothes, dental and medical care and that these were not available to her own children. Currently, it seems to be politically correct to believe that the students at these schools were routinely subjected to physical and sexual abuse. Anyone familiar with these schools when they were operating knows that that was not the case. Discipline in those days involved forms of corporal punishment—in city schools as well, which today is unacceptable. There is a side to the argument that holds that it was probably better in its results than the present hands-off regime.

Sexual abuse may have occurred in the residences, but complaints from the "victims" was not widespread until after the Mount Cashel scandal and the compensation packages it led to, jogged a lot of memories of real or imagined abuse.

It is fact, that far from being "torn from the bosoms of their families," many Indian children were annually rescued from shocking and sordid conditions at home, which included abuse and plain neglect. The annual migration by Union Steamships from the villages to the residential schools was a happy and exciting time for the Indian children that was witnessed by hundreds or thousands of fellow travellers over the years.

In 1941, J.H. Todd and Sons had decided to reopen their Klemtu Cannery and they approached Lew Hogan to rebuild it and run it. To get him, they agreed to buy the Saltery Bay machine shop from him, which they did and they operated it for two years. And this started a new phase in the family's life on the coast. An important part was that they would now spend the winters at their home in Vancouver, which had been rented out for about ten years, and to attend regular school.

Klemtu plant was a mess and Lew Hogan went to work on it. He built a cold storage plant, an ice plant for halibut fishermen and trollers, streamlined and modernized the cannery with three lines—two half pound and a tall line which could produce 70,000 cases per season—and introduced a groundfish operation. Besides salmon, he canned herring and abalone and clams and one year, even tuna. And Todds were fortunate, not only in getting an outstanding manager, but also in hiring his family members in key positions. Bob ran the electrical equipment and the refrigeration machinery. Lewis Jr. stayed at Saltery Bay and ran the machineshop for one year for Todds. He then went to Klemtu as well, and was the lineman in the cannery.

Klemtu was on land leased from the Klemtu Indian band. Most of the people worked in the cannery or fished for the company. The men went to Rivers Inlet and gillnetted for the sockeye season. When they came back they would go out as crew on the company seine boats. But there were Indians from other northern villages as well—Hartley Bay and Kitimaat. Some of these were from the Clifton family who were considered outstanding people and an important part of the history of the north coast.

Klemtu became one of the major plants in the central coast area, along with Canfisco's Butedale and B.C. Packers' Namu. And Lew Hogan expended many efforts to make it efficient and to extend its operating season. And then tragedy struck the family. Lew had gone to Klemtu in February of 1948 to ready the plant for canning clams. The clams were to come from Hartley Bay and Lew took the *Louisa Todd*, one of the company's large packers which was also used for halibut fishing, along with the skipper, Charlie Hoy and a deckhand, to Hartley Bay to finalize the arrangements for clam digging. His agent there was Chief Louie Clifton and they met to finalize arrangements. When they left Hartley Bay, there was a very strong wind blowing in Whale Channel, and as he tried to take his heading southward into the channel, the boat was turned on its beam and capsized. The vessel was found in Whale Channel after two days of searching and Lew Hogan's body was found in the rigging. The bodies of the other two men were never found.

The *Louisa Todd* was a good boat and in fact is still in service and exactly what happened that day is not known. But she was without ballast and the water tanks had been drained to prevent freezing. And with the positioning of the engine and the fuel tanks, she had a high centre of gravity, all of which probably made her unseaworthy for the weather conditions she encountered.

Lew Hogan, Jr. relates an "interesting sidelight." "When this boat was launched, Louisa Todd broke the champagne over the bow of it. Charlie Hoy had already been selected to be the skipper. He and his wife and all our family were there at the launching. Historically, when you launch a boat, the last words you say before you break the bottle are, 'God speed thee.' This is just tradition. And this girl, Louisa Todd, she didn't say that. And I remember Charlie Hoy's wife having a fit. She wanted to pull the boat back out of the water and get the girl to say that. She was really superstitious, I guess."

After the death of their father, Bob and Lew Jr. worked two more years at Klemtu and then went on to other things, Bob in Powell River and Lew in Shearwater. Mary had graduated in nursing and was a permanent resident of Vancouver.

Lew Hogan, Jr. is a natural story teller and has many vivid recollections of the days on the coast. Here are some of them in his own words:

"I was born in Rivers Inlet in 1925. There was a little hospital in Rivers Inlet. It was like a little branch of the United Church hospital at Bella Bella. Dr. Darby was running that hospital and in the summer months when all the fishermen came into Rivers Inlet, he would open this little hospital about the 1st of July, actually only for about a month, I guess. It was just south of Brunswick cannery, actually there had been a cannery there, called Green's cannery and that's where the hospital was.

"They had vicious winters in those days. Our place (at Saltery Bay) was a nice place, but the flooring had quarter inch joints between all the planking and when that wind would blow, it was really cold air coming up through these cracks. Of course, the house was all built on posts and at a high tide, there was water underneath the house and it would get blowing and get rough and logs would come in and start knocking these posts. It wasn't a very pleasurable place to live.

"There were all kinds of characters among those (Wannock) Indians. One was Tommy Highclimus. He was a real nice old guy. Incidentally, those Indians drank a lot. They drank wood alcohol, lemon extract, vanilla extract, anything like that. At some point, this Tommy Highclimus, supposedly in a drunken stupor, he put a shotgun in his mouth and he pulled the trigger and he blew the side of his face out and it blew half of his jawbone out. So his jaw hung loose and he had a rag wrapped around his jaw and around his head to keep his jaw up. But he was a nice old guy and he fished and earned a living.

"When the fishermen were there, there was lots of drinking going on in the summer months. We didn't have much drinking at our place, but down around Dawson's, there was a lot of liquor down there. If somebody had something break in their engine that was major—in the machine shop, most of the things we could rebuild. We welded up cylinders and things that nowadays, you'd just throw away. But up there, the steamboat came in once a week, so if a guy needed, like in this case, it was a piston—they didn't have any communication in those days. Like you couldn't phone Vancouver and order something—you had to send the order down on the Union Steamship and the people we dealt with in Vancouver would meet the boat and get the order and fill it and get it back on the boat before it left town. This one guy, Twenty-two-knot Pete, his piston broke and he had a 5 HP Vivian engine, one cylinder. He was at Brunswick and I guess his boat was at our place. Somebody was going from Dawson's to our place and out in the Inlet they saw this flashlight flashing around. So they went over and here was this guy, drunk of course, swimming to our place to get his piston.

"There was a fellow named Olaf Swayback and he was a really nice guy with a troller and he kept it in perfect shape. He was always a gentleman. He fished, but he'd come around the Inlet and visit people. But he had a habit of falling in love with girls and he'd start taking them chocolates and stuff and eventually he'd name his boat after them. It seemed every time you saw him, it had a different name. There were families up there, like over in Safety Cove on Calvert Island which is right across from the entrance to Rivers Inlet. There was a family in there and they had four girls and they were around 18 or 20 at that time. His boat ended up being named after each one of them, because he'd decide he was in love with one of them, then she'd tell him to leave her alone or something and he'd go for another one. Anyway, we didn't see him for a long time and nobody had heard of him or who he was in love with at the moment, but finally, after quite a few months, he showed up and his boat was called the 'Independence'!!

"Then there was a guy named Olaf Sandle. He was a Norwegian guy and he was married to an Indian woman. They drank a lot and they had a parrot. And one time, they went on a vacation and they left the parrot with us to look after for a month. That parrot would get talking and it would recite the whole evening of this Ole and his wife, drunk, arguing and fighting and him talking in Norwegian and her in Indian and then she'd cry and the parrot cried too. But it would talk for four or five hours, the whole evening's conversation.

"They had a little girl that was born without a hipbone. And Dr. Darby, he somehow or other molded a hipbone into this little girl. And it was a successful operation and it was something that was almost unheard of to the point where he was invited by the New York College of Physicians and Surgeons to bring this little girl back to New York and show what had happened. And he did. I remember her and she was getting around just like the other kids. She was about four or five years old. Then they got on a drunk and I don't know what happened, but the story is that the little girl starved to death. It was a really sad story.

"There was another character in Rivers Inlet—a lady named Mrs. Perry. And she had a logging camp in Draney Inlet. I think that she and her husband had the logging camp, but he had died so she just continued to live at the camp. She had two guys with her. The one guy looked like a logger and dressed like a logger, but the other guy, I don't know where she found him but he was an Englishman and he always wore a suit and he was very astute. All that I remember was that they had several floats and several houses. They had the donkey and the A-frame. All that I ever saw these guys do was repair things like roll new logs under the floats where they were sinking. She was a real husky woman and she was the boss. She bossed these two guys around and she was one of the Rivers Inlet characters.

"Over at Dawson's Landing there was Jimmy and Jean Dawson. They had a good-sized store on a float, and a gas station. Surprisingly, they had almost anything you could ever want at that store. The Fisheries Department had a house there and an office. Charlie Lord was the Fisheries Officer and he was the boss of the Fisheries in Rivers Inlet for years. He would usually hire four or five guys in the summer as deputies and there was always one located at RIC.

"At Dawson's, there was a guy there—these are Depression years and things are tough. In Vancouver, there were a lot of women who had trouble making a living and they did some strange things. Like a lot of them advertised as a mail-order bride, so there were a lot of these mail-order brides up there.

Almost every lighthouse keeper had a mail-order bride. But there was this fellow at Dawson's named Harry Furness. He had a boat and he'd come up there on this boat. He wasn't a fisherman or anything. He didn't work—he was probably a remittance man getting money from England, say. But anyway, he brought this beautiful woman up with him. We were at Saltery Bay then, so that would be like 1936. The manager at RIC was a guy named Hardy and he married this girl who had come up with Harry Furness. And one of my trips up there—he had a little speedboat, a little hydroplane with an outboard motor from England. I saw this thing and I was only 11 years old and I wanted that boat. I started trying to buy it from him. Finally he felt sorry for me and he gave me that boat and I fixed it all up and got the engine running and everything. In the meantime, they're catching a lot of great big spring salmon up there. I saw one that a gillnetter had caught that was 126 pounds. I thought it would be fun to catch these things, so I made a rod and reel and I went up there in this speedboat. And the first day, I caught two big springs, 55 pounds or something. And I figure I'm the first guy that sport-fished in Rivers Inlet. That would be 1937. Charlie Lord had one of his people on the dock at RIC and I guess all the commercial fishermen were complaining about me fishing in behind the boundaries. I knew that with sport fishing there were no boundaries and you didn't need a licence. The fishermen were complaining to this guy and he talked to Charlie Lord and Charlie Lord, I guess said, 'Well, there's nothing we can do about it.' But he came up to see me and I remember him telling me, 'You're not breaking any laws, I can't stop you from doing what you're doing, but please, would you not go inside the boundary, because it's not fair to these commercial fishermen.' And I did stop and that was my experience with Charlie Lord.

"There was a family, a man, his wife and son and they had a float house and he was a fisherman, but they were also bootleggers. Well, just south of Wadhams, there's a place called the Hole in the Wall and there's a river coming in there and there's a lot of salmon go up there. This guy, Jack Everett, they caught him in the Hole in the Wall with his net out on a weekend when you're not supposed to fish anyway. So they arrested him and seized his boat and they were going to auction his boat. So he and his wife came around the Inlet and she's crying, and she kept saying, 'We're just trying to make an honest living.' I remember laughing about it because you couldn't break the law any worse than he was doing. He was telling everybody, 'The auction is on a certain day and I'm going to bid a dollar. And I want everybody to know that if anybody bids over a dollar, I'm going to shoot him.' So that's what happened. He bid a dollar and nobody else bid anything and he got his boat back for a dollar.

"Across the channel from Dawson's was a logging company owned by Fred Hendricks and his family. The logging camps were all pretty well closed down because of the Depression—there was no business. They had a pretty big logging camp but they were closed down and they were tied up across from Dawson's. And they had built like a dancehall on a float, so on the weekends, there were big parties down at this place and there was lots of drinking. The Hendricks had, I guess, six kids. So those were our friends. There was one guy, Jack Hendricks, who was the same age as me. And talk about lonely. They used to come to our place—only about four or five miles—but you didn't travel around in those days. It was really a rare occasion for us to get down to Dawson's or down to see the Hendricks. But every year, this Fred Hendricks and his family would come up and Fred and our Dad would go hunting in Kildala. They'd go up there and shoot birds. That was a great place for mallards and geese. And I remember one time, they went up behind Saltery Bay, up the mountain and came back with a goat. So the family would come up there and they'd be there maybe three days. Every year. So I tell people, and it's true, that my closest friend was Jack Hendricks and I saw him for three days a year. So it was pretty lonely living. Of course, in the summer months, there were about a thousand fishermen in the Inlet. There were lots of people around, but no kids for us young people.

"The fishing was really only in July. That's when the sockeye ran. After the sockeye, there were the coho, dog salmon and pinks and of course, the run of spring salmon in the last two weeks of July. Everybody was busy while the fishing was going on, but there weren't many boats fishing after July.

With our family, we were busy working night and day during the summer when the fishermen were there because, not only were we fixing engines that broke down, but we had a hoist there. People were always getting their net caught in their propeller and we could lift the back of the boat up out of the water so they could get at it. And that thing was going steady in the summer months.

"In the cannery at Klemtu, I was the lineman, looking after all the machines past the Iron Chink. One Chinaman's job was to put lids into the clincher and to keep salt in the salter. The salt was always wet and balling up and it would plug up. I used to reach down in the salt and I'd trip the little lever and clean the hole out. So I guess this Chinaman used to watch me and I used to tell him not to do it and if there was a problem he was to call me and I'd go over and clear it up. One time, he was calling me but I was busy doing something else and the next thing I know, I see him holding his finger. I had an assistant and I told him to go over and see what was wrong. He took the guy over to the First Aid and I shut the line down because I didn't know what had happened.

But there was no blood or anything and everything looked okay, so I started the line up again. And about a half hour later, the First Aid man was over there with some paper for me to sign. I said, 'What's this all about?' He said, 'We're going to have to send this man to town, to Vancouver. He cut his finger off.' I said, 'Where's the finger?' He said, 'I thought you had it.' So the only place it could be was in a can—sealed in the can.

"I didn't know what to do. We were canning chum salmon and all the cans had the same code on them. If we had had the line number on the code, we could at least have separated those from the stack. So I got the manager to come over and I talked to him about it (this was the year after our Dad died, 1949). We didn't know what to do because there we had a whole day's run of two half-flat lines. There were a lot of cans that day and you would have had to take them all and open them or throw them away. He called head office in Victoria and they said they had already sold that pack to China and the finger would just be going back home! They said, 'Let's just forget about it.' So we did. It was cut right through the first joint.

"We used to get cans back from all over the world, usually with glove fingers—the girls were always doing something like that. Every year we'd get four or five cans back from somewhere in the world with something in it—usually just the label with the letter of complaint—but we never did get that finger back.

"There's a very interesting Japanese story in Rivers Inlet. Near the old Green's cannery there was a little Japanese settlement of four or five families. Kobayashi was the main man. They had a sawmill there and they had a wooden water wheel like the old time ones on the farms, that ran the sawmill. When our grandfather decided to build that cannery in Moses Inlet, that group of Japanese moved up into Moses Inlet right where he built the cannery. And they brought all their stuff with them including the sawmill. I remember watching these Japanese as they hand-hewed trees into beams and lumber. It was mostly all cedar and they'd bring a tree in there and take a broadaxe and cut one side of it just perfectly straight and they'd lay it over and shave that side. They used a rag with ink in it to make a chalk line. And with a broadaxe, they'd end up with an 8 x 8, just perfect and it looked like it had been planed. Anyway, they built that sawmill and of course, they cut the lumber for the cannery and for houses and sidewalks and all the lumber that was used up there."

(Mary [Hogan] White recalls that at three years old, she fell over the wharf at Moses Inlet and five of the Japanese jumped in to save her.)

"In World War I, a bunch of Germans showed up in Safety Cove and they had a settlement there, on Calvert Island. They had cattle and everything.

Jessie will tell you that there were a couple of them that fished in Rivers Inlet, but they couldn't speak English. The story is that a couple of submarines came in and picked them up, because they disappeared all of a sudden. And then Uncle Alec and Uncle Jim, Jessie's brothers, went over there to look the place over after this and they found pianos and dishes all set as if they were ready to eat, but nobody there and everybody gone. Everybody had opinions of what happened, but nobody seemed to know.

"At Klemtu, Harvey French was a guy that my Dad hired and he was a carpenter but a superintendent type and he built all those buildings at Klemtu for my Dad. He was in charge of all the construction and he was a real nice guy. His wife was a character and she was a practical joker. She used to hire on as the cook for all the crew.

"Up there, if somebody died, you couldn't just put their body in a box and ship it to Vancouver, because there was no embalming or anything. So we had to put them in a sealed metal box, solder it sealed and put that in a wooden box and ship it to Vancouver. So one of my jobs was to make these metal boxes whenever this happened and Harvey would make the wooden box for the outside. We'd put the body in the cold storage with a blanket over it or something, and once I got this metal box made, we'd take it in there and put the body in it, and I'd solder up the last seam on the box. And we'd take it out and put it in the sun so it would warm up and we could tell if there were any leaks. Then we'd put it in the wooden box that Harvey had made, nail it up and put it on the *Cardena* and send it down.

"Well, his wife talked some guy into this. We had this body in there with the blanket over it and she knew Harvey and I were going to go in and put the body in this box. So she went down there with this guy and they pulled the body out and he got under the blanket. So Harvey and I went in there, Harvey mumbling something like, 'Goddamn it, I don't know how we get mixed up in this sort of thing.' And he grabbed the blanket to pull it off the body and this guy jumps up and says, 'You ain't taking me any place.' Poor old Harvey. I think it was like three months before he recovered from that. It shook me up too, but I got over it.

"There was a fellow in the Klemtu-Butedale area. In the manager's office at Butedale, there was a picture on the wall of a big rock with five dead grizzly bears around it. There was this guy named Art Hodson. He was a really nice guy, well spoken and everything. But he was strange in that he would get somebody to take him up to Coutts Inlet—this was one inlet he really liked, right across from Butedale. They would put this guy ashore and all he appeared to have was his rifle. He never carried a blanket or sleeping bag or anything like that. Not even any food, apparently. He'd go in and disappear in the mountains for months at a time. He loved trout fishing and he'd get away back there and he'd come across a lake or a stream and he'd try trout fishing. So he knew of the best trout fishing spots. And my Dad loved trout fishing and they became real good friends. And so when this guy would come out of the woods, he would come down and he'd stay at Klemtu.

"At the same time, there was the fishery officer, the head guy out of Prince Rupert, who had a Waco airplane. It was a bi-plane and I know, I went up in it and wide open it did about 50 miles an hour. This guy also liked trout fishing. So they'd get this Art guy and they'd get in this plane and he'd show them where there was a lake with good trout fishing. There was one that I used to go into too, but we hand-carried a boat in there so we could get on the water. I used to tell people that I took in there or sent in there, that if they got a fish under 18 inches, I'd give them 10 dollars. I never had to pay off.

"This Art Hodson was somewhere back in there in the spring and he was walking across a slide and the bears were just waking up. So these five grizzlies took after him and he ran down this slide and he came to this big rock and managed to climb up on it. And all five bears were around the rock and they were clawing at him. He could just barely keep away from them all. He shot them and he killed four of them and the fifth one was still alive. He used the sixth shot to kill it.

"So he took off and went down to the ocean and somehow or other he got a ride to Butedale. He told the manager what had happened and the manager got his camera and they went back to the site and he took this picture that was famous on the B.C. coast for years. I think they got Art back up on the rock and had these five grizzlies around him. That would be around 1940 to '45. When I was at Bella Bella, he got a little house there and he retired.

"There was the story of this guy at one of the lighthouses. His wife had to go to Vancouver for something. And when she was ready to come back she wired him and said I am leaving stop. You can meet me at Namu.' (or something like that). But the operator, when he sent it made a mistake and it said, 'I am leaving you, stop.' And the guy committed suicide.

"Then there was the Moresby Island lighthouse on the southern tip of the Queen Charlottes, Cape St. James. Talk about a lonely place. The man and his wife went out fishing in a little boat and they came back and he had a heart attack and fell overboard at the dock. And she tied the boat up and tried to get him up on the float. She wasn't strong enough so she tied him to the float. It was bad, stormy weather and it was a month before a fishing boat went by and she was able to wave them in. And she lived there with her husband in the water a whole month."

Chapter 19

THE SIMPSONS

There is no one more closely associated with fish processing in the Queen Charlotte Islands than the Simpson family. They were not the first by any means, or the largest, but they were the most personally involved, the most innovative, the most persistent and they stayed with it as the leaders for three generations.

Eugene Simpson and his wife Mae moved to Vancouver in 1908 from Blaine, where he had been in charge of the salmon traps for George and Barker, a B.C. Packers Association company. He went north to Prince Rupert in 1915 and packed fish out of Langara Island. He was one of the partners who built the Lockeport cannery on Moresby Island in 1918. He was manager of the plant and also of the freezing plant at Pacofi, nearby. Lockeport had a big pack in 1918, but with the end of World War I, the markets collapsed and this operation, in common with others on the coast was immediately in financial trouble. Eugene Simpson saw it coming and loaded what he could of the canning equipment on to a seine boat and headed north to Henslung Bay on Graham Island opposite Langara Island. He and one of his partners, Capt. H. Babington, built a one-line cannery there in the spring of 1919, with the object of processing spring and coho salmon from the hand trollers.

The operation was not successful and before the season was over, the equipment was loaded on a scow again and moved to Naden Harbour. Here, on the site of the former Wallace Fisheries salmon cannery, which had been moved to Watun on Masset Inlet that year, they built the first crab cannery in British Columbia and established the Simpson family as the foremost crab canners on the B.C. coast.

Simpson had solved the major problem of canning crab—the discolouration or black smut that occurred when the crabmeat, which is alkaline, reacted with the tinplate. He had been in Japan and discovered that the canners there added mild acid to the pack to overcome this problem. He used citric acid and never had a problem with smut.

The clam cannery at Tow Hill

His crew came from the Haida villages of Masset, the men to fish and the women to pick and pack the crabmeat—a highly labour-intensive job at which they became very proficient. The Haida, famous throughout the coast for their cedar dugout canoes, were, at that time building double-ended rowboats of cedar, which were ideally suited for fishing crabs in Naden Harbour. This little cannery and its attendant village operated until 1924, Eugene Simpson in charge of the overall operation and his wife, Mae in charge of the cannery and the store. In 1924, Simpson and Babington, having obtained leases for the razor clam beaches on the north coast of Graham Island, built a clam cannery at Tow Hill and a two-line salmon cannery at Masset. They were financed by Everett Packing Co. of Everett, Washington, and were incorporated as the Langara Fishing and Packing Co. This operation was successful until 1930, when Eugene Simpson unexpectedly died.

With that, with a huge pink pack that year, and with the effects of the Depression taking hold, the Company became bankrupt. The plants were closed and taken over by the Nootka Packing Co., Ltd., which was also owned by Everett Packing Co.

The family, which was now headed by son, Sam Simpson, was left with the crab fishing vessel *Ogden*. They made a meagre living fishing crabs and in 1932, made a deal to pack crabs to Ketchikan for freezing. The Ketchikan operators failed and that venture came to a halt in the same year. So in 1933, Sam Simpson and his wife Jessie went back to Naden Harbour and, with borrowed money, built a second crab cannery on the old site and formed Queen Charlotte Canners Ltd. Jessie ran the cannery in the spring and fall and Sam

The crab cannery at George Point, Naden Harbour

ran the *Ogden*, buying troll salmon and packing them to Prince Rupert. This operation persisted for seven years and it was here that Sam's son Eugene spent his early growing up years. It provided the family with a living in the difficult thirties, supplemented by the fish and game which abounded in the area and the ability to grow garden vegetables in that favourable climate. Young Gene developed his considerable hunting skills as a kid at Naden Harbour.

The life there was, in many ways, idyllic. Except for the seasonal cannery village itself, the only other company was from the big whaling station across the harbour. But in the winter, even it was closed. Schooling for Gene and his sister was by correspondence and later they attended school in Masset where they stayed with their grandmother.

Malcolm McCallum, who later established McCallum Sales Ltd., came to Naden Harbour as a young man as junior partner and bookkeeper.

Sam pioneered the use of the deep water crab traps and established the dungeness crab fishery in Dixon Entrance and Hecate Strait. In 1940, he moved his plant again, this time, to the old salmon cannery in Old Masset. This was the Masset Canners Ltd. cannery, built in 1926 and later acquired by Nelson Brothers Fisheries Ltd. It was closed down and Nelsons agreed to lease it in return for the upkeep of the property. The main business was canning crabs from the outside crab grounds, but they also canned razor clams for the Masset Cooperative Association (which Jessie Simpson headed), and some of the Prince Rupert Fishermen's Co-op's coho. But the wartime price controls inhibited the economics of the plant and in 1944, the business shut down and the crab fishery died.

But Sam Simpson persisted and invented the first live well system for keeping crabs alive aboard the fishing vessel. In 1944/45, he built the *Tow Hill*, the first crab vessel so equipped. Son Gene, then 15, was signed on as deckhand and cook, wife Jessie readied the Old Masset plant for canning, and the fishery began. The Wartime Prices and Trade Board price restrictions were lifted providentially at this time and the crab industry suddenly became viable. The Queen Charlotte Brand for canned and frozen crabs began to gain a reputation far and wide.

In 1950, the Simpsons' Queen Charlotte Canners Ltd. built a new plant at New Masset. In 1952, they built the *Dungeness*, a state of the art crab boat which doubled as a dragger for the Prince Rupert Co-op. In 1955, Gene was made production manager for the company and, in 1956 they began canning salmon in addition to the shellfish products.

The Simpsons operated this cannery successfully until 1965, when Sam sold out and retired. He had instituted a profit-sharing plan with his employees and fishermen. This had served the whole community well and was a beneficial system for the labour-intensive process of picking crab meat. But it was anathema to the powers that be in the United Fishermen and Allied Workers Union. They managed to get the plant certified and the piece-work system scrapped. This was the beginning of the end for the canning of crabs in the Queen Charlottes. Sam Simpson sold his shares to McCallum Sales Ltd., who had been his marketing agents. Son Gene became manager of the plant for McCallums and remained a minority shareholder. His wife, Pearl, was office manager, upholding the tradition of full involvement in the business by the Simpson wives.

Sam Simpson became a fishery officer for awhile and then he and Jessie were engaged by the Department of Fisheries to instruct Atlantic coast operators in crab processing for the emerging industry in the Maritimes and Newfoundland based on the Atlantic queen crab or snow crab.

In 1968, McCallum sold the Queen Charlotte Canners to Nelson Brothers Fisheries. With Gene Simpson continuing as manager, the new owners continued to operate the plant for crabs and clams, but sent the salmon catch to Port Edward. In 1971, a disastrous fire destroyed the cannery. It was rebuilt for processing cooked frozen crabs, freezing clams and dogfish, and the troll salmon facility was expanded.

In 1971, Gene was appointed vice president of B.C. Packers and took over their northern operations from Stu Shelley who had moved to head office. (By this time, B.C. Packers ownership of Nelson Brothers Fisheries had been revealed and the operations of the two companies had been integrated.) In

Queen Charlotte Canners, Masset, 1964

1980, B.C. Packers bought the northern assets of Canadian Fishing Company, which included the New Oceanside cannery in Prince Rupert. B.C. Packers doubled the size of the plant and closed down Port Edward, Sunnyside and Rupert Cold Storage.

Sam Simpson had many innovations to his credit in the shellfish industry. At one point he had conceived the idea of a mechanized system for harvesting razor clams and had conducted many experiments. Nothing came of this, however, until in 1970, Gene Simpson convinced B.C. Packers and the Department of Fisheries to build a prototype mechanical clam digger. Mac McLean was put in charge of the project and in due course, the machine arrived on the Graham Island beaches. There were some trying times and at least one narrow escape for the crew. It was successful in digging clams, but unfortunately, it kept getting mired down in the wet sand. Some believe that with bigger wheels and tires, this problem could have been overcome, but the sponsors were not prepared to go further and the experiment was abandoned.

Gene Simpson retired at the end of 1989 after 45 years in the fishing industry.

Chapter 20

A FEW (MORE) GOOD MEN

It is impossible to adequately cover the stories of all the people who made the fishing industry what it was in its heyday. Cicely Lyons is probably the best source, but even she has missed men who made significant contributions. Here are a few of them (not covered elsewhere in this narrative), who have been chosen because of their context in the growth of the canning industry and the ancillary operations which complemented them. There are many others who could and should be recognized and no doubt they will be in some future work. The fishing industry was, throughout most of its history, a man's world. Women were involved, of course, in the canneries, the netlofts, the offices and a few were even fishermen. But it was primarily men who shaped the industry and its development, and who took the leading roles.

John M. Buchanan

B.C. Packers' various amalgamations had brought people into chief executive positions who had not had previous experience in the fishing industry—men like Aemelius Jarvis and H.R. McMillan. This was a major departure from common practice and it didn't last long, perhaps because the industry is so unique in many of its elements and the need to understand those elements over-rode other considerations. H.R. himself came to realize this in short order and groomed John Buchanan to succeed him as president of B.C. Packers.

John Buchanan was born in 1898 in Steveston, which, in itself, set him apart from most of his peers. After graduating from the University of British Columbia in 1917, he went to work for C.L. Packing Co. and worked in various Fraser River canneries. He took his accounting training and worked in several forestry companies before joining British Columbia Fishing & Packing Co. as internal auditor in March, 1928. He retained that position when B.C. Packers

Ltd. was incorporated in May of the same year.

In 1932, he was promoted to the position of secretary-treasurer and in 1935, became general manager. In 1941, he became Vice-President as well. In 1946, he succeeded H.R. McMillan as president of the company and held this position until 1956, when he was appointed chairman of the board. Robert E. Walker became president and a whole host of vice-presidents were created. John Buchanan resumed the presidency when Bob Walker retired in 1958 and held the offices of chairman and president until he retired in 1964. Thus, he was the guiding light of the company through its significant post-war period of growth.

John Buchanan's activities and achievements transcended those of B.C. Packers Ltd. He became one of the giants of the industry, both nationally and internationally, along with few others perhaps, like H.O. Bell-Irving and A.L. Hager. He was a natural diplomat and earned the respect of all who came to work with him or simply to know him.

He was the long-time chairman of the canners' organization, the Fisheries Association of B.C., and he was one of the first presidents of the Fisheries Council of Canada, the national federation of provincial fish processors' organizations. His ability to create cooperation out of strongly different interests and strongly held views, and his technique of defusing explosive situations with one of his "clever stories" were legend among his fellow members. In this position of leadership, he was appointed one of the first commissioners of the International North Pacific Fisheries Commission (Canada, Japan, United States), when it was created in 1953.

He represented the Fisheries Association of B.C. in many capacities and on many delegations over his years as chairman. In 1966, he was honoured with the appointment as Chancellor of the University of British Columbia.

John Buchanan's son Bruce later became president of B.C. Packers albeit, by that time, a very different company from that run by his father.

Robert Cunningham

Port Essington was the name given to the Skeena River estuary by Captain George Vancouver, and it was the name chosen by Robert Cunningham for his trading post at the junction of the Skeena and Ecstall Rivers in that estuary. Port Essington should probably have been called Port Cunningham, because Robert and later, his son George, were the heart and soul of the town for nearly 60 years.

Robert Cunningham was only briefly a cannery owner, but his influence, and that of his son, on the Skeena River was legendary from the time he established his trading post until George's retirement in 1930. Robert had emigrated from Ireland in 1862 to become a lay assistant to William Duncan, the missionary who established Metlakatala. By 1864, he had left the mission to work for the Hudson's Bay Company at Fort Simpson and shortly after, he became chief trader there. In 1870, he left the HBC and partnered with Thomas Hankin to establish a store at Hazelton, to service the prospectors on the Omineca goldrush. At that time, Woodcock's Landing at the mouth of the Skeena (later, the site of Inverness cannery) was the trans-shipment point for goods from Victoria destined for the Interior. The partners had a facility there, but in 1872, Cunningham arranged for a provincial grant of two sections of land at the junction of the Skeena and Ecstall Rivers, where he established a fur trading post and store to supply the Hazelton establishment. It was on the site of an ancient Native campsite known to them as Spokeshute and here the village of Port Essington was built. It became the main population centre of the north coast, taking that distinction from Fort Simpson, and the supply centre for the northern interior of the province, until the Grand Trunk Pacific railway was completed in 1914. By then, Prince Rupert had firmly become the focus of the north coast.

Robert Cunningham was primarily a trader and merchant, but he built a salmon cannery in 1883, the first in Port Essington and the third on the Skeena. He had an interest also in the Lowe Inlet cannery and possibly in others. He sold the plants to B.C. Packers Association in 1902 and left the cannery business. He died in 1905, but was the dominant commercial character throughout the heyday of Port Essington. His son George succeeded him in business and in that status until he liquidated the company firm in 1930 and retired. Port Essington was at one time the site of four different canneries—the Cunningham, the Skeena River Commercial, the British American and the Ladysmith. Two others were located across the Ecstall River from the townsite—the Balmoral and the Alexandra. The Skeena River Commercial was purchased by Anglo-B.C. Packing Co. in 1926 to replace its British American, which had been destroyed by fire. They renamed it British American and operated it until 1936, when it was the last of the Port Essington canneries to be closed.

Henry Doyle

Henry Doyle's great achievement was the creation of the British Columbia Packers Association of New Jersey in May, 1902. He was just 27 years old when he brought together this historic amalgamation of 60 percent of the canneries then operating in British Columbia. He wasn't even in the canning business at that time, but he was able to achieve what some of the leading canners had not. Henry Doyle, Sr. had come from Boston to San Francisco in

1875 and opened the first fishing supply business on the Pacific coast, just 10 years after the first canning of salmon on the Sacramento River. His company was the leading supplier of netting, cordage, twine and fishing supplies. At that time, San Francisco was the fountainhead of the industry, including British Columbia and Alaska. Henry Doyle & Co. soon moved into these more northern areas and established branch offices in Seattle and Vancouver.

The father made annual trips to all the canneries over the whole Pacific coast, and as he came to know the owners and operators, he established a reputation for fair dealing and for reliable news about the industry. Young Henry accompanied his father on these trips as a child and as a young man and came, himself, to know the key players.

When the Vancouver branch was established, Henry Jr. was put in charge and continued to build his own reputation with the salmon canners of British Columbia.

In 1902, the industry was reeling from the effects of too much product and too many plants. The Fraser had produced a big pack in 1897, good packs in 1898 and 1899, which should have been off years, and another big pack in the cycle year of 1901. The 1901 pack was somewhat reduced from what it might have been by the ugly strike of Fraser River fishermen in that year. But still, the result was huge carry-overs of canned salmon and the possibility of bankruptcy facing many of the canners.

Some of the leading canners had made attempts at convincing their competitors that an amalgamation was essential for the health of the industry as a whole, but the owners were not prepared to trust each other enough and these attempts failed. Henry Doyle was well known to the canners, was familiar with the formation of the Alaska Packers Association, had no axe to grind and he was able to pull it off.

The previous summer, 1901, Doyle had happened to meet one Aemelius Jarvis, a former banker and now a venture capitalist and broker from Toronto. Jarvis was on a pleasure trip up the B.C. coast on one of the coastal steamers and Doyle was on one of his business trips. They struck up an acquaintance that made it possible for this amalgamation to take place. The objective was to combine all the canneries into a single company, but the J.H. Todd and H. Bell-Irving interests, along with the owners of British Columbia Canning Co. declined to join, leaving some 40 percent of the canning capacity out of the merger.

Nevertheless, it was a huge achievement. Henry Doyle negotiated options in the name of himself and Jarvis. Jarvis arranged for financing and formed a syndicate of eastern bankers and investors to provide the funds. The options were taken up and the plants sold to the new company.

Alexander Ewen, whose company was one of the main participants in the merger, became president and Henry Doyle became general manager. Two of the larger banks were involved and each had a representative on the board of directors. It didn't take long for friction to develop between the management and the directors—in particular, the bankers. These were easterners and neither the first nor the last to find difficulty in understanding the peculiarities of the salmon canning industry.

In 1903, Ewen and Doyle resigned their positions. The board called in an expert to examine the situation and as a result they were asked to reconsider their resignations. Ewen did but Doyle did not. The expert was W.H. Barker of Alaska Packers Association (APA) in Astoria and, in 1904, he replaced Henry Doyle as general manager.

Doyle was not idle for long. In 1905, he was managing the Port Nelson Canning & Salting Company's plant on the Nass. In 1906, he and Daniel Drysdale of APA leased the Lighthouse cannery on the Fraser and operated as Royal Packing Co. The same year, Peter Herman had drowned on the Skeena River and his assets at Port Essington were bought from the receiver by Doyle and R.V. Winch and George Bower. They formed Skeena River Commercial Co. Ltd. and Doyle was president, secretary and general manager. It included the cannery, a store and hotel. They operated under that name until 1916 when they formed Northern B.C. Fisheries Ltd., which then took in the Port Essington operation as well as the other Doyle and Winch properties.

In 1908, Doyle bought the Mill Bay cannery and subsequently spent much of his time there as manager. In 1912, he partnered with Donald Drysdale and Donald Moore as Draney Fisheries Ltd. and bought Namu and Kimsquit from Robert Draney. They rebuilt Namu and electrified Kimsquit with water power. The same year, he added a cold storage at Mill Bay and electrified that plant. Mill Bay and Namu were some of the first on the coast to install can-making machinery. Mill Bay supplied Arrandale and Cassiar—Namu supplied Kimsquit.

In 1916, Doyle and R.V. Winch formed Northern B.C. Fisheries Ltd. and merged all of their cannery properties into the new company. But banker trouble arose again after the First World War. There was a general Depression in the wake of the armistice and many canning companies found themselves with reduced markets, carryover stocks and surplus capacity. The main banks, except for one, knowing the cyclical peculiarities of the business, carried their customers through the critical years. The exception was the banker for Northern B.C. Fisheries Ltd. Again, a new bank manager had been appointed at the wrong time, who was from central Canada and who was unacquainted with the industry. He prevented the company from packing to capacity and there were further losses. The bank took over the management and there were still further losses. In 1924, they lost their nerve altogether and offered the properties for sale. Namu was sold to Gosse Millerd for half its value; Port Edward was abandoned to the mortgagor for the $25,000 mortgage (its appraised value was $153,000); Skeena Commercial and Bella Coola were leased to competitors. Subsequent to the sale of Namu to Gosse Millerd, that company bought Kimsquit. Skeena Commercial was sold to Anglo-B.C. Packing Co., who had lost their neighbouring British American cannery to fire in 1923. Port Edward was sold to Pacific American Fisheries and Mill Bay to Wallace Fisheries.

Henry Doyle took no further part in cannery management after 1924. He did, however, keep his profound interest in the fishery resource and wrote copiously and with credibility about protection and enhancement of the salmon runs of the province. Beginning in 1948, he became a champion for the Fraser sockeye runs in the face of potential power development. He articulated most of the arguments that the industry and the Department of Fisheries would use in the Fish and Power battles of the 1950s and again in the 1960s. The high dam at Moran was his particular target and he tackled the proposition with vigour and the conviction that comes from extensive knowledge of the subject. He died in 1961, having seen both levels of government declare in favour of the Fraser salmon and having seen the work of the International Pacific Salmon Fisheries Commission bear fruit in the rehabilitation of those fabulous sockeye and pink salmon runs.

Kenneth F. Fraser

Ken Fraser was born in Vancouver in 1910 and into the fishing industry. His father, Frank Fraser was a partner with Messrs. Tom and Morris in the Princess Royal Cannery on China Hat Island, which they had built in 1900. The cannery became part of the B.C. Packers Association when that company was formed in 1902, and it was closed shortly afterward. Frank Fraser stayed on with the new company at Imperial cannery.

Ken was at university when his father died and he had to go to work. He was employed by B.C. Packers, but the Depression put a stop to that and he found a job on the construction of the railway tunnel between Vancouver harbour and False Creek.

But by 1937, he was back at B.C. Packers and his first management job was to build the new salmon cannery at Pacofi on Moresby Island in the Queen Charlottes in 1938. Pacofi had periodically been the site of a cannery and cold storage from 1910 and a salmon saltery from 1927. In 1938, Ken built the new plant which consisted of a cannery for pinks and chums and a herring reduction facility. He brought the canning equipment from the former cannery at Alliford Bay and installed it at Pacofi.

In 1943, the Pacofi installation burned and Ken was transferred to Steveston as Manager of Imperial cannery. During his 10 years in that position he made an indelible mark on the Fraser River fishery.

His strongest points were always his relationship with the fishermen and his sense of humour. One of his proud possessions was an illuminated scroll presented to him by members of the fleet which reads:

Our father who art in Steveston,
Ken Fraser be thy name.
Give us this day our 10%
And forgive us for selling for cash.
Drive us not into the hands of Canadian Fish
But deliver us from poverty
And let the buyers and packers have the glory forever.

In 1953 Ken moved to Head Office in Vancouver in charge of production. He continued to rise in the management ranks and in a sense came to define the fishing industry of the day. He became vice-president in charge of production and in addition, in 1961, became president of Western Canada Whaling Corporation, the partnership with Japan's Taiyo Gyogyo fisheries company.

He spearheaded an industry initiative to buy British products in the post war period, in order to make it possible for Britain to reestablish its market for Canadian canned salmon.

In 1964, Ken became president of B.C. Packers Ltd. But like others of his colleagues, his management style was inimical to Westons—the majority owners—and he eventually took his retirement. He became a consultant and a Director of Sealife Fisheries, which operated herring reduction facilities in Nova Scotia—and he continued in that role until his untimely death in 1977.

A.L. Hager

Alvah L. Hager was a Boston man, born there in 1876. In 1901, he began a business distributing west coast salmon to Boston and New York dealers. In 1908 he arrived in Vancouver to better supervise that business which now included halibut. The Canadian Fishing Co., Ltd. had been established in 1905 by five Vancouver men, including Capt. Absolem Freeman, to produce halibut for the New England Fish Company out of Boston.

Al Hager took over active management of The Canadian Fishing Co. in 1909 and soon had it operating a fleet of halibut fishing vessels. These were steam vessels and included the *Celestial Empire, Carlotta G. Fox, Canada,*

Pescawha, Borealis, Kingsway, Emma H., Imbrecaria, Flamingo, Capilano, and the *New England.*

In 1910, the company built the Home Plant at the foot of Gore Avenue, in Vancouver—a large freezing, cold storage and ice-making plant. But it wasn't until 1918 that Canfisco entered the salmon canning end of the industry with the construction of their first cannery at Home Plant. Al Hager steered the company through a long period of steady growth to become the second largest fishing company in British Columbia. He pioneered many new techniques in fishing and processing, particularly in freezing technology and quality control.

In 1924, B.C. Fishing and Packing Co. was assessing various companies and their management with a view to amalgamation and in regard to Al Hager, they wrote, "He is one of the best-informed fish dealers on this continent, a hard worker, of great executive capacity and is highly regarded in the business community." High praise from a competitor!!

But he is probably best remembered for his leadership in conservation of fish stocks and in the organization of international treaties with the United States. He was a driving force behind the International Pacific Halibut Treaty (1923), and the International Pacific Salmon Fisheries Treaty which was signed between the two countries in 1937 with the objects of preserving and rehabilitating the Fraser River sockeye runs and regulating the division of the catch between the fishermen of the two countries.

Along with his contemporaries, like H.O. Bell-Irving and Capt. Richard E. Gosse, he recognized the damage that was being done to the Fraser stocks with the development of the so-called Puget Sound net and trap fisheries which were able to so effectively intercept the Fraser-bound fish in U.S. waters, especially off Point Roberts. He and the others worked for many years to have the two countries cooperate for the sake of the salmon. He was the first chairman of the International Pacific Salmon Fisheries Commission (The Fraser River Commission).

Al Hager was also a keen "sportsman" and had his own private collection of big game trophies from the Pacific Northwest. That collection was donated to the province and housed at the B.C. Building in Hastings Park.

Fred Kohse

Fred Kohse was the ultimate fisherman—an innovator and a highliner (and story teller and philosopher). His whole life was the fishing industry and he was a keen and unrelenting student of the resources and where they lived. It wasn't enough to be successful at catching fish; he had to know why they were where they were and what natural systems determined their abundance or lack of it.

Fred's father and uncle had come to Canada in 1907. Their home was in East Prussia and they had trained as *maitre d*'s in Hamburg and had worked in France and England. Arriving in Canada, they worked in the CPR hotels—first the Chateau Frontenac, then Banff Springs and finally in the Empress in Victoria.

Fred was born in Victoria in 1914. When World War I was declared, because his father did not yet have his papers as a British subject he and his family were interned as enemy aliens at the Vernon military camp.

After the war, Fred's father became interested in boats and gained a reputation as being reliable. He was hired to operate boats out of Victoria for rum-running, which was a thriving industry during the 1920s. Eventually he bought land near Kelsey Bay for farming where, to quote Fred, "it pretty near broke your heart to grow radishes." They sold beef and potatoes to the logging camps and it was here that Fred grew up.

His first attempt at commercial fishing was in 1929, when he and his brother-in-law rowed to Smiths Inlet to try their hand at gillnetting. Their destination was LeRoy Bay cannery where Mr. Stump, the manager, was an acquaintance. But they arrived too late to get a net so they went over to Margaret Bay where Bill Trotter was manager. Bill Trotter had a long career in Canfisco canneries, being manager at Margaret Bay, Lagoon Bay and Gulf of Georgia, and was universally liked and respected. But he didn't make a good impression on Fred Kohse, supplying him with a leaky skiff and a rotten net. In spite of that, Fred and his brother-in-law made money on the sockeye by the simple expedient of following the highliner and setting where he did. In the fall, Fred rowed again to Smiths Inlet and fished fall fish out of LeRoy Bay.

The boys fixed up some old boats for gillnetting and trolling in the 1930s, interspersed with some stints in logging camps. And by 1941, Fred had built the *B.C. Troller* for salmon fishing. He claims that he "never got very good at salmon fishing," but he was more successful than he would admit.

In 1946, he sailed to Chile on a mission to sell a vessel belonging to Mercer Shipyards and Vivian Engine Works.

The *B.C. Troller* led to the *B.C. Producer* in 1950, with which he fished salmon and halibut and dragged for groundfish. His halibut fishing took him to the Bering Sea and he became one of the premier producers in that fishery.

He built the *Sleep Robber* in 1956, determined to get into herring seining. (The *Sleep Robber* got its name from Mao Tse Tung's Long March. His guerilla troops used to raid Chiang Kai Chek's camps at night, keeping them from getting their rest and they were called the sleep robbers. Fred thought that would be an appropriate name for a seine boat.)

"Before that, I was fishing halibut in season and I'd be out there in the winter dragging while those fat cats were on the herring, fishing in the inlets and everything. And I wanted to get in that.

"Tony Vick got me down to see Rosenberg (Canadian Fishing Co.) and I ran into Dick Jack. Old Mr. Prince claimed that he looked like one of those totem poles at Alert Bay. Anyway, I went to see him and I said, 'Gee, it's quite a change. The last time I saw you was in Bones Bay. You were looking after the store and everything. I came in with an old gillnet boat. I remember giving you a twenty dollar bill and you looked at it and whistled and you said, 'You don't see many of them around these days.'

"And I said, 'Here I am now coming up to build a ninety thousand dollar boat to go out on the herring.' He says, 'What makes you think you know anything about herring fishing?'

"So he got talking like this and I thought, 'Well, gee, there's no good to go up to see Mr. Rosenberg when Dick Jack talks that way already.' So I never got up to see Rosenberg. Tony Vick was madder than the dickens about this.

"So, I went to see Richie Nelson and asked him, if I built a boat, if I could get a net. He says, 'Sure, there's no problem there at all.' So, that's how I got started on building the *Sleep Robber* and she was finished in 1956." And that started his long association with Nelson Brothers Fisheries.

His next boat was the *Eastward Ho*. He fished it on halibut off Alaska and then in 1969, took it to Newfoundland to fish herring for Nelbro's plant in Port aux Basques. He returned to the west coast in 1973. Refrigerated seawater had been developed by the Fisheries Research Board and the *Eastward Ho* was one of the first vessels to be fully rigged with RSW.

In the meantime, he and his partners were building the *Southward Ho* for Atlantic coast herring fishing. But that fishery was depending on a single year class and was fished out in a few years with drastic results for many people who had invested in it. The *Eastward Ho* and the *Southward Ho* both fished hake for the Russian motherships. Subsequently, the *Eastward Ho* continued on the Bering Sea halibut and the *Southward Ho* went to the South China Sea for experimental fishing under the United Nations' FAO. This led to B.C. Packers tuna operation in the Philippines. Fred returned from there for the last time in 1981 and then retired. He kept his active interest in the fishery until his death in 2001 at age 87.

Ron McLeod

Ron was another one that was born with gills. His father was fishery officer at Tofino and that's where he began his days. Even as kids, he and his friends would go out on the small seiners that were based at Tofino for a week at a time. Fishing and boats were their playthings. Tofino was a Scots, Norwegian,

Japanese community—abut 160 people, plus the three Indian villages nearby at Opitsat, Clayquot and Ahousat. From here, over the next few pages, Ron tells his own story of his early days in the fishing industry.

"As kids, in the morning, it would be like a flotilla going out of Tofino, going out to catch coho or whatever, two people to a canoe or the odd one had a rowboat. One would be paddling and the other would work the lines. We were a fishing community. We had the big pilchard fleet that used to come in on west wind days because they couldn't fish in the westerlies—people like Johnny Bidland, Jimmy Goodlad, Johnny Dale and Charlie Clark. They'd let us scramble around the boats and turn the wheel and we'd have all sorts of fun.

"We had an extremely strong *el Nino* in the early '30s. The water would be covered with these Portuguese man o' war jellyfish and there would be droves of them on the beach. And when you went out fishing you were just as likely to catch a sunfish or see an elephant seal —all these exotic creatures. Tofino Inlet was full of Spanish mackerel much to the dismay of the locals. Yet there were record catches of coho and there were quotas set on chums in Barkley Sound.

"In Rivers Inlet, '36 was a record year for sockeye up to that point and there were pilchards in Hakai Pass and in Burke Channel. So even with the exotic predation, the normal stocks were strong, because there was a much wider band of genetic material and a greater diversity of stocks than there is today.

"I went fishing commercially for the first time in 1940 on a local seine boat. In Tofino, if you wanted to go to school you got sent out. I was sent to Victoria when I was 12 years old. Then the war came along and in 1939, a lot of the boys who had joined the Fishermen's navy were called up and they were looking for kids to man the seine boats. And I got a job as crewman on one of them for the summer. The next year I quit school and I fished with a local family. We started in May for sockeye in Barkley Sound and then in Nitinat and we fished until November. It was a long season and mostly 5 days a week. We were hand pulling and the gear efficiency just wasn't there.

"There were about 32 Japanese troll licences at Tofino. There was a limitation on the number that could be issued to them. There were only a handful of whites who were trolling and a few of the Indians. They were more into seining and working in the cannery. There was a cannery at the head of Tofino Inlet at the mouth of the Kennedy River.

"I joined the Fishermen's navy in '43 after working at the Tofino airport when they were clearing land there. We were still fishing and basically we were the eyes and ears. We were to observe, record and report. Some of the patrols would be around the Queen Charlottes and others down the coast, checking every inlet. There weren't all that many planes on the coast at that time. There were a few of the navy ones like the old Stranraers that would hardly buck the wind.

"There was a kind of theory that underlay the activity: that the Japanese who fished on the West Coast—Tofino and Ucluelet—and up the mainland coast, had Japanese spies—people who were trained in the Japanese navy—and they were collecting charts and information about places.

"After the war, I went to University for a couple of years, but I couldn't adjust, so I went fishing with Norm Sigmund on the *Seapride II*. We would fish salmon and halibut and then go dragging in the wintertime. But I had always had it in my mind to try the Fisheries Department and so in 1956, I joined DFO. I started in Alert Bay. I was there in 1958 when the great Adams River sockeye run came through there. That was something to behold. I'll never forget one Sunday morning, just after daybreak, we got in the plane and were flying down Johnstone Strait and everywhere you looked, there were fish jumping. The whole place seemed to be alive with fish moving through there. When the fishery started that Sunday afternoon, the seine fleet was like a wedge coming down the centre of Johnstone Strait. They were leapfrogging down the Strait—what a wonderful sight to behold!!

"From there I went to Rivers Inlet for four and a half years and lived at Dawson's Landing. There was only the storekeeper and his wife and four kids and ourselves over the winter. There were maybe forty-seven people in the whole inlet in the winter. People were scattered all around, maintaining their independence. Jim and Jessie Graham were there only in the summers by that time. The Gildersleeves had gone but there was an in-law in Smiths Inlet. There were a few at the Wannock reserve and at Takush village in Smiths.

"In the summer, Goose Bay was the only cannery operating. Stan Milne was manager. Hans Otteson was manager at Wadhams, Ole Anderson at Good Hope and Gordon Gosse at Beaver. Don Main was running Nelsons' camp at Dawson's Landing. Tulloch Western's camp was run by Don Cruikshank.

"There was a family at Takush and they would do the oddest things. They would pile a bunch of people into one of their little boats and there would always be somebody at the pump. And they'd come into Rivers Inlet and they'd be pumping away and all these people would come out of the cabin. They did this even in mid-winter. I remember being in the village once and the only ones there were two young girls about 11 or so and the old Chief who was in his '90s. I said, 'Hi, where is everybody?' 'Oh, they've gone to Alert Bay to see Elvis Presley.' An Elvis movie was playing at the Bay."

Ron went on to become assistant supervisor for District 2 (north of Cape

Caution) in Prince Rupert and then to Vancouver as assistant chief of conservation and protection and then as manager of Northern Operations. In 1974, he was put in charge of the Salmonid Enhancement program. He was in Ottawa from 1979 to 1984, when he retired from the Department of Fisheries and Oceans.

Ron saw the great changes that took place in the fishery and fisheries management from the inside and from the perspective of one who had grown up in a fishing environment, had been a fisherman himself for most species and with most types of gear. His opinions as to what went wrong are insightful. But that sad story is beyond the scope of this work and will have to wait for another one.

Ron was honoured with the Order of Canada in 2002.

Jack McMillan

J.S. McMillan Fisheries Ltd. is now a household name in the B.C. fishing industry. But its founder did it the hard way, with hard work and raw talent, learning the industry from making things happen and taking risks. Jack McMillan was born in Scotland and came to Winnipeg as a child with his parents. In the mid-1930s, he eventually made his way to B.C., where one of his first jobs was at Columbia Cold Storage (later Pacific Coast Terminals) in New Westminster. That was his introduction to the fish business. He introduced groundfish freezing and filleting at Butedale in the 1930s and, in 1940, at Namu, while an employee of Edmunds and Walker. Then, in 1942, he did the same at Klemtu when Lew Hogan built the new plant there. He became production manager for Todds based at B.C. Ice & Cold Storage. But he was happiest when he was working with the fish—his favourites were heading halibut and splitting salmon.

After Todds, he briefly joined Western Fisheries with Eddie Moir and soon after, in the late 1950s, he started his own business, principally halibut bait, and incorporated J.S. McMillan Fisheries Ltd. His strong relationship with the fishermen assured the success of this venture. And he pioneered the import of octopus for halibut bait to go with the herring and gray cod frozen for bait.

He kept track of his sales in a book in his back pocket, a remarkable feat considering the thousands of tons of bait he sold.

In the 1960s, he went into the minkfood business with salmon eggs and livers, at a time when the Japanese market for salmon roe was confined to chum salmon eggs.

As son Barry says, he always had something going.

During the war he was very much involved in the harvesting of fish livers for vitamin oil, including the dogfish, which later came to be associated with him more than anyone. He worked closely with Western Chemicals Ltd., who were major factors in that industry.

Dogfish were considered a curse by the fishermen and by the fishing companies. Dogfish are known to prey on young salmon. When synthetic vitamin A was invented at the end of World War II, the market for dogfish livers—one of the mainstays for that industry—vanished. Many attempts were made, with and without government subsidy, to find an economic use for dogfish. It was Jack McMillan who showed that if they were skinned soon after being caught, the strong ammonia smell and flavour could be avoided. Jack always believed that eventually the dogfish would have a high value. But it wasn't to be in his time. Today, however, dogfish are worth as much or more than pink salmon, for their flesh, for sharkfins, for the medicinal qualities of the cartilage.

J.S. McMillan Fisheries Ltd. was based on these enterprises, but principally on groundfish. And it is the only company in B.C. that has made a long term success of the groundfish industry.

In the 1960s, Jack and Eddie Moir formed Norpac Seafoods Ltd., and in a few years the McMillans became the sole owners. Norpac Seafoods, with its plant on Commissioner Street (the former Fishermen's Coop and Tulloch Western plant), was rolled into J.S. McMillan Fisheries Ltd. in 1980, with the two McMillan boys, Barry and Danny, as owners.

Jack was not keen on expanding his business, but his sons were. They entered the northern industry by purchasing the former Babcock plant in Prince Rupert, which was then owned by Queen Charlotte Fisheries Ltd. It consisted of a two-line cannery, cold storage and fresh fish facility. And very soon it had a groundfish line.

Their production was such that they needed a bigger plant and when, in 1993, the Prince Rupert Fishermen's Co-op plant in Rupert harbour became available, J.S. McMillan bought it. And the company is now one of the principal firms in the B.C. fishing industry.

Art Miller

Art Miller was one of those British Columbia people, literally raised "at the cannery." Art was born in New Westminster in 1913 and in 1916, he and his brothers and sister went to Ecoole in Barkley Sound with their mother who had been hired to "make fish" at that new plant. Making fish meant using the Scotch cure to preserve herring. The Miller family had come from Caithness in Scotland, where both Art's parents were involved in the fishing industry—he with boats and nets and she in processing herring.

Art's father had gone overseas at the beginning of the First World War and skippered a naval ship on convoy duty in the North Atlantic. Mrs. Miller's knowledge of fish curing was known and she was invited to Ecoole. She was also instrumental in recruiting other women—all Scottish—who knew the process as well.

At the end of the war, Art's father was hired by Gosse Packing Co. as netboss at San Mateo and the family moved there. In 1921, he was netboss at Gosse's plant at Bella Bella and Mrs. Miller was forelady. Art credits Dick Gosse, who was the manager at Bella Bella, with teaching him and his brothers the fishing industry from a very early age. Art was always an eager learner. Of course, these cannery kids grew up with fish and boats and that knowledge was always in demand.

The Bella Bella cannery burned in1923 and Gosse Packing Co. bought Namu and Kimsquit from the R.V. Winch interests. Art recalls, 'when the fire burned the cannery down in 1923, they didn't know if they were going to get it rebuilt for '24. So the Gosses bought out the cannery at Namu. My Dad went down there and was netboss at Namu until 1946. Dick Gosse came down too and Moorehouse was sent to Bella Bella because they got the cannery ready and they had the two canneries running. And Kimsquit, too, which they had bought at the same time."

Bella Bella, Namu and Kimsquit all became part of the B.C. Packers' stable of canneries when the amalgamation with Gosse Packing Co. took place in 1928.

As soon as he was old enough, Art was working in the netloft and then on the boats. He was on the packers out of Namu until 1941, when he went into the airforce. But his first job was in 1927 when he was 14. Art remembers: "I was working for my Dad and we were dyeing nets. Before that, they had the white linen nets and they fished alright at night. And my Dad said, 'If we could get a colour like the water, you could fish during the day, too.' So we were colouring them green. So we had steam tanks, and I would get that up to a rolling boil and I had a certain amount of dye to put in it and the guys would throw their nets in and we'd put a wooden deal over the top with a couple of rocks on it. And we'd let it set for so long. But if you ever bluestoned the net, you couldn't do it, because it would turn purple.

"I remember one old fellow came there and he said he wanted his net dyed. I said, 'Well, did you bluestone it?' 'Never mind, young fellow if I bluestoned it or not.' I said, 'Well, it'll turn purple.' He said, 'Never you mind, I want it dyed!' So I turned on the steam and I boiled it and I got it ready and he threw the net in. When it came out it came out purple and he looked at me, 'Young fellow, you were right.' That's all he ever said."

As in all the canneries, May 24th was a big day and the Gosse company made sure their employees had a celebration in upcoast style. And very often, they took the crew to Ocean Falls for July 4th, which was celebrated there by the company owners, who were American. Art grew up with Indian kids at Bella Bella and Namu and knew them all his life. He comments on one of the issues of today, "You know, you listen to the radio and you hear that these Indian people didn't get a chance. But now you see all these that are teachers and lawyers and those are the people that picked themselves up and went and learned. Everybody had a chance. I can remember when I was a kid and the Union steamboat used to come in and pick up these kids and take them back to school at Alert Bay or Chilliwack. Those kids were all excited. They weren't gathered up and pushed on that boat. It was the big event of the year. Now they say they were taken away from their families. I don't believe that."

Art served his time on the boats in the 1930s. He also took courses in diesel engines and was well placed when they became standard in the packing fleet. He took his high school at Duke of Connaught in New Westminster and then business college, graduating in 1930. He had intended to be a bookkeeper, but the job that was available was on the Koskeemo for Packers Steamships. Later he was 2nd Engineer on the Koprino and became a Master Mariner.

He went back to Namu in 1935. He tells of the pilchards in the mainland waters—a rarity even when they were plentiful on the west coast of the Island. "Up in Kwatna in '36, there were all kinds of pilchards. There was a gang came down from Rupert. One of the Skogs came down and I went to work with them. All they had to do was set and they'd get these big schools of pilchards. I couldn't understand it at first, but one of the scientific fellows told me that once the pilchards started to head south, they kept heading south and they won't follow a shore, so they'd get trapped in a bay. We were in Kwatna until it started to snow and the pilchards were coming belly up it was so cold. Johnny Dale and them were all up there fishing them and packing them down to the west coast. That was the year they built the reduction plant at Namu and they got the pilchards and the herring.

"When the salmon finished, I would scout the country around there for herring. I'd take the *W10* or one of those boats and scout for herring all over— into Rivers Inlet and wherever. And around Calvert Island, they could fish them night or day, they were so thick. I remember the *W8*, Sam Humschitt, he set out and put his skiff on the net and the net went down and it was down for half an hour. One of the seine boats grabbed the corkline and they still brailed 800 tons out of it.

"One year, the herring were so thick. We got all kinds one night and we got all our packers loaded and I was towing scows back and forth to Namu, keeping the plant going. Two or three scows at a time. We got everything loaded and the next morning the boats went out and not a herring. They disappeared just like that.

"But all through my career, there's been years or even two years when there's been no fish of some kind. Look at the coho. We had no coho for a couple of years and the companies started to encourage people to use pinks because they thought the cohoes were finished. And then the cohoes started to come back and they started freezing them. And the Indians told me that some of the rivers, even before the white fellows came, would be barren and they'd have to move their hunting ground to some other river to get enough for the winter."

Art served in the airforce during World War II. After discharge in 1945, he went back to Namu on the boats for about a year, where he was in charge of all the floating equipment. Then to the big boats out of head office.

In 1953, Art joined the Department of Fisheries, Protection Branch and was put in charge of Rivers Inlet. He was with the Protection Branch until 1965, when he was transferred to the Inspection Branch where he remained until his retirement in 1978—a lifetime in the B.C. fisheries.

Donovan Miller

Don Miller spent all of his working life in the B.C. fishing industry and most of that with The Canadian Fishing Co. He was primarily a head office man but, being responsible for the company's personnel and industrial relations, and later, as president of the company, he was intimately associated with the staffing and operations of the outlying plants. He even spent a year as manager of the Home Plant in Vancouver.

Anglo-B.C. Packing Co. was Don Miller's first experience in the fishing industry. He started there as office boy in 1937. As he tells it, "The reason I went there was that I had been working for Johnson Motors at $30.00 a month, and Bell-Irvings offered me $60.00 a month and I felt, 'My God, any firm that could afford double my salary must be a good outfit to stay with.'"

In 1941, he left to join the Navy, and after the war and after attaining a Bachelor of Commerce degree at the University of British Columbia, he went back to Anglo-B.C. The pay was better but the job was still office boy, so Donovan approached Canfisco in 1947 and was hired as assistant to George Clark, who was then manager of personnel and industrial relations (later to become federal Deputy Minister of Fisheries).

Don succeeded to that job and later to president of Canfisco. But he became a tireless external affairs representative of the B.C. industry and this was his principal contribution to its well-being. He and Bill Harrison of B.C. Packers, took the lead in countering the plans of B.C. Electric Company to harness the

Fraser and Thompson Rivers for hydroelectric power—a fight that took over two decades to win and the dedication of many industry and government individuals.

At one time, Gordon Shrum, who was dean of science at the University of British Columbia at the time (and later, Chairman of B.C. Hydro), proposed that B.C. Electric would be willing to provide pensions for all the fishermen who fished on the Fraser River, so that the river would be used for power production. According to Miller, Shrum also had an idea involving the pink salmon which would still spawn in the lower reaches of the river. "He would have his research staff develop a dye which would turn the flesh of the pink salmon into a more reddish-orange colour, to fool the public into thinking it was sockeye or coho."

Don Miller was a member of the Fisheries Research Board of Canada from 1959 to 1963. He developed a high regard for the scientists employed by the board and for his industry colleagues from across the country. And that regard was reciprocated. He was one of the four Canadian commissioners on the International North Pacific Fisheries Commission (Canada, Japan and United States), from 1964 to 1987. This was the commission which controlled and terminated the Japanese drift net fishery for salmon in the eastern north Pacific.

At various times, he represented the industry on the Advisory Council to the Minister of Trade and Commerce, on the Advisory Council to the federal Minister of the Environment, on the Canada-Japan Businessmen's Cooperative Committee, on the Canada-Japan Society of British Columbia, on the Science Council of British Columbia and on the Asian-Pacific Economic Cooperative Conference.

He chaired an industry-government committee that organized the first Salute to the Sockeye on the Adams River in 1958. This was the industry's Centennial Project (the centenary of the formation of the colony of British Columbia). And it has been continued every fourth year ever since on the Adams River sockeye dominant year.

Don was president of the Fisheries Council of Canada in 1964/65. Along with Bob Payne of Canfisco and one-time President of J.H. Todd and Sons, they prepared a position paper for the Fisheries Council, which eventually led to the adoption by Canada of the 12 mile territorial sea. This was a pre-omen of the United Nations Law of the Sea Conference, which resulted in international recognition of the 200 mile limit of jurisdiction.

From 1975 to 1978, Donovan served as chancellor of the University of British Columbia, the second fishing industry executive (John Buchanan being the first) to be elected to this high office. And he was one of only a very few industry people to be awarded the Order of Canada.

Ross Nicholson
Ross S. Nicholson was one of those people who saw the fishing industry as exciting and helped make it that way. He was a people person, larger than life and totally wrapped up in his vocation.

Ross was born in Vancouver in 1907. He went to Vancouver Tech and King Edward High schools and at 17, found himself in Stewart and a job in the freight office on the dock. He was interested in sports and played both baseball and basketball—Stewart against Hyder, Alaska and Premier gold mines. In fact, he became basketball coach for Premier during his first winter there.

He chose 1930 to leave Stewart, when jobs were not easy to come by, but Ross kept an income working first in Turner Valley, Alberta and then at Wallace Shipyards in North Vancouver, then in California and then at Whitehorse on the Yukon River boats and finally, selling real estate in Victoria.

Ross began his long association with B.C. Packers in 1936 at Shannon Bay cannery on Masset Inlet. In those days, the manager in Smiths Inlet (in this case, Frank Nason), was also the manager at Shannon Bay for the pink salmon fishery. Ross' first job was to prepare the cannery for processing. He speaks of H.R. McMillan arriving there by float plane. H.R. was president of B.C. Packers at the time and he must have been one of the first to use bush plane flying to keep contact with the far flung plants. But even with that, the cannery crews could not depend on outside services. Ross tells of his mechanic, a man from Queen Charlotte City, "One day, the top blew off one of the steam engines which operated the lines. Joe picked up the pieces and put it back together. If he hadn't done that, we would have been stuck as far as operating was concerned."

In those days, too, the bookkeepers and in some cases the managers were laid off at the end of the season. This happened to Ross at the end of his first season and he was lucky enough to get back on at Wallace Shipyards.

The next spring he went back to B.C. Packers and was never laid off again. He was at Sunnyside, then buying fish in the Charlottes, then to Port Edward where he worked as bookkeeper for Mac McLean.

Port Edward was a reduction-only plant. One of Ross' stories from 1940 illustrates the conditions that existed even in those days. One night, one of our crew got caught in the worm for taking the herring out of the bins. We had the RCMP bring a doctor out from Prince Rupert. In the meantime, I had my First Aid certificate, and I got a pillow under his leg and got Mac to back up the worm and we pulled him out of it. We put him on the messhouse table and put hot water bottles all around him. When the doctor arrived, he looked at it and he said, 'Ross, there's no need of taking that leg into Rupert.' He cut it off right there. We had to take him into Rupert. It was stormy and the RCMP wouldn't go out again, so we took him in one of our boats. Old George Fritz was the skipper and he said, 'I can go anyplace,' and we got him into Rupert hospital."

Ross managed the Smiths Inlet operation in 1941 and then was sent to Tofino to see why B.C. Packers were not getting their share of the pilchard catch. "We had eight seine boats. Canfisco had eight and Nelsons had eight. Nelson delivered up to Ceepeecee, Canfisco at Nootka and we had Kildonan." Fishing in the open Pacific, the seine boats had to have their nets towed off by the packers. The problem was that the packers were not being unloaded promptly at the plant and returned to the grounds and so the seiners could not fish. Ross, ignoring the niceties of diplomacy, got the problem solved.

In 1942, Ross became manager at Port Edward and was responsible for buying halibut for the company at the Prince Rupert Halibut exchange—a unique auction system where the members of the exchange bid each day on the catches of the halibut vessels as they came into port. Doug Souter, Sr. was his bookkeeper and between the two of them, they ran Port Edward and Pacofi in the Charlottes.

Ross tells us something of wartime conditions at Pacofi. "There was that big army deal at Sandspit. Down comes this big speedboat with this general or major, whatever he was, from the Canadian army. We talked for a minute and he said, 'You know, we're putting on a big dance and I would like very much if you and your wife came up to it.' Now I had all the girls from Skidegate and Queen Charlotte City working down at the cannery—every one of them. So I said, 'My wife isn't with me and besides, it's those girls you want, isn't it?' He laughed and he said, 'You're not so dumb. What about it?' I said, 'I'm sure that they would like to go.'

"So I called Becky Pearson in, she was in charge of the girls, and told her what the proposition was. She was from Skidegate and a real nice person. She said, 'Holy gosh, that sounds wonderful; you grab it.'

"So Saturday night, down came these two big speedboats. They loaded all the girls on and they were all dolled up and they had a wonderful time.

"But I used to have a dance most every Saturday night—in the netloft. And the loggers would come over. We had to prohibit smoking because of all the nets and oil, etc. One night these two loggers were smoking inside and when I challenged them, they said, 'We'll smoke where we want,' and they got pretty snotty. So I closed down the dance and announced why and told them that in the future there would be no loggers allowed. So that was it and boy, was everybody after those two guys."

In 1943, Ross was put in charge of acquiring fish out of head office, succeeding Ken Fraser, who had become Manager of Imperial plant. But the Company had bought Albert & McCaffery in Prince Rupert to acquire the majority interest in the Northern Fishermen's Cold Storage which McCaffery owned and Ross was asked to take over the operation. And he built the fish shed and unloading facilities under difficult wartime conditions when everything in Rupert was controlled by the U.S. armed forces.

In 1945, he returned to head office as acquiring manager and held that position until he retired in 1969. During those years, Ross was involved in many of the innovations that took place—the first seine boat catches of Adams River sockeye off Port Renfrew; the daily conference calls by radiotelephone with the plants and the fleet; the Canadian fishery for pinks on the west coast which forced the Americans to agree to include pink salmon in the International Pacific Salmon Fisheries Convention; the installation of echo sounders on the seine boats; the introduction of lights or pitlamps for fishing herring; the development of drum seining; and the first commercial herring roe operation.

Ross was a people person and his ability to have good relations with his people, particularly the fishermen, was his strongest asset as a company manager. He was especially well-liked by the Indian people of the north coast and the Queen Charlotte Islands. He was actually a blood brother of the Kincolith band on the Nass River—an honourific title, but one rarely given.

John and Peter Wallace

The Wallace brothers came from Blackwater Foot, a small village on the Isle of Arran in Scotland, to Astoria on the Columbia River in the 1880s. They entered the fish business primarily for sturgeon and became the main producers. But they and those who emulated them soon fished out the sturgeon and the Wallaces turned to the famed Columbia River Spring salmon from which they made salted salmon and mild cure. They were singularly successful in this and developed their own markets in Chicago and New York to which they shipped over the new railroads.

The sturgeon of the Fraser River drew them north and they established John Macmillan there to buy sturgeon on the Fraser and Pitt Rivers and to prepare them for shipment to the eastern United States. Macmillan used space in the Bon Accord cannery for his production. Very soon, the Fraser sturgeon were fished out as well, and Macmillan turned to spring salmon and the production of mild cure.

Around 1900, he heard of the great redsprings on the Skeena River and advised the Wallaces to have a look. In no time they were making mildcure in

Cunningham's plant at Port Essington which had a small cold storage. The Wallaces reorganized themselves, moved their operations to the Skeena and in 1900, bought Claxton cannery. They upgraded the cannery and built a cold storage plant.

In 1905, John Wallace bought the Pacific Northern cannery on Observatory Inlet and moved the machinery to the lower Nass River and built his Arrandale cannery.

In 1909, Wallace Brothers Fisheries Ltd. purchased Alberni Packing Co.'s Uchucklesit cannery. They renamed it Kildonan and it became part of the transfer to Wallace Fisheries Ltd. when that company was formed in 1910.

The Wallace brothers had, at some point, ceased to work well together, and in December of 1910, they sold out to Alexander D. McRae, who formed Wallace Fisheries Ltd. and was its principal shareholder. Peter Wallace was also a major shareholder and was its first president. John sold his Arrandale cannery to Anglo-B.C. Packing Co. in 1911 and built Butedale. (Thus his home islands of Arran and Bute were memorialized in British Columbia.) Western Packers Ltd. bought Butedale from him in 1917 and John retired to Scotland. Peter's son Tom became Manager of Claxton and after the amalgamation of Wallace Fisheries with B.C. Fishing and Packing Co. in 1928, he became B.C. Packers Ltd.'s northern manager based at Sunnyside. He was an icon of the Skeena River until he retired in the 1960s.

Chapter 21

GLIMPSES OF CANNERY LIFE

Everyone who worked in the outlying canneries has memories and stories to tell. Surprisingly, most don't see their experiences as anything out of the ordinary. But they were. Here are a few of them.

Joe Antonelli
"When we were going to high school in Prince Rupert in the '30s, during the summer holidays in July and August, I went up to North Pacific cannery with a bunch of other kids and I got a job there pughing fish for 20 cents an hour—sometimes for 14 hours a day.

"At Canadian Fish and Cold Storage in Seal cove, Harry Jr. and I were loading the fresh rail cars with fresh halibut in big crates, loaded with halibut and ice. And we loaded five or six cars at a time. We'd then go on the top of the cars and open the trap door and we'd break up the 300 pound block of ice and put in 125 pounds of salt (the salt bags weighed just as much as I did) with it and that's how we bunkered the cars. It took about six days to get to New York.

"Once we were hauling nets over the roller and here was a big shark about nine feet long. Everybody whooped and hollered because shark liver at that time was about six or seven dollars a pound (during the war). And we prayed that it was a female—if it was a male, it was useless, they have small livers—because the female's liver was maybe three feet long and one liver used to more or less fill a can. That's 240 bucks and that was a hell of a lot of money in those days. We were getting about 40 cents a pound for dogfish livers. Doug Souter gave us slips and every so often, paid us with a cheque."

Bill Babcock
"I was working in a furniture factory on 2nd Avenue (in Vancouver) and

I cut my finger off. My Dad was fishing halibut on the Annie Tuck and when he saw this he made me get out of it. And he took me down to Gosse Packing Co. and they sent me to San Mateo cannery in Barkley Sound with another chap by the name of Billy Malcolm. That was 1928 and I was 16. Billy was the storekeeper and I was his assistant. The following winter, they sent me to Kildonan, which was a cannery and next door to it was Green Cove Salteries. They used to pack chum salmon in 300- or 400-pound boxes.

"I fished on a seine boat called the Skill in Nitinat Lake. And there were some cabins at the head of lake. So I took what little money I had (it was the Depression), and bought shells for the shotgun and flour and milk and so on, and I got a ticket on the *Maquinna* to Clo-oose, where they used to stop. And I went to the head of the lake and to my surprise there were three other guys there that I knew. We stayed there all winter. I made a net and fished that early run of sockeye at the Hobart River. Johnny Clark was the production manager for Nelson Brothers and he came in there with his camp to buy the sockeye. I went to work for him on the camp buying fish.

"The cannery at Nitinat only operated the one year I was there. It originally belonged to an American.

"About Joe Babcock. The *Annie Tuck* was built right here in Burrard Inlet in 1919. It was built by three Newfoundlanders who used the Atlantic coast style of vessel. That's why she had that long prow—schooner style. The story of why he wore the bowler hat fishing—it was a result of a fire that burnt all the hair off his head. And he couldn't find a hat that would give him comfort, so he bought a bowler. The top was hard and light and it didn't come in contact with this head except at the brim."

Epp Arbeider

"When I was at Goose Bay, the Indians on the seine boats, they were the music people—guitars and brass instruments. We had Saturday night dances when the girls were there. They were in the girls' bunkhouse, which was the biggest place. At that time, the fishermen were fishing five days a week, so they just had Saturday. And Sunday, they had to get ready to go out again; they had to bluestone all the nets and all that.

"We sometimes had a picnic on the 24th of May just at the mouth of Schooner Pass. There was a nice big sandy beach there. I remember once we found a skull there. The Indians had had a war—the Bella Bellas and the Owikenos—and they had a big battle there around the turn of the century and just about wiped out all the Owikenos.

"You could go a long way up the river at Kildala in a speedboat. But later they logged in there and ruined it. They also started running logs through the

Wannock River to salt water and that was the downfall of Rivers Inlet.

"At Goose Bay, the machines were run by steam engine. There was one upstairs for the reform line and the main one for the cannery. That ran the main shaft and all the belts came off that.

"We used to have an RCMP guy posted at Goose Bay during the canning season. He was from the Vancouver detachment. We supplied him with a house and he stayed around the plant most of the time."

Marvin Eckert

"When we fished with the sailboats, we got the boats for nothing. If you wanted to take a company net, they used to give us 30 cents apiece for sockeye and 2½ cents apiece for humps and 7½ cents for dog salmon—this was in the early days. And spring salmon, it didn't matter if it weighed 50 pounds or 10 pounds, you only got 50 cents for it. If you had a company net, that's what you got, but if you bought the net, they'd give you 5 cents more for your fish.

"On Sundays, the packers would all line up in front of the canneries and you'd row out and get on the towline and then they'd take off. You could get off whenever you wanted to. One guy would get in the stern and the other guy would be up in the bow and when you wanted to get off, you'd let the bow go first and the boat would swing out and the guy would let the stern line go and that would shoot you off to the side so you would clear the other boats. And in the river (Skeena), they used to have the boats running up and down and towing you back for the sets. They'd come right down by Oceanic and they'd pick you up and tow you way upriver if you wanted to go upriver. We did lots of rowing too. And especially night times or early morning if we wanted to get back in around Lawyer Light or any of those places. If the wind was blowing right, we'd put the sail up. There's all kinds of guys that drowned with those things, off those old sailboats.

"They converted all the sailboats into gas boats. Most of them was 5-horse Easthopes and Vivians. They were one-cylinder. Then we got two-cylinder Easthopes and they called them 10-horse. Then they made 3-cylinder ones. The sailboats were 28 feet long and most of them had 8 feet beam. They made a nice gasboat. Usually it was the Japs that were converting them at the cannery because some of the Japs stayed there all winter, at Carlisle.

"The first boat I bought, the Sakamoto boys made it. That was just about when the war broke out. It was at Carlisle and it wasn't quite finished yet when they came and took all the Japs out of there. The navy came and took all the Japs out. I felt sorry for those Japanese—the guys had their god-damned guns with the bayonets on and everything. All they could take with them was a suitcase and a blanket."

Ed Eyford
"The kids used to have to walk the tracks from Cassiar to Sunnyside because that's where the school was.

"One year there was a strike and my Dad and the white guys and the Japanese guys were all worried about when they were going to go back to work. They were all stressed out about it, but the Natives were all out playing basketball—they weren't too worried.

"At times, at Port Edward, the Japanese people would invite you up to their house for a drink. It was Scotch on the rocks and if it wasn't a small glass, it was a job to get away. All the races got along. But you always had to be careful. If you said the wrong thing at the wrong time, if you were alone, things could happen.

"I was sent to Port Simpson when they were building that new cannery there. That plant was really political. There was a bunch of government funding but the funding was set up so that all these different tribes had to have x number of people working at the plant and they didn't get along.

"The Rupert Co-op built the crab cannery in 1961. Then they added a half-pound salmon line in 1963.

"When I was in the canneries, American Can owned all the canning machinery and it was part of your tinplate contract. They used to do all the major overhauls. We used to haul a whole line out of the cannery, crate it all up and the steamer would come in and we'd load it up and send it down to Vancouver. It would come back up in the spring and we'd put it all back in place. We would do a line a year."

Eric Kremer
"At Namu, we would get a tremendous amount of people. We'd have a payroll of about 400 to 500 people in the summertime at the peak. That pink run up there always has a lead time. It's either the last two weeks of July and the first two of August, depending of the year. And we'd have Rivers and Smiths sockeye. We'd get into chums with the pinks—particularly in the Bella Coola area, they'd come with the pinks and extend out longer. That's when they still canned chums.

"We had a two-room school that had two teachers on a year-round basis. We had a bowling alley and a rec committee, which was a volunteer function, to look after it. We had basketball in the gym and dances there in the summer. You went to bed Saturday night and shut the door and hoped everything was still standing Sunday morning.

"One of the big things in the summer would be the annual visit by Bing Crosby and Phil Harris. They would hire a yacht and cruise the coast, fishing.

They'd park their yacht in front of the cannery. You could just forget about work for awhile. Instead of a 15 minute coffee break, it might be 30 or 45 by the time everybody shakes their hands and says hello and gets an autograph (and Bing sings Indian Love Call).

"There were lots of characters. Usually one of the characistics was too much to drink. There were a couple of fellows in the village who worked in the reduction plant. We had one seine boat, maybe two, that had found herring about half an hour away. But we didn't know that. It was just around the corner at a place called Second Bay. It opened a 2 o'clock Sunday afternoon in those days. This guy's in at 4 o'clock with a load. He was back in again at 7 and this went on all night. So I went over to chase the unloaders out at 4 o'clock. And I knew that there was a party going in the village. They all sing songs and clap hands and drink their brew. These guys were sitting around and singing and doing their thing and I was banging on the door and calling them out. They don't want to go to work. So I continued on down the walkway to get some more people out and came back again and here they are trying to get into their rubber pants and swearing away at me for calling them to work. They did come.

"The store had a staff of about ten or twelve. A butcher and a helper, a hardware guy and a helper, somebody in dry goods, a couple in the grocery, a couple more part time. The store was year round, but only a few working there in the winter. The restaurant only ran in the summer. It had half a dozen people attached to it. There was always a problem getting staff because they could get more hours and do better in the plant.

"We had a stand-by boat for the hospital. We had an old character on it, Oscar Hansen—standby Oscar. That's all he did and that's all the boat did. It had bunks and first aid and a stretcher, etc."

Art Nielsen
"At Butedale, there were activities you did in the winter time. There was a hall where we played badminton, there were weekly poker games in the time between salmon and herring. It was a good life and you got to meet a lot of people.

"There was a group called the tallymen who would tally and weigh the fish as they came off the boat. They had a little clique of their own and they would challenge the rest of the people sometimes to a water fight. One night after the cannery was shut down and everything washed down, there was a little feud set up to take place and it was the tally dock people against the rest of us. We got in there with the hoses and everything was wet. I was even hung up on a hook and raised so I couldn't touch the floor and my pants were filled with ice. It was all in reasonably good fun.

"During the summer seasons there was a RCMP constable stationed there. One of his duties was confiscating liquor from those that shouldn't have it. And he would take it and put it in the back of his little office. We'd break up into two groups and one group would engage him in conversation and the other half of the group would go in and repossess what had just been taken from them or from somebody else. It wasn't that he didn't know who did it; he just couldn't pin it down.

"The whole place was very well-maintained. It had other attractions. Like for recreation times, you had the lake which was fantastic—628 steps, but good fishing and lovely swimming. We had free power from the waterfall and they had flood lights on all the buildings and on the waterfall.

"We had two seiners that came up from Bella Bella. The rest were Kitimaats. They used to make their own brew. They would get in on Thursday night and they would get hold of whatever vegetables or fruit that were over-ripe and they would start this brew and it would be ready by late Saturday and they would be into it.

"The Saturday night dance was the big thing, of course. Everybody would be in on the weekend, the packers and the seiners and everybody and there were the ladies from the cannery crew. We had a Native band and they were damned good. The hall had a hardwood floor and it was marked out for badminton. There was very good badminton played there."

Don McKay

"The girls at the cannery (Butedale) came from all over. There were a couple from Squirrel Cove, which is as much of an Indian village as you'll find anywhere. They had a Spanish-sounding name and they passed themselves as having Spanish blood. They were cannery workers, but they didn't want to stay in the Native village, they wanted to stay in the white girls' bunkhouse. They claimed they were from Chile and they weren't part of the coastal tribes. But when it came to swinging on a Saturday night, they swung with the best of them.

"Our peak employment was in the salmon season—maybe more than 300. On the weekends, there would be a tremendous transient population when the seiners were in our area. There could be thirty or forty seiners in there with six or seven guys per boat.

"They had a truck there, a fair sized one—two or three ton with a flat deck on it. It would run around to the cold storage and to the reduction plant and there were roads up by where the families lived. And to go down between the bunkhouse and the messhouse, there was a ramp and you were supposed to stop before you got to the bullrail. That didn't happen one day and the guy driving it went over the end with the truck and everything. He had on these big gumboots and he just about didn't come up.

"There was the "Toonerville Trolley" which was one of the ways to make it more attractive for the tourists. These would be from the Corvettes of the Union Steamships or the Alaska cruise trips that would stop and take on salmon on their way south. It was just these little cannery dollies, outfitted with seats and pulled by the lift truck."

Toonerville Trolley, Butedale, 1948

Don Main

"My Dad's first job in the industry (Don Main Sr.) was at Porcher Island in 1933 or 1934. He was the netboss and winter watchman, too. We lived there year round. The cannery had closed down. He stayed there two or three years and then he moved to B.C. Packers at Sunnyside. I remember a bit about Porcher. We had a dog, an Alsatian. We used to have a boat anchored out in the bay and we'd row out to the boat. One time we were rowing out with the dog in the skiff and these wolves were howling on the shore. The dog jumped overboard and swam ashore—that was the end of the dog.

"I was manager at Mill Bay from '56 to '59 when they closed it down. We had 75 gillnetters fishing for us from Kincolith, Greenville and Aiyansh. We worked 7 days a week and there was little time for leisure. But from Sunnyside, we used to go to Kitson Island for picnics—especially the 24th of May. There's a nice sandy beach there.

"I went on the *Samson IV* as manager. That was the original, the old paddle wheel snag boat from the Fraser. I had a crew of 14 on her and she was quite cramped. So we decided to buy a ferry, the old *Kahloke*. She was three storeys high and 150 feet long. We built a boat hoist on the stern and a machine shop, a netloft, electronics shop, office, store, rooms for the crew. We'd tie up at Everett's Landing in Rivers Inlet, in May until the end of July and then we'd move to Seaforth Channel, just north of Bella Bella, for a couple of months and then to Port Harvey in Johnstone Strait for the fall fishing.

"When I was at Rivers Inlet (on the *Samsons*), we used to go up each year to Owikeno Lake with the Fishery officer and inspect all the streams. There were about a dozen streams and we were in there most of a week. They used to blame a lot of the problem on the logging. Both Rivers and Smiths have collapsed since then. The Department did a pretty good job of controlling the fishery when I was there."

Peter Matthews

"My Dad, Bill Matthews was the manager at Glendale Cannery in Knight Inlet. I spent my summers up there as a kid, so I entered the fishing industry at a very early age. I think the happiest times of our lives were up there. We were as free as birds and we had a wonderful time as kids. There were other families up there too with kids that were within a few years of each other in age. We used to play together and got lots of exercise rowing boats, climbing mountains, picking berries and doing all those kid things.

"When we were 12 or 13, we would get jobs when they were busy, piling cans up. There was a special way to pile them and to us, being small, these piles looked like mountains.

"In the inlets, they still had a lot of sailboats for gillnetting. They used to tow them out on Sunday morning. They had a long towline and they had little rings spliced into it. The painter of the skiff went through this ring and they'd feed it back to where the guy was sitting in the middle of the skiff and he'd just put a slip knot in it. Then when he wanted to leave the tow, he'd pull the slip knot undone, put some pressure on one oar and it would steer him away from the rest of the fleet.

"At Glendale, we had a badminton court and that would be the only recreational facility. Wind was a problem! We used to have dances in the netloft. There was one fellow from Kingcome Inlet and he had a bit of a band. And there would be other people who were talented in one way or another. The plant workers and the fishermen would come. There wasn't a great deal organized. We played a lot of cards and dominoes and checkers, and all those board games.

"I worked with a Japanese fellow who owned his own collector. And I knew all his family. They were harmless people, as most of them were, and wouldn't hurt a fly. They were herded out to Hastings Park and then from there they were doled out to various places. They were in Steveston when this happened early in 1942. I felt sorry for the families, the innocent people. They were quite progressive and would have been quite uncomfortable in the conditions in the camps. But they were targets and it wouldn't have taken very much to set some of the white people off like when Estevan was shelled. When they came back, I was in Port Edward. That was in 1948. They all came back and they all seemed to find houses to live in. They were industrious people and it didn't take them long to get back on their feet again. It was remarkable how they did come back after being downtrodden for so many years.

"Two of our A.B.C. seine boats went into the airforce. I was skipper on the *Anna M*. We were supplying all the bases up the coast. I don't know of any of the boats that were armed except maybe the odd one that went around to the west coast. But I know that when I was with the Waterhouse Company, we used to get extra pay for going around the west coast even though the war was officially over. There were mines around, and of course, the Japanese had shelled Estevan, and they thought that was a dangerous run and they paid everybody extra.

"I got a job with Nelson Brothers in the office at Port Edward. My wife came up—we had just been married. She had been a city girl all her life and had spent three years during the war in Washington D.C. with the British government. She had never seen a place like this before. She came up with cocktail dresses and high heels thinking she was going to a big city. But there were boards for sidewalks and gravel for roads.

"It used to be, in the fish business, that everything you did was fun. There were always new adventures. You had loyalty to the company and vice versa.

"All the school children and the mothers used to go to the various canneries in June, either on the old *Venture* or the *Chelohsin* or whatever ship happened to be on that run. And they'd all come home to Vancouver, the last week in August just in time for school. And they got to know each other even though they were at different canneries."

Stan May

"I was 15 years old when I went up the coast to Walker Lake. That was 1926. We got off the CPR boat, the *Princess Mary* and they took us into little two room shacks. I was the youngest kid there and I did all the joe-jobs, like sweeping and cleaning and scraping. I was there one year and I got moved to Namu where I became assistant lineman and then lineman. Then I went to

Arrandale with ABC in '34 or '35. I worked in American Can in the winters, overhauling machines. The Arrandale season was about five months. I was there five or six years then they shut down the cannery.

"Then to Namu with Moorehouse, and then to Carlisle with Clare Salter and I worked at Home Plant in the winters. Then to Butedale as foreman—Lloyd Stewart was the manager. I quit Canadian Fish and went as lineman at Phoenix and became foreman there for fifteen years.

"ABC was the best company I worked for. They were a good outfit. They didn't pay any more money but you were respected and they looked after you.

"We used to go to Port Essington from Carlisle—a whole bunch of us in a boat on Saturday night. And we'd come home with a dozen of those big beer bottles to last you through the week. But we didn't drink much then. If we had a bottle of rum, we used to divide it up between five or six of us at a Saturday dance—but it was overproof, of course.

"I put some time in at Butedale. Winter and summer. That's what finished me there. That whole cannery was pretty shaky. We had it tied to the beach with cables that went right through the rafters, six big cables, to hold it from sliding out to sea. The base was bad too. For two months at a time, I'd have a gang of five or six men just putting piles under there. We used to reform cans. These heavy cases would come in. I was piling them alongside the posts. I couldn't pile them off to the side because I was afraid it would go over. I kept mothering that old cannery as best I could.

"I got lost one time at the top of that creek behind Butedale. It was a hell of a trip in that salal. We used to go hunting on a Sunday after deer. We'd go down the channel and they'd be sitting there with their noses poking out of the bushes. The Indians and all the whites—they slaughtered them.

"The Indians were a problem. You'd get a dozen of them to work but they never did anything. And they drank a lot—home brew. One time, the manager brought the police down to clean out the home brew. There were six of them and he was going to take them to Prince Rupert. They said, 'We'll go; we don't mind.' So they got a free ride on the police boat to Rupert and they really enjoyed it.

"But Salter was a good guy to work for. He was a go-getter, no flies on him. He looked after his fishermen.

"I'll never forget sports day over there at Bella Bella. I outran a bunch of the Indians and got a bunch of prizes. They didn't like it very much. Some of them were good fellows. And they were good shots. They got 5 bucks a nose for seals. They would shoot them when they came up and took air. Not a very big target from a boat.

"Moorehouse would have us all go to church at Bella Bella from Namu. We would stay there for four or five hours and have dinner there. We had to listen to Dr. Darby preach—he spoke partly in Chinook. One young fellow from the Queen Charlottes was there and he knew Chinook and he taught us to sing Nellie Gray in Chinook. I've never forgotten it.

"At Arrandale, the cook was old Tom. The food we used to get was terrible. One of the guys asked, "Why don't you put beans on the table?" So all we got was beans for two solid weeks, every meal."

Don Miller

"Clare Salter was manager at Carlisle, a typical hard nut guy of a cannery manager. I remember once visiting Clare and he was visited by a salesman selling engines for gillnetters. This was a typical salesman type who'd come up the coast to sell the various cannery managers these engines. Clare needed three or four engines so he was entertaining this fellow and the fellow gave his sales pitch and finally Clare said, 'Alright put me down for six.' So the fellow said, 'That's very nice, now can I buy you a drink?' And Clare of course, said yes and the fellow brought out a bottle of rye which was about 2/3 full. He passed it around and everybody had a drink and it was down to about ¼ full. He was going next to Cassiar to try to sell Ewen Macmillan some of these engines. Before he went, he asked Clare if there was a washroom handy. It was adjacent to the office and the door didn't close properly and we saw this fellow filling up the bottle from the tap to 2/3 again (the water was cedar coloured). Clare said, 'You son of a bitch, did you fill that bottle up with cedar water?' Clare said, 'Cancel the order!' Then he got on the radiophone and warned Ewen and asked him to get hold of everybody in the area and let them know this guy feeds you watered-down whisky. That was a big no-no."

Stan Milne

"Quisenberry was quite a guy. One day, he was fixing up the telephone line—we used to have a sort of jury-rigged telephone line that went to Bella Coola from Tallheo, a single line that went right around the bay right on the cliffs. Quis was up the pole and he was pretty cranky in those days. Anyway, Charlie Nappy, who was one of the cultus Indians around there, was drunk. He stood at the bottom of Quisenberry's ladder and was nattering at him. Quis turns and says, 'Charlie, if you don't get the hell out of here, I'm coming down and I'm going to cut you up for the can with these pliers.' Charlie left in a hurry.

"Dick Wagner used to be foreman for Francis Stone at Goose Bay. When Francis quit the fishing industry, Dick went as manager.

"The Islands was an interesting operation (Lagoon Bay). We used to have our crew come down from Skidegate, all the women, they used to have the cannery houses there. They were a different Indian altogether than what the mainland coast Indians were. For example, I came to the office one day and Trotter hands me a note. It's addressed to Stan, bookkeeper and it says Mrs. Frank Jones is having a tea and would be pleased to have your presence. You went into their houses and they were scrubbed clean and curtains up and white tablecloths and everything else. Whereas if you walked into the Indian houses at Margaret Bay, the first thing you would probably see is a seal lying on the table, split with the guts rolling out.

"There's only about four or five left of the Owikeno tribe now. You know, it's a funny thing—they were sort of lazy guys, but they could sure build floats or pile driving or anything like that. They were like cats on logs. And they did good work.

"I never saw Kildala when it was canning. It was just used as a netloft when I was manager. One winter the roof caved in and all those brand new linen nets were in the main building. Some wizard at head office said to go up and chop the roof off and take those nets out and we'll take them down and dry them. It was cold weather and the snow was right level with the tops of the netrack rails. We did as we were told but it was the worst thing we could have done. We should have left it until spring, because they were nice and dry. When we got them out, they were full of shingle nails and pieces of wood.

"When I first started with the company, one of my jobs was to go and spray out the craphouse and the urinal which was an old water tank cut in half. And at the end of the dock was the toilets and they were just planks taken out of the wharf and a rail put up to sit on. The wind used to come up through there doing about 90 miles an hour so you sure as hell didn't waste any time in there.

"The dog salmon used to come into the Lagoon Bay cannery so fresh that you'd have to wait days before you canned them. They had those plunger filling machines there and if they were too fresh, they'd bounce out of the can."

George Olsen

"This guy was working on his engine. There was a part he had to move and he couldn't do it alone, so he called the campman over to give him a hand. The campman said, 'Oh, no, this is my day off.' Some time later, the skipper on the boat got tight. They went to tie up alongside the float there and they got the tie-up line tangled up with the toilet at the end of the float and dumped it overboard with the campman in it. He hollered, 'Give me a hand to get out of here.' And the guy says, 'Oh, no, it's my day off.'

"They were repairing the oil dock. After the piles were driven, they had to be cut off so they could be pulled under the caps and fastened. In this case, Mr. Quisenberry asked Tom Donald to get out on the plank and he would stand on the other end to counteract Tom's weight. Tom wasn't pleased with this deal and told Quisenberry, 'You'll see something wrong and you'll walk off the plank and I'll be in the chuck.' Everything was going great when the dinner bell went. Quis yells, 'Okay boys, twelve o'clock.' And he walks off the plank and Tom, saw and all, went in the chuck.

"Charlie Draney who was manager at Tallheo at the time (c.1930), used to take a run out among the fishermen on Sunday evenings to see how they were making out. This Sunday he was taking the *Kano* out, but couldn't get the engine started. So handyman Bill Julian was called on to get things going. The *Kano* at the time had a gas engine, and when Bill went to start the engine, he forgot to retard the ignition. When he turned the engine over with a bar in the flywheel, it backfired, threw Bill up against the deck, pushing his bowler hat down over his eyes. Back on his feet again, he pulls his hat up and says to Charlie, 'That's the way you start 'er.'

"One day, several of the women hand fillers were missing, so Quisenberry takes a walk to the village to see what gives. He finds several of the women celebrating. 'Where is the home brew?' But none of the women seemed to know where it was. He noticed one of the women sitting in an odd way, so he grabs her by the hand and pulls her to her feet. Here she was sitting on a six-gallon crock of home brew with her skirt draped over the crock. They all laughed when he discovered this but he wasn't long disposing of it.

"One day, Joe Edgar came to Quisenberry to tell him he should do something about this Amos, a fisherman from Kitimaat who was getting involved with his daughter who one of the local boys was courting—and there would be trouble if something wasn't done about it. A week or so later, Joe comes to Quisenberry on the run and tells him that David, the local fellow, is up in the bush with a rifle to shoot Amos who at the time was sitting on the cabin of his boat, happily plunking away on his ukulele, not knowing that David was lining up on him with a rifle. Quisenberry got it all sorted out."

Audrey Pearson

"The first year we worked at Carlisle—1945—we rolled cans. The second year we worked on the reform line and in the third year, we got down in the fish. We were big shots. We stood on the lines where the cans come out of the filling machine. We had white gloves on and white uniforms and our hair done up in bandanas and we had big butcher knives. And when the cans came by, if they weren't full enough or if there was skin showing, we had to take them off and patch them.

"And our hands used to stink something awful when we wore those gloves. You couldn't get your hand up to your face, it stunk so bad. I couldn't eat. By the next week, I'd be fine but everybody else at the table couldn't eat.

"We had a good time going up on the *Cardena* or *Catala*. We had fun playing shuffleboard on deck and going to the dining room and getting invited to the captain's table. I guess we were the only young girls on the ship.

"One big thing in the week at Carlisle was going down to meet the steamship. It didn't matter if it was 2 or 3 o'clock in the morning, you got up and went down there. We were getting the mail and buying a chocolate bar or a magazine. The purser would have his little news stand open.

"It was beautiful at night. We used to call it the city of lights because all the lights from the boats and nets were out there. It was just one big lit-up river. And you could hear the boats—putt, putt, putt."

Gwen Pearson

"There were some sad times. We had a lady drown. She was drinking and she fell off the wharf and nobody missed her. They found her clothing. And there was the little Dutch boy. He was just five years old and he went missing and he was found under the houses. That was really, really sad for that family. We were friends with them because they were our age and they worked in the cannery with us.

"We used to walk up to the dam and roast weiners. It was a long boardwalk and it wasn't very wide. We also walked to Claxton on the boardwalk and trail. It was all falling apart. Claxton was closed by then.

"We had a rec hall we could go up to—ping pong and a record player there.

"They had a good cannery crew and they and the management people were really good to us kids. And the young people from Rupert, we had a lot of fun together. Like there was Jack Banner, Harold Britton, Norm Christensen, Clare Salter, Alan Hale, Bill Ross, we were all one big family. It was a nice experience.

"A lot of the Indian women came from Terrace and Kitwanga and Kitwancool. It was always the same women and their husbands worked on packers or fished. They looked after themselves and cared how they looked. They were very clean and put out a wash that was bright and clean and their houses were kept swept. They were really nice. There were some that smelled of oulichan oil which was very important to them. They ate with it, cooked with it and they rubbed it on their skin and in their hair. It was an acquired taste and smell."

Peter Seifert
"I went with Canadian Fishing Co. in 1947, after I came out of the airforce. I went to Bones Bay as junior bookkeeper with Charlie Birch. I was with the company for 33 years, and that was the start of a wonderful, wonderful life.

"When I was at Tallheo, alcohol was a very powerful factor up there during the season—on the weekends. We used to have a little lady called Annie. She was the mother of all of them. She was born many, many moons. She was a real charmer and she was head of all the ladies there. She would get all the bad oranges and other fruit from the store and they would buy lots of sugar. And by Friday at 4:30 when everything quit, they'd march down from the cannery to their village and get ready to head home to Bella Coola. Everybody would be soused up on the home brew and they would stagger down to the boats and make the trip home. Annie looked after the whole thing. Sunday nights they'd come back and you could see they were really hung over. By Monday morning, when they'd go to work, all they had to do was drink a little water and shake themselves up and they were on another toot. They did this every week. And it was just rotten fruit and yeast and sugar. Some of that fruit used to be pretty high by the time it arrived on the *Cardena*. That was the only sad part of the fishing industry—that alcohol controlled a lot of people through all those years.

"On May 24th, we always used to go across to Bella Coola and up to Stuie Lodge, about 20 miles past Hagensbourg. There were about five of us would go up there just to get away from the cannery. It was a nice outing. The 24th of May was the holiday for the canneries because you didn't have time to do anything once the season started.

Eric Turnill
"While on the Skeena, at Sunnyside, in 1938, Doug Souter and I were required, because of our First Aid certificates to attend at the birth by an Indian woman, whose midwife had not arrived. So we threw in the towel and became midwives ourselves. Doug had the sense to take a bottle of brandy along with us, which was a lifesaver because I damned near fainted. Somebody had told me, I think it was St. John's Ambulance, that I had to tie a knot at some point. Well, this confused the entire situation. However, we managed to survive, thanks to the mother and so did the baby, and there were no complications.

"I organized basketball games between the Natives and the whites. And we had marvelous fun. One of my opponents was Roy Vickers, who is the father of the famous artist, Roy Henry Vickers.

"After the war and my stint in the navy where I had managed to become the skipper on a corvette, I went back to B.C. Packers in the insurance department. Bill Harrison, who was personnel manager asked me to join him and I became employment manager. One of my first challenges was a panic call from Kildonan, requiring 20 or 30 women workers for the cannery. I took out ads and I scrounged around Vancouver and I wasn't getting anywhere. No one answered the ads. Eventually I had the bright idea of phoning the John Howard Society and it worked wonders. I got 30 of the most marvelous first-class prostitutes in British Columbia and I sent them off to Kildonan.

"When I was posted to Port Edward, Mac McLean was manager there. This was about 1939. Our communication with Prince Rupert, which was very important, depended on using a company speeder—a device with a little motor in it and you putt along the railway tracks. But in order to make sure there wasn't any train traffic expected, because it was a one-way street, you had to phone the CN headquarters in Rupert and say you would like to go into Prince Rupert and would there be any trains on the track? And they would give you permission. However, this particular day, Mac and I decided to go into Rupert, I think it was to take some money to the bank. So we got the speeder out and Mac forgot, or I forgot to phone Canadian National. So off we went. And where the Columbia Cellulose Company is now ensconced, was a sort of a viaduct, a fill with gravel down about 20 feet on each side and this was where the rails ran. And lo and behold, when we got there, a freight train was coming towards us from Prince Rupert. Now this created a difficulty for us. We had to abandon the speeder somehow or other and there was no place to put it on a side track. Luckily, we had a rope, so we quickly lowered it to the bottom of the bank and Mac and I went over on our stomachs and held on for dear life while the train went by above us. At first I had tied the rope to the rail. Mac pointed out to me that that was not a good thing to do, so we tied it to the tie. The train went by and we had to get the speeder back up this 20-foot slope. A speeder is quite a heavy piece of equipment. I don't know when I've put so much strength into anything—Mac was heavier, bigger and stronger than I was—and between the two of us, we finally got it up on the rails and off we went. It was one of those dumb experiences, but also a rather scary one."

Anonymous
"Bob Payne Jr. was a competent pilot and sometimes he would pilot himself on his upcoast business trips. He loved to fly and he loved the coast with its awesome scenery and its dozens of small outpost communities. And if he had a passenger, he delighted in treating him to the vantage of in-air viewing. I made several trips with him, up the mainland coast and down the

west coast of Vancouver Island and each one was memorable.

"On one of these, we had flown to Rivers Inlet where we had overnighted, probably at Goose Bay or Wadhams, and were flying to Bella Coola via Owikeno Lake. What wonderful scenery and the spectacle of all the sockeye rivers flowing into the lake! Of course, float planes are supposed to fly over water, but we had to cross the height of land between the head of the lake and South Bentinck Arm. And Bob chose that point in the trip to change over from one gas tank to the second one. He didn't tell me he was doing this and when the engine cut out my heart hit my mouth. It was probably just for a few seconds but it was long enough for me to imagine a crash landing in that unforgiving wilderness below.

"I made a number of trips upcoast with Ralph Hansen, Nelson Brothers' venerable pilot. He was the ultimate in caution and good flying skills. Those trips were always enjoyable and educational. Ralph spent most of his time in the air until his retirement and logged thousands of miles and hours. Probably no one was as familiar with the B.C. coast as he was. So far as I know, he never had a serious mishap.

"I was working one summer as head bookkeeper at Margaret Bay in Smiths Inlet. It was just a gillnet camp then and a small one at that —a netloft and machineshop, office and store. When the fleet was out during the week, the evening entertainment was cribbage or poker. At one point, one of the Fisheries Research Board ships was scouting Smiths Inlet to see if there was a commercially viable shrimp population. There wasn't, but they caught enough beautiful prawn-sized shrimps to keep the camp in gourmet feeds for a week or so.

"It was a pretty lonely place. The weekend entertainment was a case of beer in the sauna—most of the fishermen were from Sointula and the sauna was a must. Awhile in the sauna with the beer to keep you hydrated and then, for the brave, a run to the end of the dock and a jump into the saltchuck, then back to the sauna.

"The Margaret Bay season was short—just the sockeye run—and ended in August. Then the whole crew would go to Bones Bay in Johnstone Strait for the fall fishing. Harold Malm was the manager—himself a Sointula man—and a prince of a guy. After we closed the camp, we made a trip to Rivers Inlet in his dispatch boat, the *Camp Point* and fished for those big springs outside Kildala at the head of the Inlet. It was a perk of working for a fish company and a taste of what the elite on the nearby yachts were paying thousands of dollars to enjoy.

"We then set course for Bones Bay, with an overnight stop at Sointula, where I stayed at the local boarding house, and where we made contact again with our gillnetters, who were also heading for the Strait. It was like a paid vacation.

"Namu was the largest fishing operation on the coast. I spent part of one summer there, dispatching boats for Canadian Fishing Co. This was a bit of an anomaly, seeing that Namu was a B.C. Packers plant, but the two companies and Nelson Brothers had a loose joint packing arrangement in progress.

"I had an "apartment" in Toonerville and my wife and two kids came up for a few weeks. The Canfisco packer would pick me up at Namu, and we would head out to anchor in Fishegg Inlet, or Koeye or Port John, to receive the seine boats when they came in to deliver at the end of the fishing day.

"We would load salmon all night from the seiners and once the packer was loaded, I would shift to another one or get back to Namu the best way I could and the packer would head to Vancouver.

"These days and nights in those isolated anchorages had a surreal quality about them and were unique to fishing industry experiences. The big packers would be surrounded by seiners waiting their turn to be unloaded. The packer's flood lights lit up the deck and the adjacent boats, but barely pierced the gloom of the night beyond. Each fish would be tallied as it was pitched into the brailer and each brailer load weighed before being dumped into the hold where the packer crew iced down the layers of salmon. The hum of the diesel engines was the background white noise over which the chatter of the fishermen's band and music on short wave radios brought the outside into the harbour.

As each boat was unloaded, it would drift off to anchor in a corner of the bay and the crew would bunk down for a much needed rest until daylight."

Appendix 1

1923 SURVEYS

British Columbia Fire Underwriters Association

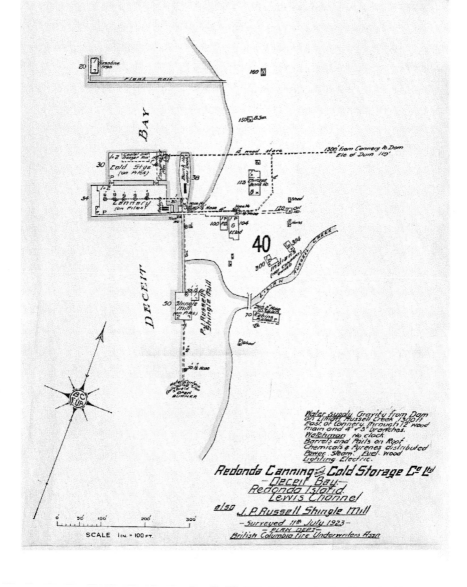

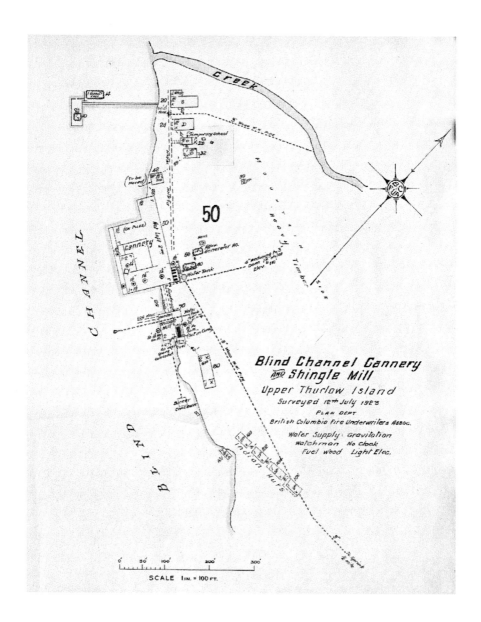

Appendix 1 - 1923 Surveys BCFUA 303

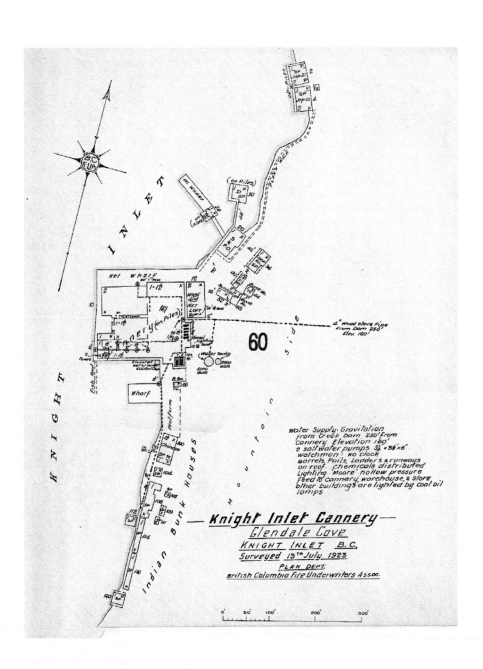

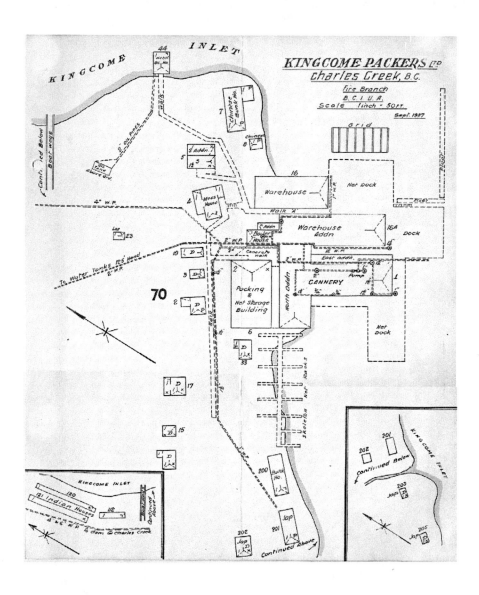

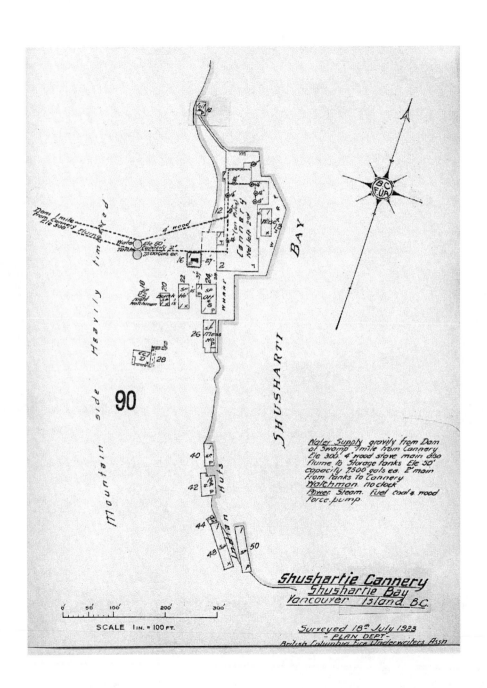

306 Cannery Village—Company Town

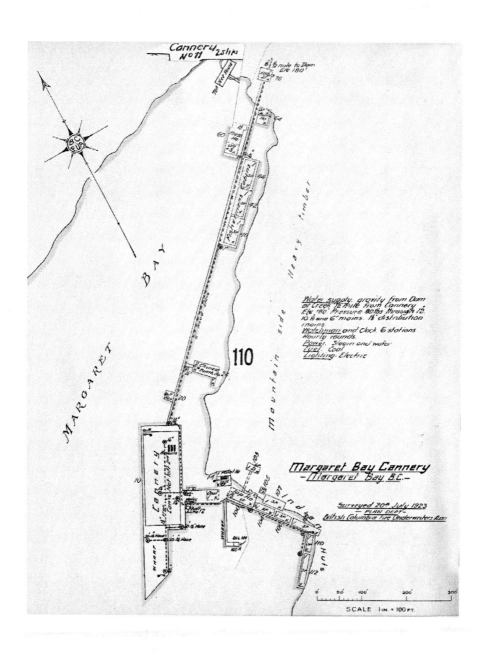

Appendix 1 - 1923 Surveys BCFUA 307

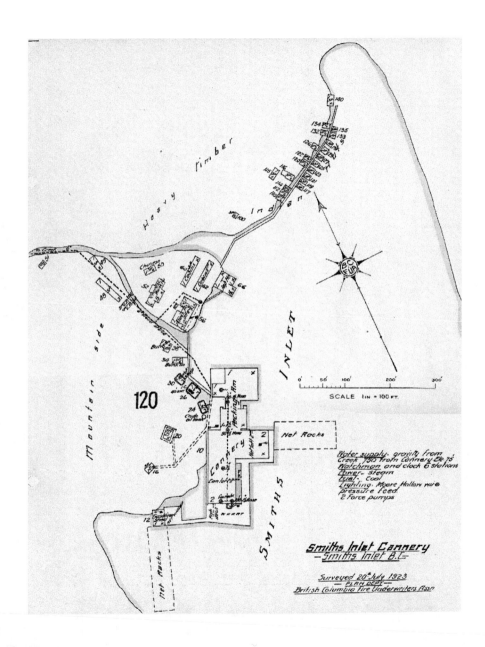

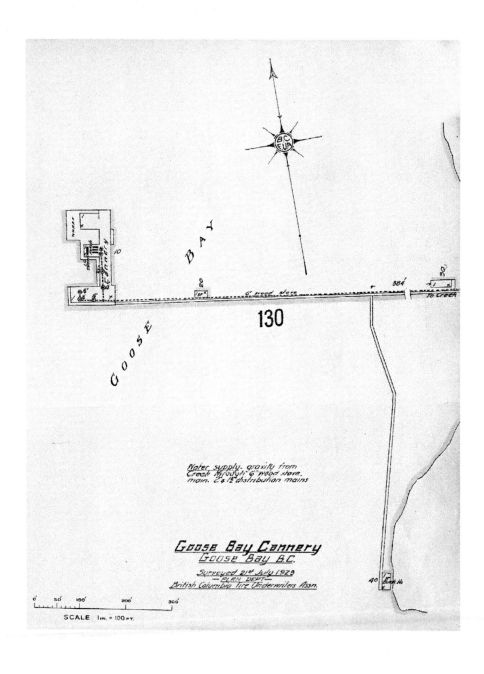

Appendix 1 - 1923 Surveys BCFUA 309

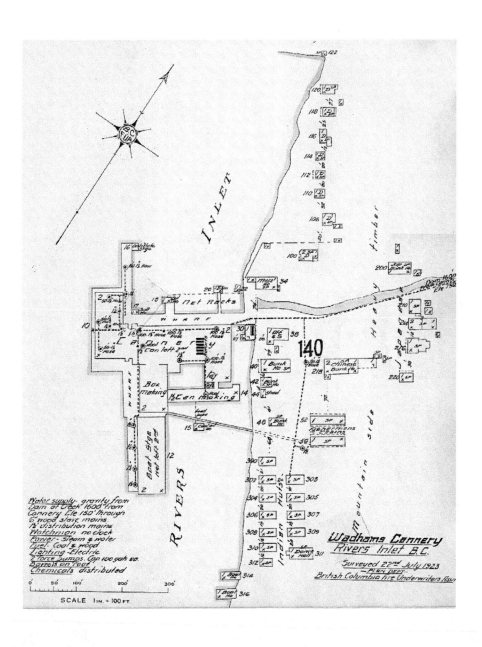

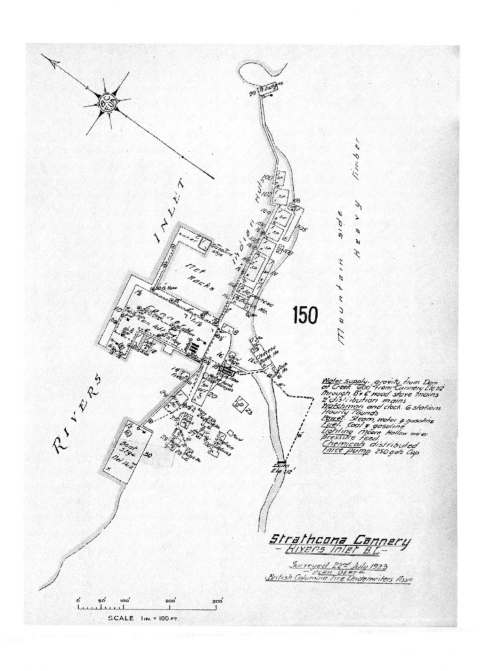

Appendix 1 - 1923 Surveys BCFUA 311

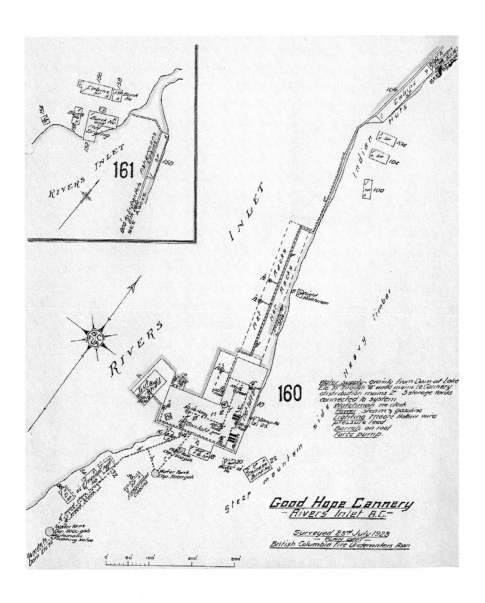

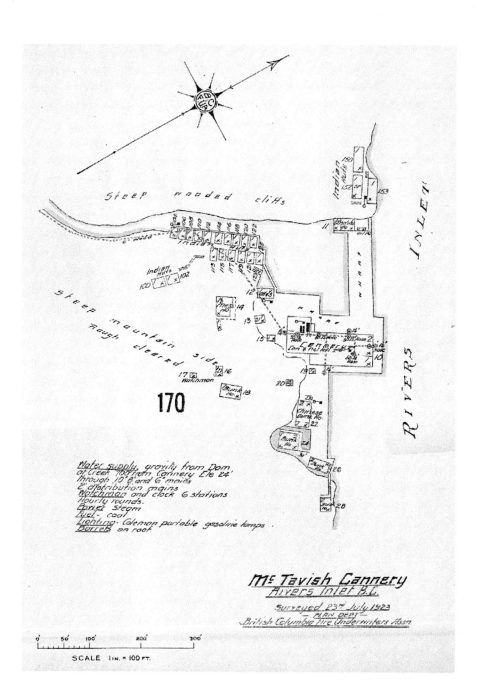

Appendix 1 - 1923 Surveys BCFUA 313

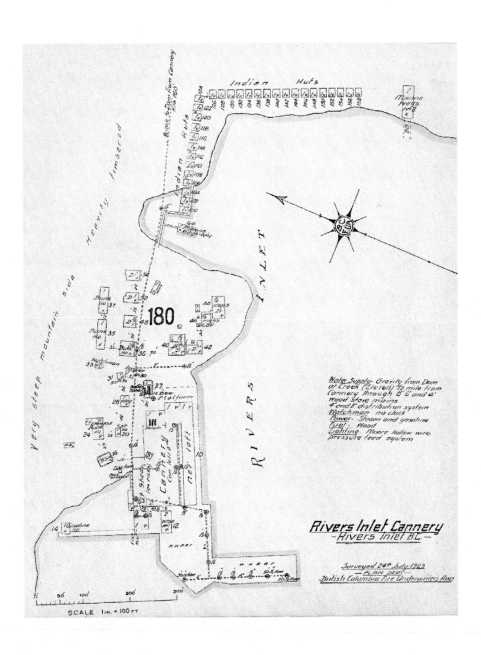

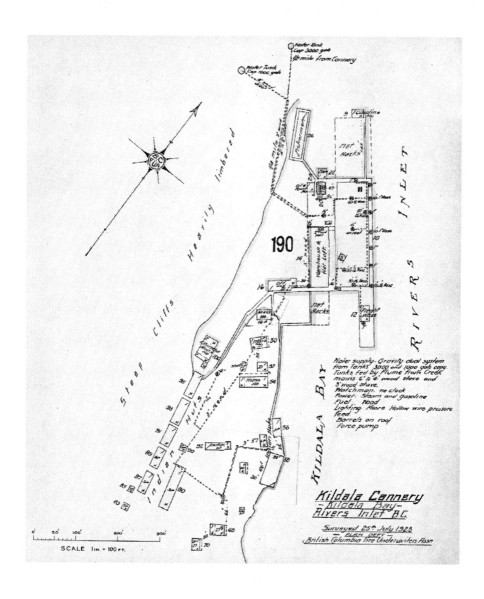

Appendix 1 - 1923 Surveys BCFUA 315

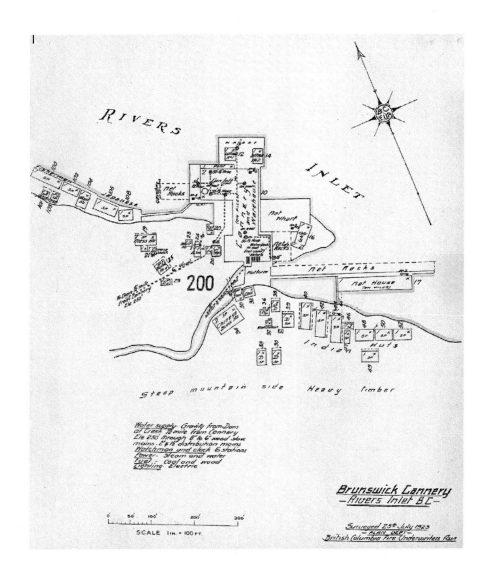

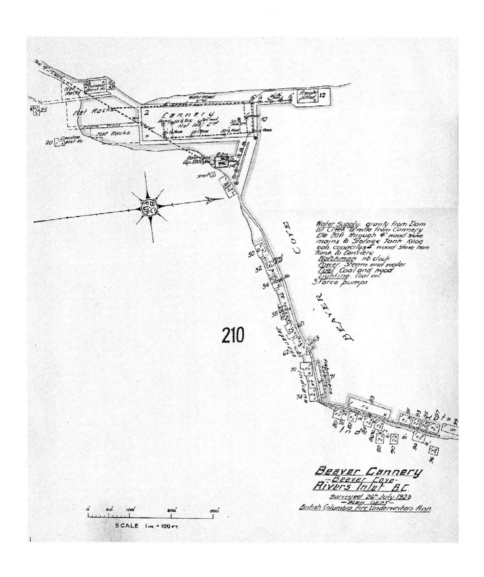

Appendix 1 - 1923 Surveys BCFUA 317

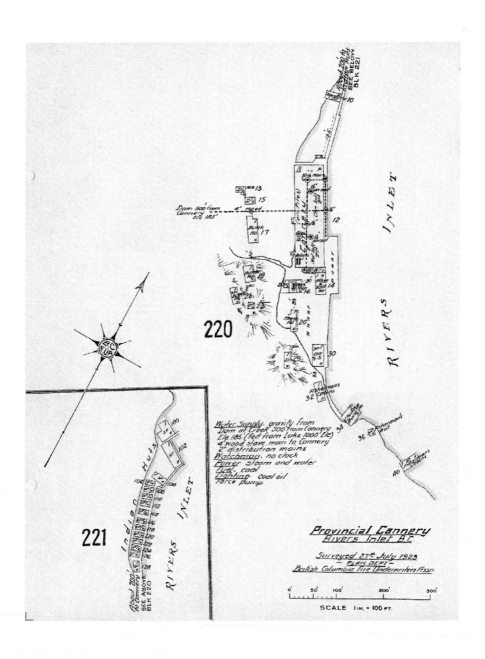

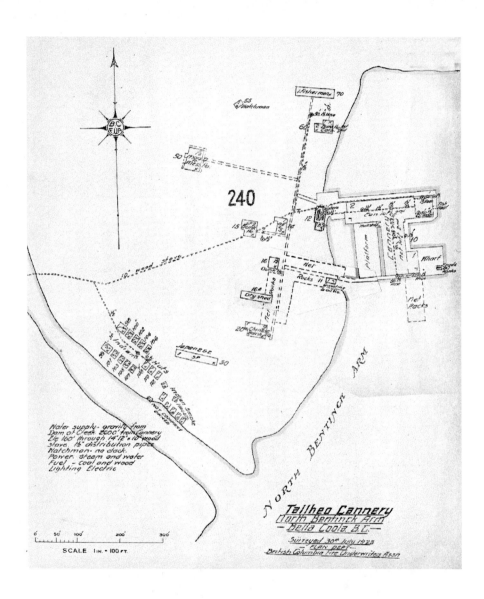

Appendix 1 - 1923 Surveys BCFUA 319

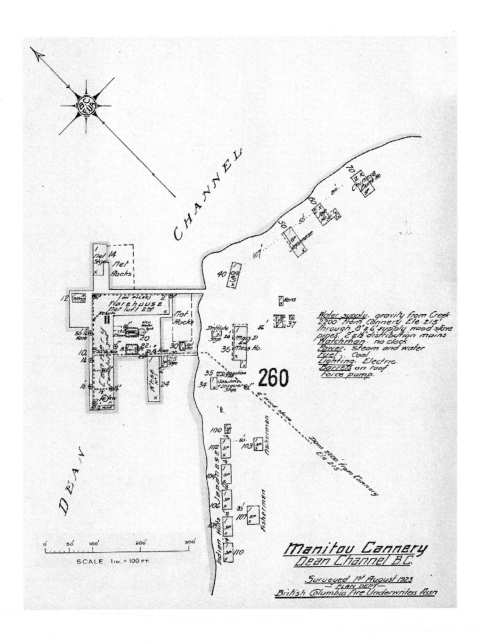

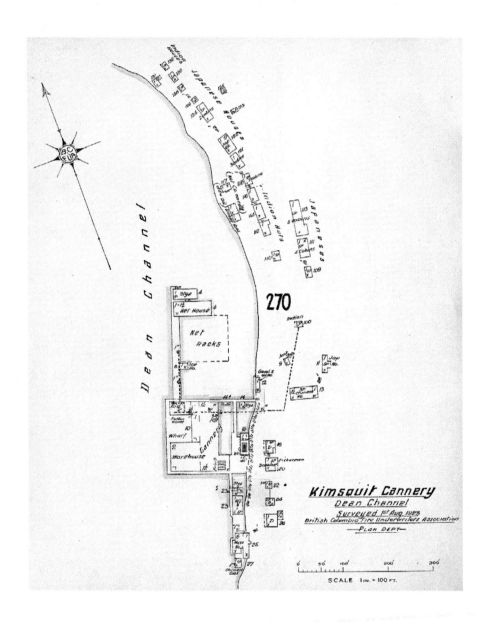

Appendix 1 - 1923 Surveys BCFUA 321

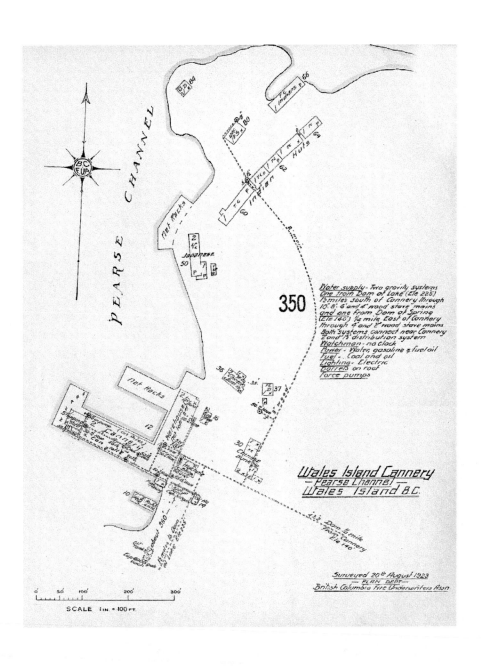

322 Cannery Village—Company Town

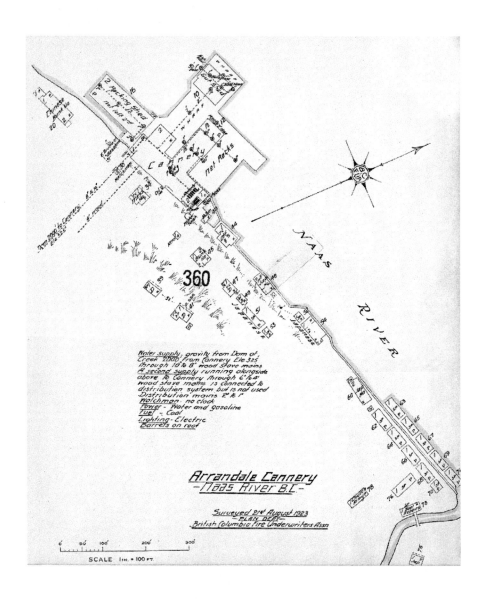

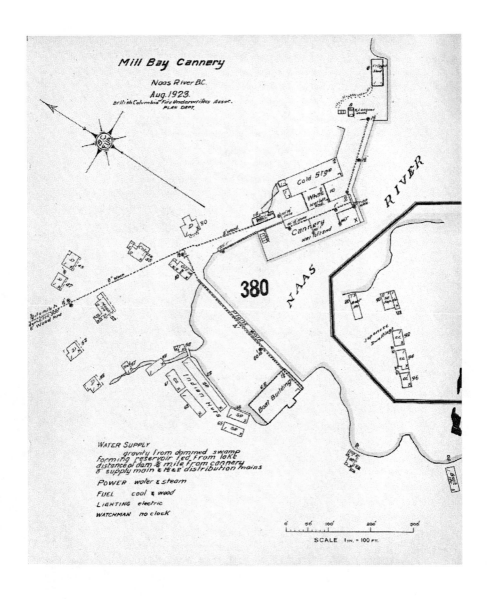

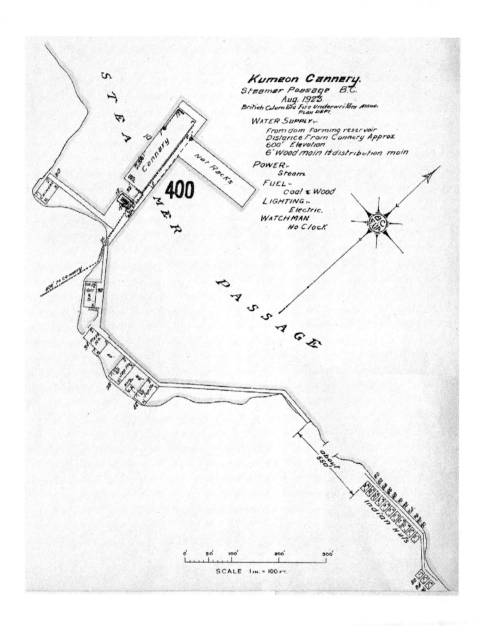

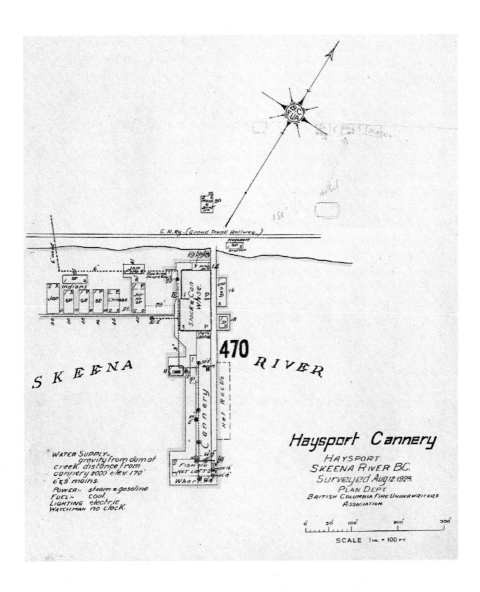

326 Cannery Village—Company Town

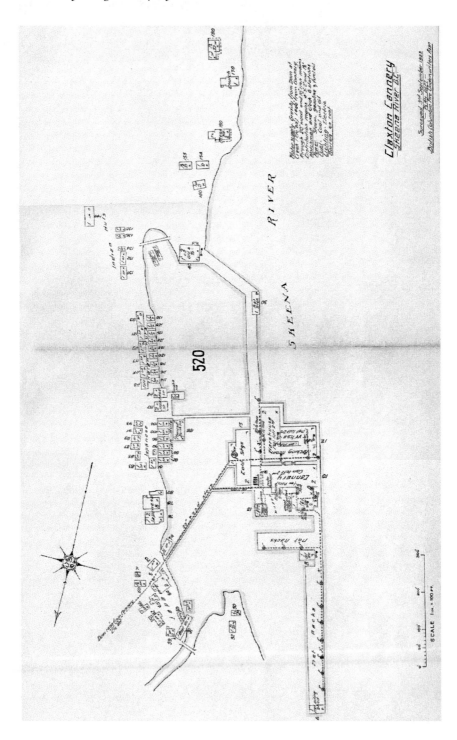

Appendix 1 - 1923 Surveys BCFUA 327

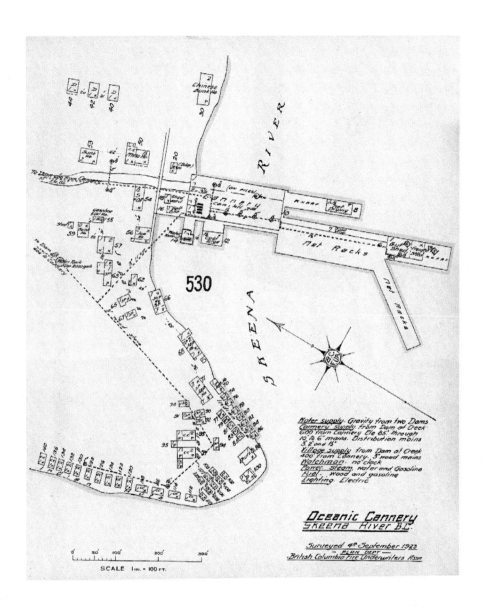

328 Cannery Village—Company Town

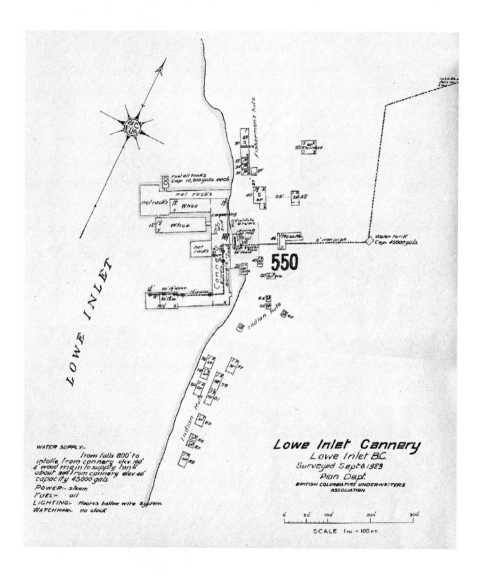

Appendix 1 - 1923 Surveys BCFUA 329

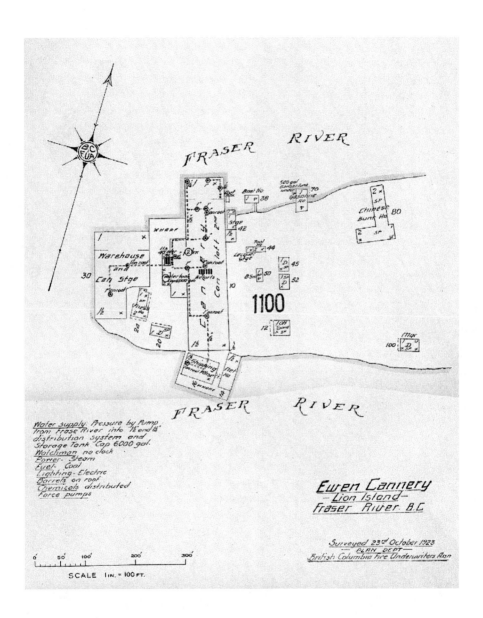

Appendix 2

Canneries and Fish Hatcheries on the British Columbia Coast

1932

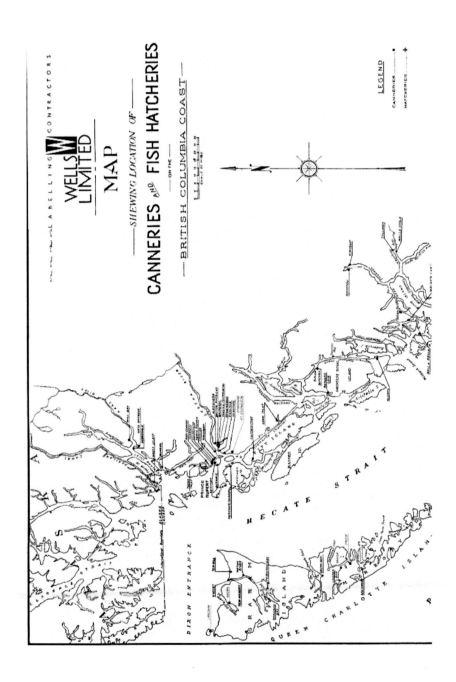

Appendix 2 – Canneries and Fish Hatcheries on the British Columbia Coast 333

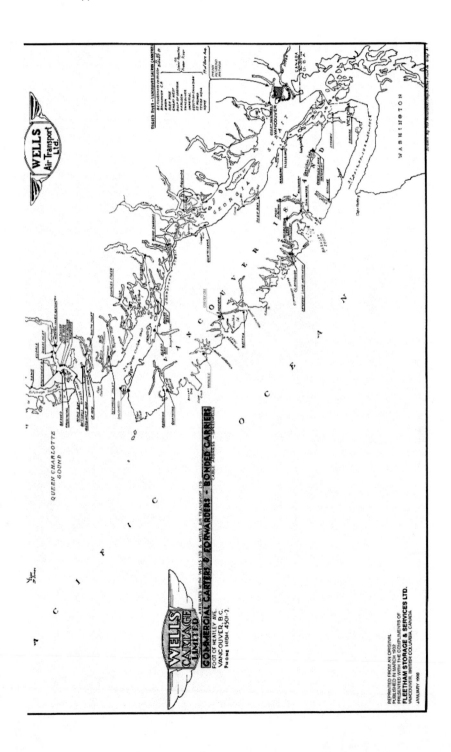

Bibliography

Beard, Harry R. *Story of Canfisco*, The Canadian Fishing Co., Ltd., Vancouver, B.C., 1937.

Bloom, Alder. *Salmon Canning in British Columbia*, self-published, 1994.

Boam, Henry J. *BRITISH COLUMBIA, Its History, People, Commerce, Industries, and Resources*, Sells Ltd., London, England, 1912.

Blyth, Gladys Young. *History of Port Edward, 1907–1970*, self-published, undated.

Blyth, Gladys Young. *Salmon Canneries, British Columbia North Coast*, Oolichan Books, Lantzville, B.C., 1991.

Canadian Fishing Co. Ltd. *Canfisco – From Sea to Shelf*, The Canadian Fishing Co., Ltd., 1947.

Carrothers, W.A. *The British Columbia Fisheries*, University of Toronto Press, Toronto, 1941.

Hacking, Norman. *Prince Ships of Northern B.C.*, Heritage House Publishing Co., Surrey, B.C., 1995.

Hacking, Norman and Lamb, W.K. *The Princess Story*, Mitchell Press, Vancouver, B.C., 1974.

Harris, E.A. *Spokeshute*, Orca Book Publishers, Vancouver, B.C., 1990.

Henry, Tom. *The Good Company*, Harbour Publishing, Madeira Park, B.C., 1994.

Hill, Beth. *The Remarkable World of Frances Barkley, 1769 – 1845*, Gray's Publishing Ltd., Sidney, B.C., 1978.

Hutchinson, W. *Landing at Ladner*, Carlton Press, New York, 1982.

Kennedy, Liv. *Coastal Villages*, Harbour Publishing, Madeira Park, B.C., 1991.

Large, Dr. R.G. *The Skeena – River of Destiny*, Mitchell Press, Vancouver, B.C., 1957.

Large, Dr. R.G. *Drums and Scalpel*, Mitchell Press, Vancouver, B.C., 1968.

Lyons, Cicely. *Salmon: Our Heritage*, Mitchell Press, Vancouver, B.C. 1969

Maclachlan, Morag. *The Fort Langley Journals, 1827-30*, University of British Columbia Press, 1998.

Macmillan, Lt. Col. John. *Unpublished memoir*, 1950.

McKervill, Hugh M. *The Salmon People*, Gray's Publishing, Ltd., Sidney, B.C., 1967.

Meggs, Geoff. *Salmon – The Decline of the B.C. Fishing Industry*, Douglas & McIntyre, Vancouver, B.C., 1995.

Meilleur, Helen. *A Pour of Rain*, Raincoast Books, Vancouver, B.C., 2001.

Nicholson George. *Vancouver Island's West Coast 1762 –1962*, Morriss Printing Co., Ltd., Victoria, B.C., 1962.

Rushton, Gerald A. *Whistle Up the Inlet*, J.J. Douglas Ltd., Vancouver, B.C., 1974.

Simpson, Sam L. and James E. *The Clam Story*, self-published, 2002.

Smith, Dorothy B. *The Reminiscences of Dr. John Sebastian Helmcken*, University of British Columbia Press, 1975.

Sutherland, Eileen. *My Skeena Childhood*, British Columbia Historical News 6(2), Spring 2003.

Turner, Robert D. *Those Beautiful Coastal Liners – The Canadian Pacific Princesses*, Sono Nis Press, Victoria, B.C., 2001.

Weicht, Chris. *Jericho Beach and the West Coast Flying Boat Stations*, Morriss Printing Co., Ltd., Victoria, B.C., 1997.

White, Howard and Spilsbury, Jim. *Spilsbury's Coast*, Harbour Publishing, Madeira Park, B.C., 1987.

Williams, David R. *Mayor Gerry*, Douglas & McIntyre, Vancouver, B.C., 1986.

Anglo-British Columbia Packing Co., Ltd., Advisory Board Meeting Minutes, 1895 – 1903.

British Columbia Packers Ltd. records, Steveston, B.C.

Henry Doyle Papers, Special Collections, University of British Columbia Library.

H. Bell-Irving & Co., Ltd., Minute Books, 1901 – 1972.

H.O. Bell-Irving Journals, Vancouver Archives.

Norman R. Christensen papers.

The Canadian Fishing Co., Ltd., records, Vancouver, B.C.

PERSONAL INTERVIEWS

Antonelli, Joe, 1996
Babcock William, 2001
Arbeider, Epp, 1997
Bell-Irving, Ian, 1996
Dorman family:
  David Dorman, Shirley Dorman Coates, Patricia Dorman Horne, John Horne, 1997 and 1998
Dorman, Garth, 1997
Christensen, Norman, 1996
Eckert, Marvin, 1996
Elsey, Jack, 2001
Eyford, Ed, 1996
Fleetham, Stan, 2002
Fraser, John, 2001
Graham, Jessie, 1996
Gray, Sandy, 1996
Gregory, Richard, 2001
Harrison, E.L. (Bill) 1997
Hogan, Lew and Mary Hogan White, 1998
Hogan, Robert, 1998
Kohse, Fred, 1996
Kremer, Eric, 1998
Levelton, Clifford, 1995
Lindsay, Robert, 1996
Lloyd, David L., 1995

MacLean, Milton (Mac), 1996
McLeod, Ron, 1998
MacKay, Don, 1998
Macmillan, A. Ewen, 1996
Macmillan, Kathryn, 1996
Main, Don, 2001
Matthews, Peter, 1998
May, Stan, 1998
McMillan Barry, 2002
Miller, Art, 1998
Miller, Donovan, 1996
Millerd, Frank, 1996
Milne, Stan, 1996
Nelson, Norman (Sonny), 1996
Nelson, R.I., (Dick), 1996
Nicholson, Ross, 1995
Nielsen, Art, 1998
Olsen, George, 1996
Payne, Robert L., 1998
Pearson, Audrey and Gwen, 1998
Rothery, Tom, 1997
Russell, Don, 1996
Seifert, Peter, 1996
Turnill, Eric, 1996
Van Snellenberg, Ben, 2001
Wilson, Peter, 1997

ISBN 1412009065-0